D1173853

Life And Works Of Alexander Csoma De Körös

TRÜBNER'S ORIENTAL SERIES.

"A knowledge of the commonplace, at least, of Oriental literature, philosophy, and religion is as necessary to the general reader of the present day as an acquaintance with the Latin and Greek classics was a generation or so ago. Immense strides have been made within the present century in these branches of learning; Sanskrit has been brought within the range of accurate philology, and its invaluable ancient literature thoroughly investigated; the language and sacred books of the Zoroastrians have been laid bare; Egyptian, Assyrian, and other records of the remote past have been deciphered, and a group of scholars speak of still more recondite Accadian and Hittite monuments; but the results of all the scholarship that has been devoted to these subjects have been almost inaccessible to the public because they were contained for the most part in learned or expensive works, or scattered throughout the numbers of scientific periodicals. Messrs. TRÜBNER & CO., in a spirit of enterprise which does them infinite credit, have determined to supply the constantly-increasing want, and to give in a popular, or, at least, a comprehensive form, all this mass of knowledge to the world."—*Times.*

NOW READY,

Post 8vo, pp. 568, with Map, cloth, price 16s.

THE INDIAN EMPIRE : ITS HISTORY, PEOPLE, AND PRODUCTS.

Being a revised form of the article "India," in the "Imperial Gazetteer," remodelled into chapters, brought up to date, and incorporating the general results of the Census of 1881.

By W. W. HUNTER, C.I.E., LL.D.,

Director-General of Statistics to the Government of India.

"The article 'India,' in Volume IV., is the touchstone of the work, and proves clearly enough the sterling metal of which it is wrought. It represents the essence of the 100 volumes which contain the results of the statistical survey conducted by Dr. Hunter throughout each of the 240 districts of India. It is, moreover, the only attempt that has ever been made to show how the Indian people have been built up, and the evidence from the original materials has been for the first time sifted and examined by the light of the local research in which the author was for so long engaged."—*Times.*

THE FOLLOWING WORKS HAVE ALREADY APPEARED:—

Third Edition, post 8vo, cloth, pp. xvi.—428, price 16s.

ESSAYS ON THE SACRED LANGUAGE, WRITINGS, AND RELIGION OF THE PARSIS.

By MARTIN HAUG, Ph.D.,

Late of the Universities of Tübingen, Göttingen, and Bonn ; Superintendent of Sanskrit Studies, and Professor of Sanskrit in the Poona College.

EDITED AND ENLARGED BY DR. E. W. WEST.

To which is added a Biographical Memoir of the late Dr. HAUG by Prof. E. P. EVANS.

I. History of the Researches into the Sacred Writings and Religion of the Parsis, from the Earliest Times down to the Present.
II. Languages of the Parsi Scriptures.
III. The Zend-Avesta, or the Scripture of the Parsis.
IV. The Zoroastrian Religion, as to its Origin and Development.

" ' Essays on the Sacred Language, Writings, and Religion of the Parsis,' by the late Dr. Martin Haug, edited by Dr. E. W. West. The author intended, on his return from India, to expand the materials contained in this work into a comprehensive account of the Zoroastrian religion, but the design was frustrated by his untimely death. We have, however, in a concise and readable form, a history of the researches into the sacred writings and religion of the Parsis from the earliest times down to the present—a dissertation on the languages of the Parsi Scriptures, a translation of the Zend-Avesta, or the Scripture of the Parsis, and a dissertation on the Zoroastrian religion, with especial reference to its origin and development."—*Times.*

Post 8vo, cloth, pp. viii.—176, price 7s. 6d.

TEXTS FROM THE BUDDHIST CANON

COMMONLY KNOWN AS "DHAMMAPADA."

With Accompanying Narratives.

Translated from the Chinese by S. BEAL, B.A., Professor of Chinese, University College, London.

The Dhammapada, as hitherto known by the Pali Text Edition, as edited by Fausböll, by Max Müller's English, and Albrecht Weber's German translations, consists only of twenty-six chapters or sections, whilst the Chinese version, or rather recension, as now translated by Mr. Beal, consists of thirty-nine sections. The students of Pali who possess Fausböll's text, or either of the above-named translations, will therefore needs want Mr. Beal's English rendering of the Chinese version; the thirteen above-named additional sections not being accessible to them in any other form ; for, even if they understand Chinese, the Chinese original would be unobtainable by them.

" Mr. Beal's rendering of the Chinese translation is a most valuable aid to the critical study of the work. It contains authentic texts gathered from ancient canonical books, and generally connected with some incident in the history of Buddha. Their great interest, however, consists in the light which they throw upon everyday life in India at the remote period at which they were written, and upon the method of teaching adopted by the founder of the religion. The method employed was principally parable, and the simplicity of the tales and the excellence of the morals inculcated, as well as the strange hold which they have retained upon the minds of millions of people, make them a very remarkable study."—*Times.*

" Mr. Beal, by making it accessible in an English dress, has added to the great services he has already rendered to the comparative study of religious history."—*Academy.*

" Valuable as exhibiting the doctrine of the Buddhists in its purest, least adulterated form, it brings the modern reader face to face with that simple creed and rule of conduct which won its way over the minds of myriads, and which is now nominally professed by 145 millions, who have overlaid its austere simplicity with innumerable ceremonies, forgotten its maxims, perverted its teaching, and so inverted its leading principle that a religion whose founder denied a God, now worships that founder as a god himself."—*Scotsman.*

Second Edition, post 8vo, cloth, pp. xxiv.—360, price 10s. 6d.

THE HISTORY OF INDIAN LITERATURE.

By ALBRECHT WEBER.

Translated from the Second German Edition by JOHN MANN, M.A., and
THÉODOR ZACHARIAE, Ph.D., with the sanction of the Author.

Dr. BUHLER, Inspector of Schools in India, writes:—"When I was Professor of Oriental Languages in Elphinstone College, I frequently felt the want of such a work to which I could refer the students."

Professor COWELL, of Cambridge, writes:—"It will be especially useful to the students in our Indian colleges and universities. I used to long for such a book when I was teaching in Calcutta. Hindu students are intensely interested in the history of Sanskrit literature, and this volume will supply them with all they want on the subject."

Professor WHITNEY, Yale College, Newhaven, Conn., U.S.A., writes:—"I was one of the class to whom the work was originally given in the form of academic lectures. At their first appearance they were by far the most learned and able treatment of their subject; and with their recent additions they still maintain decidedly the same rank."

"Is perhaps the most comprehensive and lucid survey of Sanskrit literature extant. The essays contained in the volume were originally delivered as academic lectures, and at the time of their first publication were acknowledged to be by far the most learned and able treatment of the subject. They have now been brought up to date by the addition of all the most important results of recent research."—*Times.*

Post 8vo, cloth, pp. xii.—198, accompanied by Two Language
Maps, price 12s.

A SKETCH OF
THE MODERN LANGUAGES OF THE EAST INDIES.

By ROBERT N. CUST.

The Author has attempted to fill up a vacuum, the inconvenience of which pressed itself on his notice. Much had been written about the languages of the East Indies, but the extent of our present knowledge had not even been brought to a focus. It occurred to him that it might be of use to others to publish in an arranged form the notes which he had collected for his own edification.

"Supplies a deficiency which has long been felt."—*Times.*

"The book before us is then a valuable contribution to philological science. It passes under review a vast number of languages, and it gives, or professes to give, in every case the sum and substance of the opinions and judgments of the best-informed writers."—*Saturday Review.*

Second Corrected Edition, post 8vo, pp. xii.—116, cloth, price 5s.

THE BIRTH OF THE WAR-GOD.

A Poem. By KALIDASA.

Translated from the Sanskrit into English Verse by
RALPH T. H. GRIFFITH, M.A.

"A very spirited rendering of the *Kumárasambhava*, which was first published twenty-six years ago, and which we are glad to see made once more accessible."—*Times.*

"Mr. Griffith's very spirited rendering is well known to most who are at all interested in Indian literature, or enjoy the tenderness of feeling and rich creative imagination of its author."—*Indian Antiquary.*

"We are very glad to welcome a second edition of Professor Griffith's admirable translation. Few translations deserve a second edition better."—*Athenæum.*

Post 8vo, pp. 432, cloth, price 16s.

A CLASSICAL DICTIONARY OF HINDU MYTHOLOGY AND RELIGION, GEOGRAPHY, HISTORY, AND LITERATURE.

By JOHN DOWSON, M.R.A.S.,
Late Professor of Hindustani, Staff College.

"This not only forms an indispensable book of reference to students of Indian literature, but is also of great general interest, as it gives in a concise and easily accessible form all that need be known about the personages of Hindu mythology whose names are so familiar, but of whom so little is known outside the limited circle of *savants*."—*Times.*

"It is no slight gain when such subjects are treated fairly and fully in a moderate space; and we need only add that the few wants which we may hope to see supplied in new editions detract but little from the general excellence of Mr. Dowson's work."—*Saturday Review.*

Post 8vo, with View of Mecca, pp. cxii.—172, cloth, price 9s.

SELECTIONS FROM THE KORAN.

By EDWARD WILLIAM LANE,
Translator of "The Thousand and One Nights;" &c., &c.
A New Edition, Revised and Enlarged, with an Introduction by
STANLEY LANE POOLE.

". . . Has been long esteemed in this country as the compilation of one of the greatest Arabic scholars of the time, the late Mr. Lane, the well-known translator of the 'Arabian Nights.' . . . The present editor has enhanced the value of his relative's work by divesting the text of a great deal of extraneous matter introduced by way of comment, and prefixing an introduction."—*Times.*

"Mr. Poole is both a generous and a learned biographer. . . . Mr. Poole tells us the facts . . . so far as it is possible for industry and criticism to ascertain them, and for literary skill to present them in a condensed and readable form."—*Englishman, Calcutta.*

Post 8vo, pp. vi.—368, cloth, price 14s.

MODERN INDIA AND THE INDIANS,

BEING A SERIES OF IMPRESSIONS, NOTES, AND ESSAYS.

By MONIER WILLIAMS, D.C.L.,

Hon. LL.D. of the University of Calcutta, Hon. Member of the Bombay Asiatic Society, Boden Professor of Sanskrit in the University of Oxford.

Third Edition, revised and augmented by considerable Additions, with Illustrations and a Map.

"In this volume we have the thoughtful impressions of a thoughtful man on some of the most important questions connected with our Indian Empire. . . . An enlightened observant man, travelling among an enlightened observant people, Professor Monier Williams has brought before the public in a pleasant form more of the manners and customs of the Queen's Indian subjects than we ever remember to have seen in any one work. He not only deserves the thanks of every Englishman for this able contribution to the study of Modern India—a subject with which we should be specially familiar—but he deserves the thanks of every Indian, Parsee or Hindu, Buddhist and Moslem, for his clear exposition of their manners, their creeds, and their necessities."—*Times.*

Post 8vo, pp. xliv.—376, cloth, price 14s.

METRICAL TRANSLATIONS FROM SANSKRIT WRITERS.

With an Introduction, many Prose Versions, and Parallel Passages from Classical Authors.

By J. MUIR, C.I.E., D.C.L., LL.D., Ph.D.

". . . An agreeable introduction to Hindu poetry."—*Times.*

". . . A volume which may be taken as a fair illustration alike of the religious and moral sentiments and of the legendary lore of the best Sanskrit writers."—*Edinburgh Daily Review.*

Second Edition, post 8vo, pp. xxvi.—244, cloth, price 10s. 6d.

THE GULISTAN;

Or, ROSE GARDEN OF SHEKH MUSHLIU'D-DIN SADI OF SHIRAZ.

Translated for the First Time into Prose and Verse, with an Introductory Preface, and a Life of the Author, from the Atish Kadah,

By EDWARD B. EASTWICK, C.B., M.A., F.R.S., M.R.A.S.

"It is a very fair rendering of the original."—*Times.*

"The new edition has long been desired, and will be welcomed by all who t ke any interest in Oriental poetry. The *Gulistan* is a typical Persian verse-book of th· highest order. Mr. Eastwick's rhymed translation ... has long established itself in a secure position as the best version of Sadi's finest work."—*Academy.*

"It is both faithfully and gracefully executed."—*Tablet.*

In Two Volumes, post 8vo, pp. viii.—408 and viii.—348, cloth, price 28s.

MISCELLANEOUS ESSAYS RELATING TO INDIAN SUBJECTS.

By BRIAN HOUGHTON HODGSON, Esq., F.R.S.,

Late of the Bengal Civil Service; Corresponding Member of the Institute; Chevalier of the Legion of Honour; late British Minister at the Court of Nepál, &c., &c.

CONTENTS OF VOL. I.

SECTION I.—On the Kocch, Bódó, and Dhimál Tribes.—Part I. Vocabulary—Part II. Grammar.—Part III. Their Origin, Location, Numbers, Creed, Customs, Character, and Condition, with a General Description of the Climate they dwell in.—Appendix.

SECTION II.—On Himalayan Ethnology.—I. Comparative Vocabulary of the Languages of the Broken Tribes of Nepál.—II. Vocabulary of the Dialects of the Kirant Language.—III. Grammatical Analysis of the Váyu Language. The Váyu Grammar.—IV. Analysis of the Báhing Dialect of the Kiránti Language. The Báhing Grammar.—V. On the Váyu or Háyu Tribe of the Central Himaláya.—VI. On the Kiránti Tribe of the Central Himaláya.

CONTENTS OF VOL. II.

SECTION III.—On the Aborigines of North-Eastern India. Comparative Vocabulary of the Tibetan, Bódó, and Gáró Tongues.

SECTION IV.—Aborigines of the North-Eastern Frontier.

SECTION V.—Aborigines of the Eastern Frontier.

SECTION VI.—The Indo-Chinese Borderers, and their connection with the Himalayans and Tibetans. Comparative Vocabulary of Indo-Chinese Borderers in Arakan. Comparative Vocabulary of Indo-Chinese Borderers in Tenasserim.

SECTION VII.—The Mongolian Affinities of the Caucasians.—Comparison and Analysis of Caucasian and Mongolian Words.

SECTION VIII.—Physical Type of Tibetans.

SECTION IX.—The Aborigines of Central India.—Comparative Vocabulary of the Aboriginal Languages of Central India.—Aborigines of the Eastern Ghats.—Vocabulary of some of the Dialects of the Hill and Wandering Tribes in the Northern Sircars.—Aborigines of the Nilgiris, with Remarks on their Affinities.—Supplement to the Nilgirian Vocabularies.—The Aborigines of Southern India and Ceylon.

SECTION X.—Route of Nepalese Mission to Pekin, with Remarks on the Water-Shed and Plateau of Tibet.

SECTION XI.—Route from Káthmándú, the Capital of Nepál, to Darjeeling in Sikim.—Memorandum relative to the Seven Cosis of Nepál.

SECTION XII.—Some Accounts of the Systems of Law and Police as recognised in the State of Nepál.

SECTION XIII.—The Native Method of making the Paper denominated Hindustan, Népálese.

SECTION XIV.—Pre-eminence of the Vernaculars; or, the Anglicists Answered; Being Letters on the Education of the People of India.

"For the study of the less-known races of India Mr. Brian Hodgson's 'Miscellaneous Essays' will be found very valuable both to the philologist and the ethnologist."—*Times.*

Third Edition, Two Vols., post 8vo, pp. viii.—268 and viii.—326, cloth,
price 21s.

THE LIFE OR LEGEND OF GAUDAMA,

THE BUDDHA OF THE BURMESE. With Annotations.

The Ways to Neibban, and Notice on the Phongyies or Burmese Monks.

BY THE RIGHT REV. P. BIGANDET,

Bishop of Ramatha, Vicar-Apostolic of Ava and Pegu.

"The work is furnished with copious notes, which not only illustrate the subject-matter, but form a perfect encyclopædia of Buddhist lore."—*Times.*

"A work which will furnish European students of Buddhism with a most valuable help in the prosecution of their investigations."—*Edinburgh Daily Review.*

" Bishop Bigandet's invaluable work."—*Indian Antiquary.*

"Viewed in this light, its importance is sufficient to place students of the subject under a deep obligation to its author."—*Calcutta Review.*

"This work is one of the greatest authorities upon Buddhism."—*Dublin Review.*

Post 8vo, pp. xxiv.—420, cloth, price 18s.

CHINESE BUDDHISM.

A VOLUME OF SKETCHES, HISTORICAL AND CRITICAL.

BY J. EDKINS, D.D.

Author of "China's Place in Philology," "Religion in China," &c., &c.

"It contains a vast deal of important information on the subject, such as is only to be gained by long-continued study on the spot."—*Athenæum.*

"Upon the whole, we know of no work comparable to it for the extent of its original research, and the simplicity with which this complicated system of philosophy, religion, literature, and ritual is set forth."—*British Quarterly Review.*

The whole volume is replete with learning. . . . It deserves most careful study from all interested in the history of the religions of the world, and expressly of those who are concerned in the propagation of Christianity. Dr. Edkins notices in terms of just condemnation the exaggerated praise bestowed upon Buddhism by recent English writers."—*Record.*

Post 8vo, pp. 496, cloth, price 18s.

LINGUISTIC AND ORIENTAL ESSAYS.

WRITTEN FROM THE YEAR 1846 TO 1878.

BY ROBERT NEEDHAM CUST,

Late Member of Her Majesty's Indian Civil Service; Hon. Secretary to
the Royal Asiatic Society;
and Author of "The Modern Languages of the East Indies."

" We know none who has described Indian life, especially the life of the natives, with so much learning, sympathy, and literary talent."—*Academy.*

"They seem to us to be full of suggestive and original remarks."—*St. James's Gazette.*

" His book contains a vast amount of information. The result of thirty-five years of inquiry, reflection, and speculation, and that on subjects as full of fascination as of food for thought."—*Tablet.*

" Exhibit such a thorough acquaintance with the history and antiquities of India as to entitle him to speak as one having authority."—*Edinburgh Daily Review.*

" The author speaks with the authority of personal experience. . . . . It is this constant association with the country and the people which gives such a vividness to many of the pages."—*Athenæum.*

Post 8vo, pp. civ.—348, cloth, price 18s.

BUDDHIST BIRTH STORIES; or, Jataka Tales.

The Oldest Collection of Folk-lore Extant:

BEING THE JATAKATTHAVANNANA,

For the first time Edited in the original Pâli.

By V. FAUSBOLL;

And Translated by T. W. RHYS DAVIDS.

Translation. Volume I.

"These are tales supposed to have been told by the Buddha of what he had seen and heard in his previous births. They are probably the nearest representatives of the original Aryan stories from which sprang the folk-lore of Europe as well as India. The introduction contains a most interesting disquisition on the migrations of these fables, tracing their reappearance in the various groups of folk-lore legends. Among other old friends, we meet with a version of the Judgment of Solomon."—*Times.*

"It is now some years since Mr. Rhys Davids asserted his right to be heard on this subject by his able article on Buddhism in the new edition of the 'Encyclopædia Britannica.'"—*Leeds Mercury.*

"All who are interested in Buddhist literature ought to feel deeply indebted to Mr. Rhys Davids. His well-established reputation as a Pali scholar is a sufficient guarantee for the fidelity of his version, and the style of his translations is deserving of high praise."—*Academy.*

"No more competent expositor of Buddhism could be found than Mr. Rhys Davids In the Jâtaka book we have, then, a priceless record of the earliest imaginative literature of our race; and . . . it presents to us a nearly complete picture of the social life and customs and popular beliefs of the common people of Aryan tribes, closely related to ourselves, just as they were passing through the first stages of civilisation."—*St. James's Gazette.*

Post 8vo, pp. xxviii.—362, cloth, price 14s.

A TALMUDIC MISCELLANY;

OR, A THOUSAND AND ONE EXTRACTS FROM THE TALMUD, THE MIDRASHIM, AND THE KABBALAH.

Compiled and Translated by PAUL ISAAC HERSHON,

Author of "Genesis According to the Talmud," &c.

With Notes and Copious Indexes.

"To obtain in so concise and handy a form as this volume a general idea of the Talmud is a boon to Christians at least."—*Times.*

"Its peculiar and popular character will make it attractive to general readers. Mr. Hershon is a very competent scholar. . . . Contains samples of the good, bad, and indifferent, and especially extracts that throw light upon the Scriptures."— *British Quarterly Review.*

"Will convey to English readers a more complete and truthful notion of the Talmud than any other work that has yet appeared."—*Daily News.*

"Without overlooking in the slightest the several attractions of the previous volumes of the 'Oriental Series,' we have no hesitation in saying that this surpasses them all in interest."—*Edinburgh Daily Review.*

"Mr. Hershon has . . . thus given English readers what is, we believe, a fair set of specimens which they can test for themselves."—*The Record.*

"This book is by far the best fitted in the present state of knowledge to enable the general reader to gain a fair and unbiassed conception of the multifarious contents of the wonderful miscellany which can only be truly understood—so Jewish pride asserts—by the life-long devotion of scholars of the Chosen People."—*Inquirer.*

"The value and importance of this volume consist in the fact that scarcely a single extract is given in its pages but throws some light, direct or refracted, upon those Scriptures which are the common heritage of Jew and Christian alike."—*John Bull.*

"It is a capital specimen of Hebrew scholarship; a monument of learned, loving, light-giving labour."—*Jewish Herald.*

Post 8vo, pp. xii.—228, cloth, price 7s. 6d.

THE CLASSICAL POETRY OF THE JAPANESE.

By BASIL HALL CHAMBERLAIN,

Author of "Yeigo Heñkaku Shiran."

"A very curious volume. The author has manifestly devoted much labour to the task of studying the poetical literature of the Japanese, and rendering characteristic specimens into English verse."—*Daily News.*

"Mr. Chamberlain's volume is, so far as we are aware, the first attempt which has been made to interpret the literature of the Japanese to the Western world. It is to the classical poetry of Old Japan that we must turn for indigenous Japanese thought, and in the volume before us we have a selection from that poetry rendered into graceful English verse."—*Tablet.*

"It is undoubtedly one of the best translations of lyric literature which has appeared during the close of the last year."—*Celestial Empire.*

"Mr. Chamberlain set himself a difficult task when he undertook to reproduce Japanese poetry in an English form. But he has evidently laboured con amore, and his efforts are successful to a degree."—*London and China Express.*

Post 8vo, pp. xii.—164, cloth, price 10s. 6d.

THE HISTORY OF ESARHADDON (Son of Sennacherib),

KING OF ASSYRIA, B.C. 681-668.

Translated from the Cuneiform Inscriptions upon Cylinders and Tablets in the British Museum Collection; together with a Grammatical Analysis of each Word, Explanations of the Ideographs by Extracts from the Bi-Lingual Syllabaries, and List of Eponyms, &c.

By ERNEST A. BUDGE, B.A., M.R.A.S.,

Assyrian Exhibitioner, Christ's College, Cambridge.

"Students of scriptural archæology will also appreciate the 'History of Esarhaddon.'"—*Times.*

"There is much to attract the scholar in this volume. It does not pretend to popularise studies which are yet in their infancy. Its primary object is to translate, but it does not assume to be more than tentative, and it offers both to the professed Assyriologist and to the ordinary non-Assyriological Semitic scholar the means of controlling its results."—*Academy.*

"Mr. Budge's book is, of course, mainly addressed to Assyrian scholars and students. They are not, it is to be feared, a very numerous class. But the more thanks are due to him on that account for the way in which he has acquitted himself in his laborious task."—*Tablet.*

Post 8vo, pp. 448, cloth, price 21s.

THE MESNEVI

(Usually known as THE MESNEVIYI SHERIF, or HOLY MESNEVI)

OF

MEVLANA (OUR LORD) JELALU 'D-DIN MUHAMMED ER-RUMI.

Book the First.

Together with some Account of the Life and Acts of the Author, of his Ancestors, and of his Descendants.

Illustrated by a Selection of Characteristic Anecdotes, as Collected by their Historian,

MEVLANA SHEMSU-'D-DIN AHMED, EL EFLAKI, EL 'ARIFI.

Translated, and the Poetry Versified, in English,

By JAMES W. REDHOUSE, M.R.A.S., &c.

"A complete treasury of occult Oriental lore."—*Saturday Review.*

"This book will be a very valuable help to the reader ignorant of Persia, who is desirous of obtaining an insight into a very important department of the literature extant in that language."—*Tablet.*

Post 8vo, pp. xvi.—280, cloth, price 6s.

EASTERN PROVERBS AND EMBLEMS

ILLUSTRATING OLD TRUTHS.

BY REV. J. LONG,

Member of the Bengal Asiatic Society, F.R.G.S.

"We regard the book as valuable, and wish for it a wide circulation and attentive reading."—*Record.*

"Altogether, it is quite a feast of good things."—*Globe.*

"It is full of interesting matter."—*Antiquary.*

Post 8vo, pp. viii.—270, cloth, price 7s. 6d.

INDIAN POETRY;

Containing a New Edition of the "Indian Song of Songs," from the Sanscrit of the "Gita Govinda" of Jayadeva; Two Books from "The Iliad of India" (Mahabharata), "Proverbial Wisdom" from the Shlokas of the Hitopadesa, and other Oriental Poems.

BY EDWIN ARNOLD, C.S.I., Author of "The Light of Asia."

"In this new volume of Messrs. Trübner's Oriental Series, Mr. Edwin Arnold does good service by illustrating, through the medium of his musical English melodies, the power of Indian poetry to stir European emotions. The 'Indian Song of Songs' is not unknown to scholars. Mr. Arnold will have introduced it among popular English poems. Nothing could be more graceful and delicate than the shades by which Krishna is portrayed in the gradual process of being weaned by the love of

'Beautiful Radha, jasmine-bosomed Radha,'

from the allurements of the forest nymphs, in whom the five senses are typified."—*Times.*

"No other English poet has ever thrown his genius and his art so thoroughly into the work of translating Eastern ideas as Mr. Arnold has done in his splendid paraphrases of language contained in these mighty epics."—*Daily Telegraph.*

"The poem abounds with imagery of Eastern luxuriousness and sensuousness; the air seems laden with the spicy odours of the tropics, and the verse has a richness and a melody sufficient to captivate the senses of the dullest."—*Standard.*

"The translator, while producing a very enjoyable poem, has adhered with tolerable fidelity to the original text."—*Overland Mail.*

"We certainly wish Mr. Arnold success in his attempt 'to popularise Indian classics,' that being, as his preface tells us, the goal towards which he bends his efforts."—*Allen's Indian Mail.*

Post 8vo, pp. xvi.—296, cloth, price 10s. 6d.

THE MIND OF MENCIUS;

OR, POLITICAL ECONOMY FOUNDED UPON MORAL PHILOSOPHY.

A SYSTEMATIC DIGEST OF THE DOCTRINES OF THE CHINESE PHILOSOPHER MENCIUS.

Translated from the Original Text and Classified, with Comments and Explanations,

By the REV. ERNST FABER, Rhenish Mission Society.

Translated from the German, with Additional Notes,

By the REV. A. B. HUTCHINSON, C.M.S., Church Mission, Hong Kong.

"Mr. Faber is already well known in the field of Chinese studies by his digest of the doctrines of Confucius. The value of this work will be perceived when it is remembered that at no time since relations commenced between China and the West has the former been so powerful—we had almost said aggressive—as now. For those who will give it careful study, Mr. Faber's work is one of the most valuable of the excellent series to which it belongs."—*Nature.*

Post 8vo, pp. 336, cloth, price 16s.

THE RELIGIONS OF INDIA.

By A. BARTH.

Translated from the French with the authority and assistance of the Author.

The author has, at the request of the publishers, considerably enlarged the work for the translator, and has added the literature of the subject to date ; the translation may, therefore, be looked upon as an equivalent of a new and improved edition of the original.

" Is not only a valuable manual of the religions of India, which marks a distinct step in the treatment of the subject, but also a useful work of reference."—*Academy.*

"This volume is a reproduction, with corrections and additions, of an article contributed by the learned author two years ago to the 'Encyclopédie des Sciences Religieuses.' It attracted much notice when it first appeared, and is generally admitted to present the best summary extant of the vast subject with which it deals."—*Tablet.*

"This is not only on the whole the best but the only manual of the religions of India, apart from Buddhism, which we have in English. The present work . . . shows not only great knowledge of the facts and power of clear exposition, but also great insight into the inner history and the deeper meaning of the great religion, for it is in reality only one, which it proposes to describe."—*Modern Review.*

"The merit of the work has been emphatically recognised by the most authoritative Orientalists, both in this country and on the continent of Europe, But probably there are few Indianists (if we may use the word) who would not derive a good deal of information from it, and especially from the extensive bibliography provided in the notes."—*Dublin Review.*

"Such a sketch M. Barth has drawn with a master-hand."—*Critic (New York).*

Post 8vo, pp. viii.—152, cloth, price 6s.

HINDU PHILOSOPHY.

The SĀNKHYA KĀRIKA of IS'WARA KRISHNA.

An Exposition of the System of Kapila, with an Appendix on the Nyāya and Vais'eshika Systems.

By JOHN DAVIES, M.A. (Cantab.), M.R.A.S.

The system of Kapila contains nearly all that India has produced in the department of pure philosophy.

"The non-Orientalist . . . finds in Mr. Davies a patient and learned guide who leads him into the intricacies of the philosophy of India, and supplies him with a clue, that he may not be lost in them. In the preface he states that the system of Kapila is the 'earliest attempt on record to give an answer, from reason alone, to the mysterious questions which arise in every thoughtful mind about the origin of the world, the nature and relations of man and his future destiny,' and in his learned and able notes he exhibits 'the connection of the Sankhya system with the philosophy of Spinoza,' and 'the connection of the system of Kapila with that of Schopenhauer and Von Hartmann.' "—*Foreign Church Chronicle.*

"Mr. Davies's volume on Hindu Philosophy is an undoubted gain to all students of the development of thought. The system of Kapila, which is here given in a translation from the Sānkhya Kārikā, is the only contribution of India to pure philosophy. . . . Presents many points of deep interest to the student of comparative philosophy, and without Mr. Davies's lucid interpretation it would be difficult to appreciate these points in any adequate manner."—*Saturday Review.*

"We welcome Mr. Davies's book as a valuable addition to our philosophical library."—*Notes and Queries.*

Post 8vo, pp. x.—130, cloth, price 6s.

A MANUAL OF HINDU PANTHEISM. VEDÂNTASÂRA.

Translated, with copious Annotations, by MAJOR G. A. JACOB,
Bombay Staff Corps ; Inspector of Army Schools.

The design of this little work is to provide for missionaries, and for
others who, like them, have little leisure for original research, an accurate
summary of the doctrines of the Vedânta.

"There can be no question that the religious doctrines most widely held by the
people of India are mainly Pantheistic. And of Hindu Pantheism, at all events in
its most modern phases, its Vedântasâra presents the best summary. But then this
work is a mere summary : a skeleton, the dry bones of which require to be clothed
with skin and bones, and to be animated by vital breath before the ordinary reader
will discern in it a living reality. Major Jacob, therefore, has wisely added to his
translation of the Vedântasâra copious notes from the writings of well-known Oriental
scholars, in which he has, we think, elucidated all that required elucidation. So
that the work, as here presented to us, presents no difficulties which a very moderate
amount of application will not overcome."—*Tablet.*

"The modest title of Major Jacob's work conveys but an inadequate idea of the
vast amount of research embodied in his notes to the text of the Vedantasara. So
copious, indeed, are these, and so much collateral matter do they bring to bear on
the subject, that the diligent student will rise from their perusal with a fairly
adequate view of Hindû philosophy generally. His work . . . is one of the best of
its kind that we have seen."—*Calcutta Review.*

Post 8vo, pp. xii.—154, cloth, price 7s. 6d.

TSUNI—||GOAM :

THE SUPREME BEING OF THE KHOI-KHOI.

BY THEOPHILUS HAHN, Ph.D.,

Custodian of the Grey Collection, Cape Town ; Corresponding Member
of the Geogr. Society, Dresden ; Corresponding Member of the
Anthropological Society, Vienna, &c., &c.

"The first instalment of Dr. Hahn's labours will be of interest, not at the Cape
only, but in every University of Europe. It is, in fact, a most valuable contribution
to the comparative study of religion and mythology. Accounts of their religion and
mythology were scattered about in various books ; these have been carefully collected by Dr. Hahn and printed in his second chapter, enriched and improved by
what he has been able to collect himself."—*Prof. Max Müller in the Nineteenth
Century.*

"Dr. Hahn's book is that of a man who is both a philologist and believer in
philological methods, and a close student of savage manners and customs."—*Saturday Review.*

"It is full of good things."—*St. James's Gazette.*

In Four Volumes. Post 8vo, Vol. I., pp. xii.—392, cloth, price 12s. 6d.,
and Vol. II., pp. vi.—408, cloth, price 12s. 6d.

A COMPREHENSIVE COMMENTARY TO THE QURAN.

TO WHICH IS PREFIXED SALE'S PRELIMINARY DISCOURSE, WITH
ADDITIONAL NOTES AND EMENDATIONS.

Together with a Complete Index to the Text, Preliminary
Discourse, and Notes.

By Rev. E. M. WHERRY, M.A., Lodiana.

"As Mr. Wherry's book is intended for missionaries in India, it is no doubt well
that they should be prepared to meet, if they can, the ordinary arguments and inter-
pretations, and for this purpose Mr. Wherry's additions will prove useful."—*Saturday
Review.*

Post 8vo, pp. vi.—208, cloth, price 8s. 6d.

THE BHAGAVAD-GÎTÂ.

Translated, with Introduction and Notes

By JOHN DAVIES, M.A. (Cantab.)

"Let us add that his translation of the Bhagavad Gîtâ is, as we judge, the best that has as yet appeared in English, and that his Philological Notes are of quite peculiar value."—*Dublin Review.*

Post 8vo, pp. 96, cloth, price 5s.

THE QUATRAINS OF OMAR KHAYYAM.

Translated by E. H. WHINFIELD, M.A.,
Barrister-at-Law, late H.M. Bengal Civil Service.

Omar Khayyám (the tent-maker) was born about the middle of the fifth century of the Hejirah, corresponding to the eleventh of the Christian era, in the neighbourhood of Naishapur, the capital of Khorasán, and died in 517 A.H. (=1122 A.D.)

"Mr. Whinfield has executed a difficult task with considerable success, and his version contains much that will be new to those who only know Mr. Fitzgerald's delightful selection."—*Academy.*

"There are several editions of the Quatrains, varying greatly in their readings. Mr. Whinfield has used three of these for his excellent translation. The most prominent features in the Quatrains are their profound agnosticism, combined with a fatalism based more on philosophic than religious grounds, their Epicureanism and the spirit of universal tolerance and charity which animates them."—*Calcutta Review.*

Post 8vo, pp. xxiv.—268, cloth, price 9s.

THE PHILOSOPHY OF THE UPANISHADS AND ANCIENT INDIAN METAPHYSICS.

As exhibited in a series of Articles contributed to the *Calcutta Review.*

By ARCHIBALD EDWARD GOUGH, M.A., Lincoln College, Oxford;
Principal of the Calcutta Madrasa.

"For practical purposes this is perhaps the most important of the works that have thus far appeared in 'Trübner's Oriental Series.' . . . We cannot doubt that for all who may take it up the work must be one of profound interest."—*Saturday Review.*

In Two Volumes. Vol. I., post 8vo, pp. xxiv.—230, cloth, price 7s. 6d.

A COMPARATIVE HISTORY OF THE EGYPTIAN AND MESOPOTAMIAN RELIGIONS.

By DR. C. P. TIELE.

Vol. I.—HISTORY OF THE EGYPTIAN RELIGION.

Translated from the Dutch with the Assistance of the Author.

By JAMES BALLINGAL.

"It places in the hands of the English readers a history of Egyptian Religion which is very complete, which is based on the best materials, and which has been illustrated by the latest results of research. In this volume there is a great deal of information, as well as independent investigation, for the trustworthiness of which Dr. Tiele's name is in itself a guarantee; and the description of the successive religion under the Old Kingdom, the Middle Kingdom, and the New Kingdom, is given in a manner which is scholarly and minute."—*Scotsman.*

Post 8vo, pp. xii.—302, cloth, price 8s. 6d.

YUSUF AND ZULAIKHA.

A POEM BY JAMI.

Translated from the Persian into English Verse.

By RALPH T. H. GRIFFITH.

" Mr. Griffith, who has done already good service as translator into verse from the Sanskrit, has done further good work in this translation from the Persian, and he has evidently shown not a little skill in his rendering the quaint and very oriental style of his author into our more prosaic, less figurative, language. . . . The work, besides its intrinsic merits, is of importance as being one of the most popular and famous poems of Persia, and that which is read in all the independent native schools of India where Persian is taught. It is interesting, also, as a striking instance of the manner in which the stories of the Jews have been transformed and added to by tradition among the Mahometans, who look upon Joseph as ' the ideal of manly beauty and more than manly virtue ; ' and, indeed, in this poem he seems to be endowed with almost divine, or at any rate angelic, gifts and excellence."—*Scotsman.*

Post 8vo, pp. viii.—266, cloth, price 9s.

LINGUISTIC ESSAYS.

By CARL ABEL.

CONTENTS.

Language as the Expression of National Modes of Thought.	The Connection between Dictionary and Grammar.
The Conception of Love in some Ancient and Modern Languages.	The Possibility of a Common Literary Language for all Slavs.
The English Verbs of Command.	The Order and Position of Words in the Latin Sentence.
Semasiology.	The Coptic Language.
Philological Methods.	

The Origin of Language.

" All these essays of Dr. Abel's are so thoughtful, so full of happy illustrations, and so admirably put together, that we hardly know to which we should specially turn to select for our readers a sample of his workmanship."—*Tablet.*

" An entirely novel method of dealing with philosophical questions and impart a real human interest to the otherwise dry technicalities of the science."—*Standard.*

" Dr. Abel is an opponent from whom it is pleasant to differ, for he writes with enthusiasm and temper, and his mastery over the English language fits him to be a champion of unpopular doctrines."—*Athenæum.*

" Dr. Abel writes very good English, and much of his book will prove entertaining to the general reader. It may give some useful hints, and suggest some subjects for profitable investigation, even to philologists."—*Nation (New York).*

Post 8vo, pp. ix.—281, cloth, price 10s. 6d.

THE SARVA-DARSANA-SAMGRAHA ;

OR, REVIEW OF THE DIFFERENT SYSTEMS OF HINDU PHILOSOPHY.

By MADHAVA ACHARYA.

Translated by E. B. COWELL, M.A., Professor of Sanskrit in the University of Cambridge, and A. E. GOUGH, M.A., Professor of Philosophy in the Presidency College, Calcutta.

This work is an interesting specimen of Hindu critical ability. The author successively passes in review the sixteen philosophical systems current in the fourteenth century in the South of India ; and he gives what appears to him to be their most important tenets.

" The translation is trustworthy throughout. A protracted sojourn in India, where there is a living tradition, has familiarised the translators with Indian thought."—*Athenæum.*

Post 8vo, pp. xxxii.—336, cloth, price 10s. 6d.

THE QUATRAINS OF OMAR KHAYYAM.

The Persian Text, with an English Verse Translation.

By E. H. WHINFIELD, late of the Bengal Civil Service.

Post 8vo, pp. lxv.—368, cloth, price 14s.

TIBETAN TALES DERIVED FROM INDIAN SOURCES.

Translated from the Tibetan of the KAH-GYUR.

BY F. ANTON VON SCHIEFNER.

Done into English from the German, with an Introduction,

BY W. R. S. RALSTON, M.A.

"Mr. Ralston adds an introduction, which even the most persevering children of Mother Goose will probably find infinitely the most interesting portion of the work." —*Saturday Review.*

"Mr. Ralston, whose name is so familiar to all lovers of Russian folk-lore, has supplied some interesting Western analogies and parallels, drawn, for the most part, from Slavonic sources, to the Eastern folk-tales, culled from the Kahgyur, one of the divisions of the Tibetan sacred books."—*Academy.*

"The translation . . . could scarcely have fallen into better hands. An Introduction . . . gives the leading facts in the lives of those scholars who have given their attention to gaining a knowledge of the Tibetan literature and language."—*Calcutta Review.*

"Ought to interest all who care for the East, for amusing stories, or for comparative folk-lore. Mr. Ralston . . . is an expert in story-telling, and in knowledge of the comparative history of popular tales he has few rivals in England."—*Pall Mall Gazette.*

Post 8vo, pp. xvi.—224, cloth, price 9s.

UDÂNAVARGA.

A COLLECTION OF VERSES FROM THE BUDDHIST CANON.

Compiled by DHARMATRÂTA.

BEING THE NORTHERN BUDDHIST VERSION OF DHAMMAPADA.

Translated from the Tibetan of Bkah-hgyur, with Notes, and Extracts from the Commentary of Pradjnavarman,

By W. WOODVILLE ROCKHILL.

"Mr. Rockhill's present work is the first from which assistance will be gained for a more accurate understanding of the Pali text; it is, in fact, as yet the only term of comparison available to us. The 'Udanavarga,' the Thibetan version, was originally discovered by the late M. Schiefner, who published the Tibetan text, and had intended adding a translation, an intention frustrated by his death, but which has been carried out by Mr. Rockhill. . . . Mr. Rockhill may be congratulated for having well accomplished a difficult task."—*Saturday Review.*

"There is no need to look far into this book to be assured of its value."—*Athenæum.*

"The Tibetan verses in Mr. Woodville Rockhill's translation have all the simple directness and force which belong to the sayings of Gautama, when they have not been adorned and spoiled by enthusiastic disciples and commentators."—*St. James's Gazette.*

In Two Volumes, post 8vo, pp. xxiv.—566, cloth, accompanied by a Language Map, price 25s.

A SKETCH OF THE MODERN LANGUAGES OF AFRICA.

By ROBERT NEEDHAM CUST,

Barrister-at-Law, and late of Her Majesty's Indian Civil Service.

"Any one at all interested in African languages cannot do better than get Mr. Cust's book. It is encyclopædic in its scope, and the reader gets a start clear away in any particular language, and is left free to add to the initial sum of knowledge there collected."—*Natal Mercury.*

"Mr. Cust has contrived to produce a work of value to linguistic students."— *Nature.*

"Mr. Cust's experience in the preparation of his previous work on the indigenous tongues of the East Indies was, of course, of great help to him in the attempt to map out the still more thorny and tangled brake of the African languages. His great support, however, in what must have been a task of immense labour and care has been the unflagging enthusiasm and gusto with which he has flung himself into his subject."—*Scotsman.*

Post 8vo, pp. xii.—312, with Maps and Plan, cloth, price 14s.
A HISTORY OF BURMA.
Including Burma Proper, Pegu, Taungu, Tenasserim, and Arakan. From
the Earliest Time to the End of the First War with British India.
By Lieut.-Gen. Sir ARTHUR P. PHAYRE, G.C.M.G., K.C.S.I., and C.B.,
Membre Correspondant de la Société Académique Indo-Chinoise
de France.

"Sir Arthur Phayre's contribution to Trübner's Oriental Series supplies a recognised want, and its appearance has been looked forward to for many years. . . . .
General Phayre deserves great credit for the patience and industry which has resulted,
in this History of Burma."—*Saturday Review.*

"A laborious work, carefully performed, which supplies a blank in the long list of
histories of countries, and records the annals, unknown to literature, of a nation
which is likely to be more prominent in the commerce of the future."—*Scotsman.*

Third Edition. Post 8vo, pp. 276, cloth, price 7s. 6d.
RELIGION IN CHINA.
By JOSEPH EDKINS, D.D., Peking.
Containing a Brief Account of the Three Religions of the Chinese, with
Observations on the Prospects of Christian Conversion amongst that
People.

"Dr. Edkins has been most careful in noting the varied and often complex phases
of opinion, so as to give an account of considerable value of the subject."—*Scotsman.*

"As a missionary, it has been part of Dr. Edkins' duty to study the existing
religions in China, and his long residence in the country has enabled him to acquire
an intimate knowledge of them as they at present exist."—*Saturday Review.*

"Dr. Edkins' valuable work, of which this is a second and revised edition, has,
from the time that it was published, been the standard authority upon the subject
of which it treats."—*Nonconformist.*

"Dr. Edkins . . . may now be fairly regarded as among the first authorities on
Chinese religion and language."—*British Quarterly Review.*

Third Edition. Post 8vo, pp. xv.-250, cloth, price 7s. 6d.
OUTLINES OF THE HISTORY OF RELIGION TO THE SPREAD OF THE UNIVERSAL RELIGIONS.
By C. P. TIELE,
Doctor of Theology, Professor of the History of Religions in the
University of Leyden.
Translated from the Dutch by J. Estlin Carpenter, M.A.

"Few books of its size contain the result of so much wide thinking, able and laborious study, or enable the reader to gain a better bird's-eye view of the latest results
of investigations into the religious history of nations. As Professor Tiele modestly
says, 'In this little book are outlines—pencil sketches, I might say—nothing more.'
But there are some men whose sketches from a thumb-nail are of far more worth
than an enormous canvas covered with the crude painting of others, and it is easy to
see that these pages, full of information, these sentences, cut and perhaps also dry,
short and clear, condense the fruits of long and thorough research."—*Scotsman.*

Post 8vo, pp. x.-274, cloth, price 9s.
THE LIFE OF THE BUDDHA AND THE EARLY HISTORY OF HIS ORDER.
Derived from Tibetan Works in the Bkah-hgyur and Bstan-hgyur.
Followed by notices on the Early History of Tibet and Khoten.
Translated by W. W. ROCKHILL, Second Secretary U.S. Legation in China.

"The volume bears testimony to the diligence and fulness with which the author
has consulted and tested the ancient documents bearing upon his remarkable subject."—*Times.*

"Will be appreciated by those who devote themselves to those Buddhist studies
which have of late years taken in these Western regions so remarkable a development. Its matter possesses a special interest as being derived from ancient Tibetan
works, some portions of which, here analysed and translated, have not yet attracted
the attention of scholars. The volume is rich in ancient stories bearing upon the
world's renovation and the origin of castes, as recorded in these venerable authorities."—*Daily News.*

In Two Volumes, post 8vo, pp. cviii.-242, and viii.-370, cloth, price 24s.
Dedicated by permission to H.R.H. the Prince of Wales.

BUDDHIST RECORDS OF THE WESTERN WORLD,

Translated from the Chinese of Hiuen Tsiang (A.D. 629).

By SAMUEL BEAL, B.A.,

(Trin. Coll., Camb.); R.N. (Retired Chaplain and N.I.); Professor of Chinese,
University College, London; Rector of Wark, Northumberland, &c.

An eminent Indian authority writes respecting this work :—"Nothing
more can be done in elucidating the History of India until Mr. Beal's translation of the 'Si-yu-ki' appears."

" It is a strange freak of historical preservation that the best account of the condition of India at that ancient period has come down to us in the books of travel
written by the Chinese pilgrims, of whom Hwen Thsang is the best known."—*Times.*

" We are compelled at this stage to close our brief and inadequate notice of a book
for easy access to which Orientalists will be deeply grateful to the able translator."—
Literary World.

" Full of interesting revelations of the religious feelings, fables, and superstitions, manners and habits of peoples inhabiting a vast region, comprising North
and North-Western India and contiguous countries in that remote and obscure
period."—*Daily News.*

Third Edition. Post 8vo, pp. viii.-464, cloth, price 16s.

THE SANKHYA APHORISMS OF KAPILA,

With Illustrative Extracts from the Commentaries.

Translated by J. R. BALLANTYNE, LL.D., late Principal of the Benares
College.

Edited by FITZEDWARD HALL.

Post 8vo, pp. xlviii.-398, cloth, price 12s.

THE ORDINANCES OF MANU.

Translated from the Sanskrit, with an Introduction.

By the late A. C. BURNELL, Ph.D., C.I.E.

Completed and Edited by E. W. HOPKINS, Ph.D.,
of Columbia College, N.Y.

" This work is full of interest; while for the student of sociology and the science
of religion it is full of importance. It is a great boon to get so notable a work in so
accessible a form, admirably edited, and competently translated."—*Scotsman.*

" Few men were more competent than Burnell to give us a really good translation
of this well-known law book, first rendered into English by Sir William Jones.
Burnell was not only an independent Sanskrit scholar, but an experienced lawyer,
and he joined to these two important qualifications the rare faculty of being able to
express his thoughts in clear and trenchant English. . . . We ought to feel very
grateful to Dr. Hopkins for having given us all that could be published of the translation left by Burnell."—F. MAX MÜLLER in the *Academy.*

LONDON: TRÜBNER & CO., 57 AND 59 LUDGATE HILL.

500—16/2/85—K.

TRÜBNER'S

ORIENTAL SERIES.

ALEXANDER CSOMA DE KÖRÖS.

NÖRÖ

. . LI KA . . . . .
. . . .
. . . .
. . . .
. . . . IS OF . . . .

. . CO., L. . . ATE HILL.

18..

LIFE AND WORKS

OF

ALEXANDER CSOMA DE KÖRÖS.

A Biography compiled chiefly from hitherto
Unpublished Data;

WITH

*A BRIEF NOTICE OF EACH OF HIS PUBLISHED WORKS
AND ESSAYS, AS WELL AS OF HIS STILL
EXTANT MANUSCRIPTS.*

BY

THEODORE DUKA, M.D.

FELLOW OF THE ROYAL COLLEGE OF SURGEONS OF ENGLAND;
SURGEON-MAJOR HER MAJESTY'S BENGAL MEDICAL SERVICE, RETIRED;
KNIGHT OF THE ORDER OF THE IRON CROWN;
CORRESPONDING MEMBER OF THE ACADEMY OF SCIENCES OF HUNGARY.

LONDON:
TRÜBNER & CO., LUDGATE HILL.
1885.

𝕭𝖆𝖑𝖑𝖆𝖓𝖙𝖞𝖓𝖊 𝕻𝖗𝖊𝖘𝖘
BALLANTYNE, HANSON AND CO.
EDINBURGH AND LONDON

PREFACE.

SCANTY as are the authentic data from which this biography was compiled, they form, nevertheless, a connected narrative of the chief events in the life of a remarkable man of science, who, although a foreigner, never published anything but in the English tongue. Few, if any, foreign savants have been honoured by Englishmen as he was; a fact to which the memorial standing over his grave bears ample testimony.

It is hoped that the reader will follow with sympathy the details of an arduous scientific career, the best years of which were offered to the service of the British Government, and will agree with us also in thinking that Alexander Csoma de Körös attained in some measure the reward he looked for, in so far that his name will never be omitted from any work bearing upon Tibetan literature or Buddhistic learning.

This biography is herewith presented to the reader in the sincere hope of a generous indulgence for its many shortcomings, although the production of it, imperfect as it is, has, in the circumstances under which it was prepared, necessitated the attention of many years before it could be brought to its present state of completion.

When the late Mr. Nicholas Trübner first saw the manuscript of this book, he at once kindly expressed his readiness to undertake its publication, and even suggested the desirability of editing a complete collection of all the works and essays of Csoma de Körös, which, at the present time, are only to be found scattered over many volumes of publications, extending over a period of more than thirty years. Perhaps Mr. Trübner's successors may see their way to carry out the project he had in view, and to rescue, for the benefit of European students, the important work in manuscript which is noticed in the Appendix xvi. at page 207 of this volume.

The reader will observe that a certain latitude has been permitted in the spelling of Indian names and Tibetan words occurring in this work. In the text Dr. Hunter's system has been generally followed, but in the quotations, both from print and manuscripts, the ancient forms of spelling have in most cases been retained. As to the Tibetan words Csoma's authority was decisive; moreover, instead of adhering invariably to the strict rules of Tibetan orthography, with its frequent use of mute letters, the abbreviated forms have been preferred. The strict rendering of accents and diacritical marks seemed hardly requisite in a work like this.

The author desires to express his acknowledgments to Mr. Frederic Pincott, M.R.A.S., for important assistance rendered by him in reviewing and passing through the press the Sanskrit and Hindi part of the vocabulary at the end of the volume.

LONDON, 55 NEVERN SQUARE,
SOUTH KENSINGTON, *February* 1885.

CHAPTER V.

PAGES

Embarrassing situation — Csoma petitions Government to be
allowed to visit Calcutta, or to go to Tibet for three years
more to complete his studies 73–78

CHAPTER VI.

Government orders on Csoma's last application—Third journey
into Tibet to Upper Besarh—Dr. Gerard's visit to Kanum,
and his letter to Mr. W. Fraser on the subject . . . 79–98

CHAPTER VII.

Csoma completes his Tibetan studies at Kanum—Correspondence
with Dr. Horace Hayman Wilson, Captain Kennedy, and
Mr. Brian H. Hodgson 99–111

CHAPTER VIII.

Csoma's arrival in Calcutta—Resolution of Government of India
as to the publication of his works—Was elected Honorary
Member of the Asiatic Society of Bengal 112–118

CHAPTER IX.

The Tibet Grammar and Dictionary are published at Government
expense—Mr. Prinsep's letter to Government on the subject
—Prince Eszterházy to Mr. James Prinsep—Mr. Döbrentei,
of Pest, to the same 119–130

CHAPTER X.

Csoma applies for a passport in November 1835 to enable him to
travel in Hindustan — Leaves Calcutta—His last letters to
Mr. Prinsep — Return to Calcutta in 1837 — Dr. Malan,
Secretary of the Asiatic Society of Bengal 131-142

CHAPTER XI.

PAGES

Csoma's stay in Calcutta as Librarian to the Asiatic Society
of Bengal from 1837-1842—Last arrangements—His be-
quest to the Asiatic Society of Bengal—Leaves Calcutta
for the last time—Sets out on his journey to Lassa—Death
at Darjeeling—Dr. Archibald Campbell's report to the Secretary of Government—Csoma's grave and tombstone . . 143-162

CHAPTER XII.

Prince Eszterházy's inquiries regarding Csoma's papers—List of
some of them—Renewal of his tombstone at Darjeeling,
which is placed on the list of public monuments by Government—His portrait—Conclusion 163-167

APPENDIX.

PAGE

List of Csoma's works 169

I. Analysis of the Kahgyur and Stangyur 170

II. Geographical notice of Tibet 176

III. Translation of a Tibetan fragment 179

IV. Note on Kala-Chakra and Adi-Buddha Systems . . . 181

V. Translation of a Tibetan passport 182

VI. Origin of the Shakya race 182

VII. Mode of expressing numerals in Tibetan 186

VIII. Extracts from Tibetan works 189

IX. Interpretation of the Tibetan inscription on a Bhotian banner
taken in Assam 193

X. Note on the white satin-embroidered scarfs of the Tibetan
priests 194

XI. Notices on different systems of Buddhism extracted from
Tibetan authorities 195

PAGE

XII. Enumeration of historical and grammatical works to be met
with in Tibet 198

XIII. Remarks on amulets in use by the Trans-Himalayan Buddhists 199

XIV. Review of a Tibetan medical work 201

XV. Brief notice of Subháshita Ratna Nidhi of Saskya Pandita 205

XVI. A Manuscript Dictionary of Sanskrit and Tibetan words,
phrases, and technical terms 207

XVII. A Comparative Vocabulary of Sanskrit, Hindi, Hungarian,
&c., words and names. A fragment 217

LIFE OF

ALEXANDER CSOMA DE KÖRÖS.

———•———

CHAPTER I.

Introduction—Csoma's birthplace, parentage, and early childhood—
Studies at Nagy Enyed in Transylvania, and at the University
of Göttingen in Hanover—Plans and preparations for the journey—Departure for the East.

TOWARDS the end of 1843 Dr. Archibald Campbell, the
Government Agent of British Sikkim, wrote as follows :—
"Since the death of Csoma de Körös I have not ceased to
hope that some member of the Asiatic Society (of Bengal)
would furnish a connected account of his career in the
East. It is now more than a year and a half since we lost
him, but we are as yet without any such record in the
Journal of the Society, to show, that his labours were valuable to the literary Association, he so earnestly studied to
assist in its most important objects."

It was Dr. Campbell who, in April 1842, watched the
closing scenes of Csoma's life at Darjeeling, and his was
the friendly hand, which performed the last services at
his grave.

The 4th of April 1884 was the hundredth anniversary
of Csoma's birthday, and the Hungarian Academy of
Sciences thought this a fitting occasion to render homage
to that distinguished man of science, who was a Fellow
of their Society. The method of commemoration which

A

suggested itself was the publication of a collected edition of his scattered works and essays, translated into the Hungarian language, and accompanied by a biographical sketch. In the compilation of this sketch, advantage has been taken of the disjointed and imperfect data which have as yet appeared on the subject; and at the same time important facts have been brought forward which had previously remained unknown.

In the archives of the Foreign Office in Calcutta, many letters are to be found which refer to Csoma de Körös and to his Tibetan labours, during the prosecution of which he enjoyed the support of the Supreme Government of India. Copies of these letters have been placed at the writer's service by the courtesy of Mr. Durand, under-secretary of that department. Six original letters of Csoma have also been found in the library of the Asiatic Society of Bengal, which will be noticed in due course.

The narrative as it now stands will, it is hoped, make those interested in philological science better acquainted with the details of Csoma's early years, and enable them to follow without interruption the steps of his long and arduous wanderings. These were for the most part accomplished on foot, and extended from Europe across Central Asia, Bokhara, through Afghanistan, the Panjab, and Kashmir towards the borders of China, and afterwards into Tibet and Hindustan down to Calcutta.

The motives which led him to devote himself to these literary and historical researches, and the causes which induced him to sacrifice so many years of his life to the study of the Tibetan language and literature, will be set forth on the authority of hitherto unpublished data; and it is confidently expected, that they will clear up many still obscure points in the career of this remarkable student, and dispel the erroneous, and sometimes even unjust, judgments which have been formed regarding his works and merits.

Of Alexander Csoma's early years but few data exist.

According to the parish register he was born on the 4th
of April 1784, in the village of Körös, in the county of
Háromszék, in Transylvania. Körös is situated in a beautiful valley below the town of Kovászna, and its inhabitants carry on a flourishing trade in the manufacture of
sieves (for which there is a special demand), and various articles of fancy woodwork. Körös is a pure Székely
village, where the occupier and the proprietor are one
and the same, where landlords and subject-cultivators
of the soil were never known. It is the only frontier
community in which no Wallachian ever settled.[1] The
house in which Alexander first saw the light was destroyed
by fire, but it is known that the dwelling which at present
bears the number 143 on the village register, was built on
the same plot of ground as the house stood in which
Csoma was born.[2] His father's name was Andrew, and the
mother's Ilona Göcz. His family was poor, but belonged
to the military nobles called Széklers, a tribe which had
for centuries guarded the frontiers of Transylvania against
the invasions of the Turks. Csoma's family is still known
there; one of his nephews, also called Alexander, fell as a
Honvéd in the War of Independence during a street fight
at Nagy Szeben[3] in 1849. Gabriel, his only brother, left a
son, also Alexander by name, who survives. A cousin,
Joseph Csoma, was Protestant pastor in the small village
of Mono, in the county of Middle Szolnok. The proprietor
of the village, Baron Horváth, whilst residing there, met
him almost daily. We learn from this source, that our
Csoma's near relations, and those friends who knew him
in early life, are all dead, and we are therefore unable
to gather much information of the incidents of his
boyhood. Baron Horváth, however, tells us, on the
authority of Joseph Csoma,[4] that Alexander, even as a
boy, showed a keen desire for knowledge, and was of a

[1] The bulk of the people on that
frontier are Wallachians.
[2] See Orbán Balázs : Székelyföld
leirása.

[3] Hermanstadt, in German.
[4] Nemzet, 17th April 1884.

matics, and was in the habit of correcting his Latin
and Hungarian compositions. As regards intellectual
powers, Csoma was not considered in any way a genius,
but rather looked upon as an example of industry and
perseverance.

In 1807, Csoma finished his career at the Gymnasium,
and was promoted to the higher course of academical
studies. At this time the desire to travel in Asia was
kindled in him. As, while attending lectures at the
college, history happened to be a favourite branch of
study, owing to the popularity of Professor Adam Herepei,
the teacher of this subject, it was natural that frequent
and interesting debates and conversations should arise
among the students regarding the ancient history and
origin of the Hungarian people. It is recorded that
Csoma and two of his fellow-pupils had made a vow, to
undertake a scientific journey, with the object of discovering some trace of the origin of their nation. Ten
years later, we find Csoma at the German University of
Göttingen animated by the same desire. Here he came
under the influence of Professor Eichhorn, the celebrated historian and oriental scholar, and under him,
the student's long-cherished design was fully matured.
Csoma used to say that he heard from Eichhorn statements about certain Arabic manuscripts which must
contain very important information regarding the history
of the Middle Ages and of the Hungarian nation when
still in Asia, and that much of these data remained
unknown to European historians. This induced Csoma
to devote himself to the study of Arabic under Eichhorn's
guidance, and made him resolve not to proceed on his
travels until he had studied at Constantinople all the
available Arabic authors on the subject.

Theophylaktes Simocatta, the Greek historian under the
Emperor Mauritius, declares, in the course of his annals of
the war against Persia, that, after dispersing the Avar
hordes, in A.D. 597, the victorious Turks subdued the

Ugars, a brave and numerous nation. On this supposition, certain writers have come to the conclusion that, as there is a similarity in the sound of the words Ugor, Ungri, Hungar, Unger, Hongrois, &c., this long-forgotten tribe might possibly be the ancestors of the Hungarians of the present day. Other writers, again, according to Pavie, have maintained that the Hungarians are an offshoot of the ancient nation of Kiang, which took its wandering steps westward.[1]

We shall find, in Csoma's own account, the special reasons which induced him to decide on prosecuting his specific object. He was made of the right stuff for such an enterprise, for, having once taken the resolution, he was ready to face all the trials and struggles in the way, of the magnitude of which he was duly warned. He deliberately prepared himself for the task, by systematic scientific studies continued over many years, without patronage or pecuniary aid of any kind, beyond Councillor Kenderessy's promise of support, amounting to one hundred florins a-year. The entire sum of his other resources amounted to little more than two hundred florins. "Relying solely," as Hegedüs says, "on Divine Providence and on the unalterable desire to sacrifice his life in the service of his country, he started towards the distant goal," regarding which Csoma pointedly remarks that he "cannot be accounted of the number of those wealthy European gentlemen who travel at their own expense for pleasure and curiosity; being rather only a poor student, who was very desirous to see the different countries of Asia, as the scene of so many memorable transactions of former ages; to observe the manners of several peoples, and to learn their languages, . . . and such a man was he, who, during his peregrinations, depended for his subsistence on the benevolence of others."[2]

But we have still to add a few details to the history of

[1] "Revue des deux Mondes," vol. xix. p. 50 *et seqq.*

[2] Preface to the "Tibetan Dictionary."

his life at Nagy Enyed. After completing his studies there, he was elected Lecturer on Poetry, in which appointment he acquitted himself with credit, to the entire satisfaction of his superiors. On the pages of a manuscript Vocabulary in the library of the Academy of Sciences at Budapest (Appendix XVII.) there are some verses in Hungarian, which tend to show how versification remained always a favourite occupation with him; and his skill therein doubtless cheered the dreary hours during his long sojourn in the Buddhistic monasteries.

We find similar relics of Csoma in the shape of several Greek and Latin distichs, and a French quotation. They are in his handwriting, and found on the back of a portrait of Professor Mitscherlich of Göttingen. This picture, now in the possession of the Hungarian Academy of Sciences, he gave as a memento to his friend, Szabó de Borgáta, who, it is said, was instrumental in inducing Csoma to undertake a journey to the East.

The characteristic quotations are as follows :—

I.

Felix, qui potuit rerum cognoscere causas.—*Virgilius.*

II.

Σὺν Μούσαις¹ τὰ τερπνὰ καὶ τὰ γλυκία
Γίνεται πάντα βροτοῖς
Εἰ σοφὸς, εἰ καλὸς, εἴ τις ἀγλαὸς
Ἀνήρ.

—*Pind. Od.* xiv.

III.

Σμικρὸς ἐν σμικροῖς, μέγας ἐν μεγάλοις
Εστι.

—*Pind. Pyth.* iii.

IV.

C'est par le plaisir et par la vertu que la nature nous invite au bonheur.

V.

Omne tulit punctum qui miscuit utile dulci.—*Horatius.*

---

¹ γὰρ ὑμῖν. Recensione Heyne. Londini, 1823.

VI.

Omnia deficiant, virtus tamen omnia vincit
Per quodvis praeceps ardua vadit iter.
                            —*Ovidius.*

VII.

Sit tibi, quod nunc est, etiam minus ; at tibi vive,
Quod superest aevi, si quid superesse volunt Dî.
                            —*Horatius.*

Scribebam dulcis recordationis ergo,
      Göttingae, die 10° Aprilis, anni 1817.

ALEXANDER KÖRÖSI,[1]
Transylvano—Siculus.[2]

Part of his holidays Csoma was wont to spend as a
private tutor. In 1806 his friend Hegedüs left Nagy
Enyed to take up clerical duties elsewhere; but after an
absence of eight years, on returning to his former pro-
fessorial chair at the old College, he was greeted, on the
part of the students, by Csoma, who then held the
position of Senior Collegian. Hegedüs noticed then,
with much satisfaction, that besides an acquaintance
with general literature, Csoma had made marked progress in the Latin and Greek classics, and had become
familiar with the best works of French and German
authors. In 1815 he passed the public "rigorosum"
in the presence of Professor Hegedüs, by which Csoma
became qualified to continue his studies at an University
abroad.

This is a fitting place to mention a circumstance, of
which probably few Englishmen are aware. It may be

---

[1] The full name in Hungarian is
Körösi Csoma Sándor, which means
in English, Alexander Csoma *of*
Körös. The family name is *Csoma,*
and the word Körösi, meaning *of*
Körös, stands as a designation, to
show that he is a noble of Körös.
Körösi, although an adjective,
may be used either *alone* or as
above, *after* Alexander, but in that
case Csoma must be omitted; that
is to say, Alexander Csoma Körösi
would be a mistake.

The terminal *i* in Körösi means
of, hence *de* cannot stand before
Körösi. When *de* is used, Körös
mus tfollow.

[2] *Siculus* in Latin, *Székely* in
Hungarian, *Székler* in German and
other continental languages.

looked upon as another link in the bond of sympathy which still exists between Hungary and England. History tells us, that in the year 1704, during the Hungarian civil wars, the town of Nagy Enyed and its flourishing college were almost razed to the ground, the students were cut down, and one of the professors was mortally wounded. Not merely the public exchequer but private individuals and the municipal corporations became completely exhausted and ruined, by the long-continued struggle against the Imperialists, under the national leader, Rákóczy, between the years 1703 and 1711. This calamity was the reason why nothing could be done at that time by the Hungarians themselves for Nagy Enyed, and yet the necessity of taking some steps became more urgent day by day. Students in large numbers were applying for admission, but the College authorities were not even in a position to put a roof over the ruins which remained standing, still less to afford that assistance which is so much needed by the Székler youths. The prevailing distress was brought to the knowledge of Queen Anne of England and of the Archbishop of Canterbury, and through them to the English nation. And the cry for help was not in vain. The aristocracy and the citizens of London came forward most liberally, the Archbishop caused collections to be made in the churches for the relief of the distressed; and the result was that a sum, exceeding eleven thousand pounds, was collected and deposited in the Bank of England. A great part of the money remains to this day invested in the 3 per cent. Consols for the benefit of the college, and is managed by the banking firm of Messrs. Herries, Farquhar & Co.

This contribution from England was the basis on which the future material prosperity and intellectual progress of the College of Nagy Enyed was reconstructed after the great national disaster which befell Hungary at the commencement of the eighteenth century. We

may add, that the funds have been most conscientiously
administered, enabling the managers of the College to
found two travelling scholarships in 1816. Csoma de
Körös was one of the first scholars to whom an annual
subsidy of fifteen pounds sterling was allotted, to assist
him whilst studying at the University of Göttingen.
The director of the university boarding-house — the
Alumneum—was then the above-named Professor Eichhorn, and it was from this gentleman's hands that Csoma
used to receive his modest stipend. In that manner, Csoma
was brought into nearer acquaintance with Eichhorn, and
this doubtless had considerable influence over the future
career of the enthusiastic student.

Josef Szabó de Borgáta was a fellow-undergraduate
of Köıösi in Göttingen, and the two students lived in
intimate friendship with each other. This gentleman is
still alive (May 1884), and from him we learn that
they frequently interchanged ideas on their favourite
subject. He recollects that on one occasion Csoma declared before him, that he longed to attain celebrity and
renown.

In the course of this biography we shall repeatedly
have occasion to notice his striving after this worthy
aim, but nowhere more pointedly is it expressed, than in
the lines we find jotted down, in his manuscript Vocabulary already alluded to, where we read as follows:—

"Ardeo cupiditate incredibili, neque enim, ut ego
arbitror, reprehendum est, nomen ut nostrum illustretur
atque celebretur literis Tuis.

"A viro laudato laudari pulchrum est," &c.

We can never hope to discover what particular incident
suggested the above characteristic quotation ; it seems to
refer to circumstances which occurred in later years of
his life, and it is probable that a correspondence with
Wilson, Rémusat, or Klaproth, may have furnished the
occasion.

The study of the English language Csoma began at

he was wending his steps towards a long-desired goal.
We spent some time in friendly conversation, and
drank our parting glass in some old tokaji. Next day,
that is Monday, he again stepped into my room, lightly
clad, as if he intended merely taking a walk. He did not
even sit down, but said, ' I merely wished to see you once
more.' We then started along the Szentkirályi road,
which leads towards Nagy Szeben. Here, in the country
—among the fields—we parted for ever. I looked a long
time after him, as he was approaching the banks of the
Maros, and feelings roused by the words, ' Mentem mor-
talia tangunt,' filled my anxious heart."

In the thirty-sixth year of his age, not in a fit of excite-
ment, but armed with the result of special scientific pre-
paratory studies, pursued over a period of ten years, Csoma
entered on the memorable journey of his life. He saw
clearly his object, and knew what he meant to attain.
We may well say that Csoma belongs to the rank of those
noble minds who devote their lives unselfishly to a worthy,
though apparently thankless object, yet in the pursuit of
which nothing but death will stop their efforts. And if
a pioneer on the unbeaten track meets his fate, as Csoma
did, before reaching the end of his arduous path, what is
due to him from posterity is the laurel wreath, and not
commiseration, for which a man of his stamp always enter-
tains a noble disdain.

CHAPTER II.

Biographical sources — English and French authorities — Baron Hügel's data examined—First news of Csoma in India—His appearance at the frontier—Detained at Sabathú—Csoma's first letter to Captain Kennedy—Moorcroft's introduction.

WE have two main sources on which to rely for data referring to the details of our traveller's career, after he started for the East, apart from what he wrote himself on the subject.

The first source of information comprises the notices published by his English friends and by Monsieur Pavie in the "Revue des deux Mondes" for 1849. The most important among them is doubtless that, which we owe to Dr. Horace Hayman Wilson. It appeared in the "Journal of the Royal Asiatic Society" in 1834, and consists of an abridgment of the letter which Csoma addressed to Captain Kennedy in January 1825. This communication was frequently cited by his own countrymen as the earliest authentic source of information from India, concerning the Tibetan scholar, and has again recently been noticed (conjointly with Dr. Archibald Campbell's report of 1842) in one of the leading weekly journals, "The Vasárnapi Ujság" of Budapest, when reviewing Mr. Ralston's "Tibetan Tales."[1] The preface of this book contains a letter from the celebrated orientalist, Professor Arminius Vambéry, dated 20th February 1882, addressed to that author, to which we shall have occasion to refer at a later period.

[1] "Tibetan Tales," by W. R. S. Ralston, M.A. Trübner & Co., London, 1882.

which costume he wore at Sabathú, and ever afterwards, the hot Indian sun notwithstanding."

Eötvös continues to communicate other details on the strength of his information, and concludes:

" A great trial, however, was in store for Csoma in his new sphere of action at Calcutta. After having communicated the result of his labours to others, and heard from them that the Tibetan language, to the study of which he had sacrificed the best part of his life, was but a *corrupt dialect* of *the Sanskrit*, his heart was filled with undescribable anguish, and the strong man, who suffered so many privations cheerfully and without complaining, was prostrated on a bed of sickness by this new discovery."

It will be our duty to show that these allegations have no foundation whatever in fact. The same must be said of what we read further on in Eötvös's speech, namely, "that Csoma had prepared his extracts from Tibetan works in *Latin*."

Baron Hügel, we know, was in Calcutta in 1835. Csoma's Dictionary and Grammar were published in 1834; if, therefore, Baron Hügel had thought of it, he might easily have gathered correct information regarding the progress of Oriental literature. Csoma's merits were then fully acknowledged by the Government and by the learned world.

The statement that Csoma spent *eleven years in a Buddhistic monastery at Kanaur* is quite inaccurate, as appears from the following data:—

In the monastery *at Yangla* in Zanskar, Csoma lived from 20th June 1823 to 22d October 1824.

In the monastery *at Pukdal or Pukhtar*, also in Zanskar, he remained from 12th August *1825 to November 1826*.

At Kanum, in Upper Besarh, also written Bussahir, Besahir, from August 1827 to October 1830.

It is also an error to say that Tibetan is a subordinate dialect of Sanskrit. It belongs to the Chinese group of languages. This has been pointed out already by Giorgi, about the middle of the last century, in his work the "Alphabetum Tibetanum,"[1] and this was precisely the book which Moorcroft gave into the hands of the Hungarian traveller in 1823, from which Csoma obtained his first glimpses of that language.

Csoma arrived in Calcutta at the end of April 1831. In his letter to Captain Kennedy, which will be found further on, dated 25th January 1825, para. 17, we find in regard to the Tibetan works and literature the following remark : "They ALL are *taken from Indian Sanskrit, and were translated into Tibetan.*" This disposes of the charge against Csoma and his alleged ignorance as to the linguistic relationship between Tibetan and Sanskrit, the discovery of which, *eight years later,* is said to have caused him a "*dangerous illness in Calcutta.*"

The mere mention of Csoma's dressing himself up at Sabathú, at the "Governor's" request, in his national costume, will elicit a smile, and we may well ask how a poor wanderer through the immense distances of Central Asia and Tibet was able to carry with him on a journey, already of five years' duration, his Hungarian costume, in which to appear on festive occasions?

But on the matter of Csoma's dress we have the following statements :—

In the oft-quoted letter to Captain Kennedy, para. 7, he writes, "*From Teheran I travelled as an Armenian*" (in 1821). Moorcroft, in his Diary, edited by Dr. Wilson, mentions on the 16th July 1823, "On my journey to Dras, I was met by Alexander Csoma de Körös, an European, in the *garb of an Armenian,* who had travelled from Hungary to Tibet." Dr. Gerard, writing from Kanum in September 1829, says, "Csoma is poor and humbly clad, and dresses in the coarse blanket of the country." See also letter from Captain Stacy to Dr. Wilson, dated 3d August 1829. In Dr. Campbell's report on Csoma's

[1] See "Alphabetum Tibetanum, studio et labore, Fr. Augustini Antonii Georgii." Romæ, 1762, pag. 820.

of Yarkand to the borders of China, and there to become acquainted with the Mongolian languages, he thought that these latter would serve his purpose better than any other. He certainly was not *then* a master of Sanskrit, his original or final aim of research not being India, but China, especially Mongolia. But when he seriously commenced the study of Tibetan, and had also come across numerous elementary Sanskrit and Tibetan works, of which we find special mention in his writings, can it be reasonably supposed, that the ever-eager and indefatigable student, would have neglected such opportunities as presented themselves to him, and have remained entirely ignorant of the Sanskrit language for so many years, which, as he tells us at the outset of his new study, was the basis of all Tibetan learning? So far from this being the case, his letters to Captain Kennedy furnish ample proofs to the contrary. For instance, in his second letter to Captain Kennedy, para. 12, we read as follows:—"Besides the vocabulary which I have now by me, . . . I have another large collection of words in Sanskrit and Tibetan." This clearly establishes our surmise, that long before 1825 Csoma devoted serious attention to Sanskrit; indeed, how otherwise could he have written his report of 1825 to Government, through Captain Kennedy?

Csoma's principal trait of character was his regrettable diffidence—almost, we might say, an overstrained *vaunting* of ignorance—and his own too modest estimate of himself. This has often served as justification for disparaging his unique accomplishments. Of this, Prinsep, Gerard, and Campbell bear frequent testimony; and even Henry Torrens, who knew him less than those just mentioned, notices that "Csoma's exceeding diffidence, on subjects on which he might have dictated to the learned world of Europe and Asia, was the most surprising trait in him."[1] Under these circumstances, to avoid misunder-

---

[1] "Journal of the Asiatic Society of Bengal," vol. ii., 1844, note to Dr. Campbell's paper.

standing and to correct false impressions which have prevailed, it seems necessary that, instead of mere extracts, we should lay before our readers some of the correspondence and other documents without curtailment.

In November 1824, our traveller appeared on the northwest frontier of the British possessions, and reported his arrival to Captain Kennedy, the commanding officer at Sabathú. The correspondence which passed at that time between the authorities and the traveller is of much interest.

Captain Kennedy wrote to the Assistant Political Agent at Umbála, on the 28th of November, reporting that "an European traveller, who gives his name as Alexander Csoma de Körös, a subject of Hungary, has arrived at this post. He is particularly introduced to my notice by Mr. Moorcroft, whose letter I herewith enclose. Mr. Csoma de Körös remains here at present, and waits the arrival of a Lama, whom he expects in a few days, to proceed with him towards Tibet. I request your instructions regarding this gentleman's movements."

To this the following answer was received the next day:—

"Be good enough to detain the European traveller at Sabathú until instructions of the agent to the Governor-General at Delhi can be received regarding him."

From the following it will appear that Lord Amherst gave orders that Csoma be requested to give a complete account of himself and of his plans, and to submit the same through Captain Kennedy.

Csoma's letter, dated Sabathú, 28th January 1825, will be found below; it is the same as that which, in an abridged form and in a different shape, was published in the first number of the "Journal of the Royal Asiatic Society of London" in 1834, to which allusion has already been made:

" To Captain C. P. Kennedy, Assistant Political Agent
and Commanding Subathoo.

"SIR,—I beg leave to acknowledge your communication of the Secretary to Government's answer to your letter reporting my arrival at Subathoo, through the Governor-General's agent at Delhi, dated Fort William, 24th December 1824; and since, by the Government's order, it is required from me to give in writing a full and intelligible account of my history and past proceedings, and of my objects and plans for the future, as also of the length to which I propose to carry my Travels and Researches, I have the honour to state, for the information of the Governor-General of India, as follows:—

2. "I am a native of the Siculian[1] nation (a tribe of those Hungarians who settled in ancient Dacia in the fourth century of the Christian era) in the great principality of Transylvania, subject to his Majesty the Emperor of Austria.

3. "Having finished my philological and theological studies in the Bethlen College at N. Enyed in the course of three years, from 1st August 1815 to 5th September 1818, I visited Germany, and by his Imperial Majesty's permission, at the University of Göttingen in Hanover, I frequented several lectures from 11th April 1816 to the last of July 1818; and on my request to the Government of Hanover, I was also for·one year favoured there with *Libera mensa regia.*

4. "As in Transylvania there are no Sclavonick people, and the learned men of that country are generally unacquainted with that language, although it would be necessary for consulting Sclavonian authors on the ancient history of the Hungarians that are surrounded from all parts by nations of Sclavonick extraction—after being acquainted with several ancient and modern languages, I was desirous to learn the Sclavonick also. For this purpose, after my return from Germany, I went to Temeswár,

---

[1] Székler, military nobles.

in Lower Hungary; where, from 20th February to 1st November 1819, I was occupied with this language, making also a journey to Agram, in Croatia, for the acquirement of the different dialects.

5. " Among other liberal disciplines, my favourite studies were philology, geography, and history. Although my ecclesiastical studies had prepared me for an honourable employment in my native country, yet my inclinations for the studies mentioned above, induced me to seek for a wider field for their further cultivation. As my parents were dead, and my only brother did not want my assistance, I resolved to leave my native country and to come towards the East, and by some means or other procuring subsistence, to devote my whole life to researches which may be afterwards useful to the learned world of Europe in general, and, in particular, may illustrate some obscure facts in our own history. But as I could not hope to obtain, for this purpose, an Imperial passport, I did also not beg for it. I took a printed Hungarian passport at N. Enyed to come on some pretended business to Bucharest, in Wallachia, and having caused it to be signed by the General Commandant in Hermanstadt, in the last days of November 1819, passing the frontier mountains, entered Wallachia. My intention in going to Bucharest was, after some acquaintance with the Turkish language, to proceed to Constantinople. There was no opportunity for my instruction, nor could I procure any mode, to go directly to Constantinople, therefore:

6. " The 1st of January, 1820, I left Bucharest, and on the 3d, passing the Danube by Rustchuk, I travelled with some Bulgarians, who having brought cotton from Macedonia to that place, returned with unladen horses. After travelling for eight days in rapid marches, we reached Sophia, the capital of Bulgaria, whence, with other Bulgarians, I came in five days to Philipopolis, in Roumelia, or Thrace. I wished now to proceed by Adrianople to Constantinople, but the plague in that place forced me to

descend to Enos, on the coast of the Archipelago. Leaving that place on the 7th of February, I passed in a Greek ship by Chios and Rhodes, and on the last day of February I arrived at Alexandria, in Egypt. My plan was to stop for a certain time either at Alexandria or in Cairo, and to improve myself in the Arabic, with which I was already acquainted in Europe, but on a sudden eruption of the plague I left Egypt, and proceeding on a Syrian ship I came to Larnica, in Cyprus, thence to Sidon, Beyruth, and then, on another vessel, to Tripoli and Latakia, whence, travelling on foot, on the 13th of April I reached Aleppo in Syria. I left that place on the 19th of May, and travelling with various caravans in a simple Asiatic dress, on foot, by Orfa, Merdin, and Mosul, whence by water on a raft. On the 22d July I reached Baghdad. Thence, in August, I addressed a letter, written in Latin, to Mr. Rich, the English resident, who was at that time in Kurdistan, about eight days' journey from Baghdad, giving him intelligence of my arrival and design, and begging his protection. His secretary, Mr. Bellino, assisted me with a dress and with some money, through his friend, Mr. Swoboda, a native of Hungary, with whom I was then lodging, and to whom I was recommended from Aleppo. I left Baghdad on 4th September, and travelling in European costume, on horseback, with a caravan, passing by Kermanshah (where, in the service of Mahomed Ali Mirza, the eldest son of Fateh Ali Shah, king of Persia, were several European military officers), by Hamadan, on 14th October 1820, I arrived at Teheran, the present capital of Persia.

7. "On my arrival I found no Europeans in Teheran, but in the English residence a Persian servant received me with kindness, gave me lodging and some other things that I required. On the 3d of November 1820, in a letter, written in English, addressed to Mr., afterwards Sir Henry Willock, on his return from Tauris, or Tebriz, I represented to him my situation, and acquainted him with my circumstances and intentions. I begged him also for assistance. I am infi-

nitely indebted to Messrs. Henry and George Willock for their kind reception and generosity at my departure (and to them I beg to refer for my character). Through their complaisance I sojourned four months in the capital of Persia, became acquainted grammatically with the Persian, improved myself a little in English, perused several treatises for my purpose, examined many ancient silver coins of the Parthian dynasty. When I left Teheran I left also the European dress, and took the Persian. I deposited there all my books and papers, among others, my testimonial from the University of Göttingen, my passport from Transylvania, and a certificate in Sclavonick on my progress in that language. I gave also to those gentlemen a letter written in Hungarian, addressed to N. Enyed, in Transylvania, for Mr. Joseph Kováts, Professor of Mathematics and Physics, with my humblest request, in case I should die or perish on my road to Bokhara, to be transmitted. Mr. Willock favoured me with Johnson's Dictionary in miniature, and I travelled hereafter as an Armenian.

8. "The 1st of March 1821, I bid adieu to my noble benefactors, and the 18th of April arrived at Meshed, in Khorassan. On account of warlike disturbances in the neighbouring countries, it was the 20th of October ere I could leave that place to proceed in safety, and on the 18th of November I reached safely Bokhara, but, affrighted by frequent exaggerated reports of the approach of a numerous Russian army, after a residence of five days I left Bokhara, where I intended to pass the winter, and with a caravan I came to Balk, Kulm, and thence by Bamian; on 6th of January, 1822, I arrived at Kabool.

9. "As that was not a place for my purpose, and being informed by the Armenians that two European gentlemen were with Mahomed Azim Khan, between Kabool and Peshawur, and in the same time finding an opportunity to travel securely with a caravan, I left Kabool 19th January, and came towards Peshawur. At Daka, the 26th January, I met two French gentlemen, Messrs. Allard and Ventura,

whom afterwards I accompanied to Lahore, because it was not the proper season to go to Kashmir and to cross the mountains into Tibet. We arrived at Lahore the 11th of March 1822, and on the 23d of the same I left it, and going by Amritsir, Jamoo, I reached Kashmir the 17th of April, where I stopped, waiting for proper season and companions, till 9th May; when leaving that place, and travelling with four other persons, on the 9th June I arrived at Leh, the capital of Ladak; but I ascertained the road to go to Yarkand was very difficult, expensive, and dangerous for a Christian. After a sojourn of twenty-five days I resolved to return to Lahore.

10. " I was, on my return, near the frontier of Cashmere when, on the 16th of July 1822, I was agreeably surprised to find Mr. Moorcroft at Himbabs. He was alone. I acquainted him with all my circumstances and designs, and by his permission remained with him. I accompanied him on his return to Leh, where we arrived on the 26th August. In September, after Mr. Trebeck's arrival from Piti, Mr. Moorcroft gave me to peruse the large volume of the Alphabetum Tibetanum, wherein I found much respecting Tibet and the Tibetan literature, and being desirous to be acquainted with the structure of that curious tongue, at the departure of Mr. Moorcroft from Leh to proceed to Cashmere, in the last days of September, I begged leave to remain with Mr. Trebeck, who obtained for me the conversation and instruction of an intelligent person, who was well acquainted with the Tibetan and Persian languages; and by this medium I obtained considerable insight in the Tibetan.

11. "At Mr. Moorcroft's request, before his departure from Leh, I translated into Latin a letter written in Russian characters and language, procured by Meer Izzut Oollah of Delhi, the companion of Mr. Moorcroft, dated Petersburgh, 17th January 1820, and addressed to the chief prince of the Panjab (Runjeet Singh), which, as Mr. Moorcroft informed me after his arrival at Kashmir, he sent to Calcutta."

N.B.—This was the letter of Count Nesselrode; sent through the Russian Emissary, Aga Mehdi Rafael.

12. "During the winter in Kashmir, after my return with Mr. Trebeck, considering what I had read and learned on the Tibetan language, I became desirous to apply myself, if assisted to it, to learn it grammatically, so as to penetrate into the contents of those numerous and highly interesting volumes which are to be found in every large monastery. I communicated my ideas respecting this matter to Mr. Moorcroft, who, after a mature consideration, gave me his approbation, favoured me with money for my necessary subsistence, and permitted me to return to Ladak; nay, he recommended me to the chief officer at Leh, and to the Lama of Yangla, in Zanskar. Being prepared for the journey, I left Kashmir on the 2d May 1823, after I had passed five months and six days with Mr. Moorcroft.

13. "After my return to Ladak I arrived at Leh on the 1st of June 1823, delivered Mr. Moorcroft's and Meer Izzut Oollah's letters and presents to the Khalon. This Prime Minister recommended me in a letter to the Lama of Yangla; gave me a passport, and favoured me with about eight pounds of tea. From Leh, travelling in a south-westerly direction, on the ninth day I arrived at Yangla, and from 20th June 1823 to 22d October 1824 I sojourned in Zanskar (the most south-western province of Ladak), where I applied myself to the Tibetan literature, assisted by the Lama.

14. "During my residence in Zanskar, by the able assistance of that intelligent man, I learned grammatically the language, and became acquainted with many literary treasures shut up in 320 large printed volumes, which are the basis of all Tibetan learning and religion. These volumes, divided in two classes, and each class containing other subdivisions, are all taken from Indian Sanskrit, and were translated into Tibetan. I caused to be copied the contents of these immense works and

treatises in the same order as they stand in the printed indexes. Each work or treatise begins with the title in Sanskrit and Tibetan, and ends with the names of the author, translators, and place wherein the author has written or the translation was performed. As there are several collections of Sanskrit and Tibetan words among my other Tibetan writings, I brought with me a copy of the largest, taken out of one of the above-mentioned volumes, consisting of 154 leaves, every page of six lines.

15. "As I could not remain longer in that country with advantage to myself I left it, having agreed with the Lama to pass the winter, 1824–25, with him at Sultanpore, in Coolloo [1] (whereto his relations, also the wives of two chiefs of Lahool, commonly descend for every winter, and whom he was desirous to visit there), and to arrange the collected materials for a vocabulary in Tibetan and English. The Lama was detained by some business, and prevented for some days leaving Zanskar.

16. "As the winter was daily approaching, by his counsel I continued my march to pass the snowy mountains before the passage would be obstructed by the fall of any heavy snow. I arrived at Sultanpore, in Coolloo, without any danger, and from thence, passing to Mendee, Suketee, Belaspore, on the 26th of November of the last year I reached Subathoo. On my arrival I expected the Lama would follow me in about ten days. He came not, and at present I have no hope he will join me, as the pass in the Himalaya is now closed against him.

17. "At my first entrance to the British Indian territory I was fully persuaded that I should be received as a friend by the Government, because I supposed that my name, my purpose, and my engagement for searching after Tibetan literature, were well known in consequence of Mr. Moorcroft's introductions, to whom, before my return to Tibet in the last half of April 1823, when I was in Cashmere, on his writing and recommending me to the secre-

---

[1] Kulu.

tary of the Asiatic Society in Calcutta, and requesting him also to forward me some compendious works on the stated subjects, *I promised by my hand-writing in the same letter, which I beg to refer to, that I would stand faithful to my engagements, to study and to be diligent in my researches.*

18. " I think I have given, as it was required from me, an intelligible account of my history and past proceedings. For the future, as also the length to which I propose to carry my travels and researches, I beg leave to add, the civilised and learned world is indebted to Great Britain in many respects for useful discoveries, inventions, and improvements in arts and sciences. There is yet in Asia a vast *terra incognita* for oriental literature. If the Asiatic Society in Calcutta would engage for the illuminating the map of this *terra incognita*, as in the last four years of my travelling in Asia I depended for my necessary subsistence entirely upon British generosity, I shall be happy if I can serve that honourable Society with the first sketches of my researches. If this should not meet with the approbation of Government, I beg to be allowed to return to Mr. Moorcroft, to whose liberality and kindness I am at present entirely indebted for my subsistence; or, if it pleases the Governor-General of India, that I shall be permitted to remain under your protection until my patron's return from his present tour to Bokhara.

19. " After my arrival at this place, notwithstanding the kind reception and civil treatment with which I was honoured, I passed my time, although in much doubt as to a favourable answer from Government to your report, yet with great tranquillity, till 23d inst., when, on your communication of the Government's resolution on the report of my arrival, I was deeply affected, and not little troubled in mind, fearing that I was likely to be frustrated in my expectations. However, recollecting myself, I have arranged my ideas as well as my knowledge of the English language will admit, and I humbly beseech you to receive these sincere accounts of my circumstances, and if you

skin cloak, with his arms folded, and without a fire. After dark he was without a light; the ground forming his bed, and the walls of the building his protection against the rigours of the climate. He was exposed here to "privations such as have been seldom endured" without complaining.

1824, *October 22d,* he left Yangla, and on *November 20th* arrived at Sabathú.

If we glance at the map we shall find that Csoma's route was the same which, forty-two years later, was followed as far as Bokhara by his famous and enterprising countryman, Arminius Vámbéry. Csoma left no record of the hardships which he necessarily had to overcome in Central Asia; but if we scan the interesting pages of Vámbéry's autobiography, we may surmise in some degree what sufferings, dangers, and hairbreadth escapes were the accompaniments of travelling in those inhospitable regions. Csoma's lamentable reticence on the subject of his exploits and of what he experienced, deprives his biography of much that would have been most attractive. The still available correspondence, and the casual remarks of his friends and admirers, give us sufficient information as to the character of the man; but the full details, which otherwise make up the charm of the story of a life like his, are lost, and can never be made good.

In his letter to the political agent at Umbála, dated the 28th of November, quoted above, we find Captain Kennedy stating that a special introduction was brought by Csoma from Mr. Moorcroft. That letter was forwarded to the Government, and is dated Kashmir, the 21st of April 1823. This letter is worthy of being preserved, if only as a memento of the ill-fated writer. Mr. Moorcroft writes thus :—

" *To the Commandant at Sabathú.*

"SIR,—The object of this address is to bespeak your good offices for Mr. Alexander Csoma, or Sekunder Beg, of Transylvania, whom I now take the liberty to introduce.

" 2. I have known this gentleman for five months most intimately, and can give the strongest testimony to his integrity, prudence, and devotedness to the cause of science, which, if fully explained, might, in the opinion of many, be conceived to border on enthusiasm.

" 3. As well in pursuance of original plans of his own *for the development of some obscure points of Asiatic and of European history,* as of some suggestions stated by me, Mr. Csoma will endeavour to remain in Tibet until he shall have become master of the language of that country, and be completely acquainted with the subjects its literature contains, which is likely, on many accounts, to prove interesting to the European world.

" 4. Although no substantial grounds exist for suspecting that he will not succeed in accomplishing the object above stated, the recent date of European intercourse with the country of Ladakh may justify the adoption of substituting other measures, should the result of the plans contemplated not meet the present sanguine expectations of success.

" 5. If, therefore, events should arise to prevent Mr. Csoma continuing in Ladakh until he may have effected the matter alluded to, I beg leave respectfully to request that you will so far oblige me as to afford him such assistance as may be required to facilitate the prosecution of his studies, along with some well-informed Lama in the northern part of Besarh, as the Superior of the Gompa or Monastery of Palso, near Leh.

" 6. It is possible that the contingency of my death, or of delay of the present expedition beyond a certain period mentioned to Mr. Csoma, may induce the Government to desire him to proceed to Calcutta, in which case I shall feel myself personally obliged if you will be kind enough to furnish him with two hundred rupees, to meet which I now enclose my draft at sight on my agents at Calcutta."

This letter furnishes very important information in

respect to circumstances which matured into a formal compact between these two travellers. Csoma makes mention of the first meeting between them in his letter to Captain Kennedy (para. 10). Mr. Moorcroft refers to it in his journal, and adds,[1] "Csoma remained with me some time, and after I had quitted Ladakh, I obtained permission from the Khalon for him to reside in the Monastery of Yangla, in Zanskar, for the purpose of acquiring a knowledge of the Tibetan language," &c.

The two preceding letters settle, therefore, those points regarding which so much uncertainty and so many mistaken ideas have prevailed.

We know now that Csoma's original plan "for the development of some obscure points of Asiatic and European history," conceived in Hungary, was to proceed through the northern regions of Central Asia, as Hegedüs pointedly remarks, towards the "borders of the Chinese Empire and towards Mongolia;" and we can trace his steps from Persia to Khorassan and Bokhara, through Balkh, Kulm, Bamian, across the Hindu Kush, in that direction, till he reached Kabul on the 6th of January 1822. Thence, *viâ* Lahore, he travelled into Kashmir, where he arrived on the 14th of April. The journey towards China led *viâ* Turkestan, and he travelled as far as Leh on his way thither; but having ascertained, when at Leh, that the road to Yarkand was "very difficult, expensive, and very dangerous for a Christian," as he did not attempt to travel in disguise, he resolved to return towards Lahore. On this journey he met Moorcroft, who entertained him hospitably, and lent him Giorgi's "Alphabetum Tibetanum." This book Csoma studied through, and was thus induced to propose to Moorcroft that he would thoroughly master that language, if, during his studies, his daily wants could be provided for. The supposed reason, therefore, that Csoma devoted himself to Tibetan merely because he had observed a similarity between the Magyar

[1] Moorcroft's "Travels," edited by H. H. Wilson, vol. i. p. 338.

and the Tibetan languages, is not supported by any proofs. At the time we speak of, the British power was feeling its way slowly and extending its influence towards Central Asia : doubtless the Government officers on the frontier perceived the advantages that could be gained by a thorough acquaintance with the language of Tibet, which then indeed was a real *terra incognita* to Europeans. Dr. H. H. Wilson points out clearly this aim when he says : " To establish an accurate knowledge of the nations around us, and to promote a friendly intercourse with them. This will not only promote the commercial and political prosperity of Great Britain and her Indian possessions, but may effect the still more important end of teaching to yet semi-barbarous tribes the advantages of industry and civilisation." [1]

Csoma was ready to become a pioneer on this difficult road, IF his terms were accepted. A solemn agreement, therefore, was entered into between Moorcroft and Csoma : the former supplied the requisite funds, of which he gave an account to the Government,[2] and Csoma promised, by " his own handwriting," that he would faithfully abide by his engagement. No proof whatever exists in corroboration of the opinion that, previous to his meeting with Moorcroft, Csoma ever contemplated making Tibetan the study of his life. Nor is there any authentic proof to warrant the assertion that Csoma ever declared himself to be a believer in any special affinity between his mother-tongue and the Tibetan.

The concluding paragraphs of Csoma's letter will be read with sympathy even at this distant time ; great was his anxiety as to how his fate would be decided by Government. The power of Ranjit Singh was still paramount in the Punjab. Csoma's detention at Sabathú was but a natural precaution on the part of the English that any European stranger should, as a matter of prudence, be

---

[1] Preface to Moorcroft's "Travels," edited by H. H. Wilson.
[2] See Prinsep's Report, dated 5th January 1834, in chap. ix.

watched; especially after the proof the Indian Government had in their hands of the intrigues of the Russian Government, through emissaries like Aga Mahdi Rafael.[1]

Csoma's pride and highly honourable feelings were nevertheless deeply touched on finding that he had been suspected, which to the end of his life he never forgot. He had to wait for three long months before an answer reached him, as will be seen from his second letter, written in May. That letter touches on some points now out of date, but its general contents will doubtless be read with much interest. It furnishes proofs also in several passages of the fact, that Csoma was not altogether ignorant of the Sanskrit tongue when, in accordance with the order of the Governor-General, he wrote his second letter, addressed to Captain Kennedy.

---

[1] Moorcroft's Travels, vol. ii. p. 383.

CHAPTER III.

Government orders respecting Csoma's stipend—Report as to his
Tibetan studies in the past and plans for the future.

CSOMA'S first letter to Captain Kennedy was dated the
28th of January 1825. Owing to the distance and other
incidental delays, it was not till the month of May following that an answer to it, from the Calcutta Government,
reached Sabathú. This decided Csoma's fate. The Government granted a regular stipend of fifty rupees a month,
which enabled him to prosecute the Tibetan studies, and,
as regards his own position, to perpetuate his name in the
domain of science and literary research.

In the second letter, addressed to Captain Kennedy,
Csoma made known in detail all he had already learnt
of the language of Tibet, and of the religion of Buddha,
and explained his future plans, particularly in paragraphs
27 and 28. He gave a promise that he would devote
himself entirely to that special study ; he kept to the determination, and spent some of the best years of his life
(between 1825 and 1834) in the attainment of his object.
When once his task was finished, he remarked with melancholy emphasis to Dr. Gerard, as they met at the Buddhist monastery, he would then be " the happiest man
on earth, and could die with pleasure, seeing that he had
redeemed his pledge." On examining what Csoma has
written, we nowhere find the slightest trace to justify the
assumption that he believed in any particular resemblance
between the Tibetan language and his native tongue.
This, therefore, could not be the reason that urged him to
study it. Except in the case of one Tibetan word,—

Tibetan learning and literature. How far I succeeded in my purpose, I beg leave first to give a short emuneration of the materials which I have now in my possession; secondly, of the insight I acquired into the Tibetan; and, lastly, of my intention for the future. Then, firstly,

4. "It was by the medium of the Persian language that I learned so much from the Tibetan, that, after my return to Ladak, I could communicate my ideas to the Lama, and engage him to assist me in my undertaking. He writes very well both the capital and the small characters, is acquainted with the grammatical structure of the Tibetan language, with arithmetic, rhetoric, poesy, and dialectic. Medicine, astronomy, and astrology are his professions; about twenty years ago, in searching after knowledge, he visited in six years many parts of Tibet, Teshi lhunpo, Lassa, Bootan, &c., and also Nepal. He knows the whole system of their religion, has a general knowledge of everything that is contained in their books, and of customs, manners, economy, and of the polite language used among the nobility, and in the sacred volumes; speaking respectfully to superiors. He acquired a great deal of geography and history respecting the Tibetan countries. He is now about fifty-two years old; he is not a resident in a monastery, having married about twelve years ago the widow of the Yangla Raja. He is the chief physician of Ladak, and sometimes the chief secretary employed by Government in writing to Teshi lhunpo, and Lassa.

5. "It was this man I spoke of who, in the course of three months after my arrival at that place, wrote down, at my request, some thousand words arranged after certain heads, and since he had many books with him containing collections of words, and could easily procure others from the neighbouring monasteries, he gave me such account of technical terms used in arts and sciences, that I acquired sufficient information to be interested in the Tibetan literature, and to pursue in certain order the study I was engaged in.

6. "In the first place, he enumerated the names or attributes of the Supreme Intelligence, the first person in the Tibetan Trinity, in more than one hundred and ten terms, which frequently occur in their religious books, and are highly expressive of the Supreme Being respecting His perfections, and are the same as we have in our own theological systems, or in the works of the ancient Greek and Roman poets. There are, besides many others, seven chief emanations or incarnations (Nirmankaya, in Sanskrit) of this Supreme Being, called commonly Buddhas, of whom Sakya (who has more than twelve names, is addressed in the sacred volumes frequently as Gotama, principally by Brahmins), which is a very ancient family name of his ancestors, was the last in appearing in the world, and probably was the same with the most ancient Zoroaster, and must have lived some centuries before the age of Ninus, the great king of Assyria. Champa (the Clemency), Maitreya in Sanskrit, is to come hereafter.

7. "The Lama proceeded afterwards on the Second Person of the Trinity, which is called the 'Chief of Morality,' and gave me thirty names of the moral doctrine, upon which there are many treatises in the sacred volumes.

8. "The Third Person of the Trinity is called 'the Chief Collector or Promoter of Virtue' (the Holy Ghost, agreeably to our faith); such promoters of virtue are all the teachers of moral doctrine or religion. Among these the most perfect are styled in Tibetan 'Byang-chhub Sems-d'pah'; in Sanskrit, Bodhisatva, a saint. They are represented to be of ten different degrees of perfection ; to be immortal; free from passive metempsychosis ; and to possess great powers or faculties of mind for the promotion of universal happiness in the world. There are many appellative or common names, as also proper or peculiar ones, to express such imagined or supposed beings, which all have the signification of excellent qualities or virtues. There is also a list of other saints of inferior abilities.

9. "After these follows a full register of all the gods, goddesses, and their families, heroes, good and bad spirits in the upper and lower regions, with names of their habitations, of their offices, &c. There are many appellative names for the expression of a god or angel; also many attributes or names of every peculiar divinity in their mythology. The Brahma of the Indians (Uranos, Cœlum of the Greeks and Romans) in the Tibetan has more than twenty names. Vishnoo (Chronos, Saturn), twenty-five, among which is Narayana, the most beloved son; Titan, his brother, has ten. For Iswar or Iswara (Zeus, Jupiter), thirty; and so on for Indra and the other imagined guardians of the ten corners of the world. For the Rirap (Sumeru, Olympus) and the whole system of the ancient mythology there are hundreds of names; also for the phenomena or meteors in the atmosphere; among the planets, the sun has more than one hundred and twenty names or attributes; and so on the others also have many appellations, which in poetical works and astronomy are often introduced. There is also an exact description of the twelve zodiacal signs, of twenty-eight constellations, and of everything belonging to astronomy. Further—

10. "He has given a complete account of the human body, specifying every member, articulation, fluid substances and distempers thereof, so fully as it is required for an intelligent physician to know the structure of our body. There is a full enumeration of all the good qualities, as also of all the defects and diseases. Afterwards follow the faculties or powers of our mind, with their opposite defects; then are classified the virtues and vices. There is also a very copious enumeration of everything relating to our dresses, furniture, victuals, family, parentage, &c., &c.

11. "Then follows the enumeration of all quadrupeds, birds, amphibious animals, fishes, conchs or shells, insects, and worms, with several designations. Vegetables and

trees, shrubs, plants, all sorts of corn, pulse, flowers, herbs, &c. Minerals, and different kinds of earth or soil, stones (common and precious), salts, metals, &c. &c. Words for all sorts of instruments employed in farming, manufactures, and every kind of workmanship; arms and everything relating to war. All sorts of pronouns, numbers, adjectives, with their opposites. Inward and outward properties of bodies, colours, figures, technical terms, with several distinctions in arts and sciences. Names of officers, civil and military. Ecclesiastical persons, orders, dignities, and different sects in Tibet; their great names and their titles; monasteries or convents, and their buildings; respecting religion and superstition. Verbs, participles. In a word, there is a full enumeration of whatever we can meet within the region of the elements, as they are called, namely, the earth, water, fire, air, ether, and in the intellectual kingdom. These all were arranged after my direction and plan.

12. "Besides this vocabulary of the most necessary words which I have now with me, written all by the same Lama in the Tibetan capital character, I have another large collection in Sanskrit and Tibetan (the Sanskrit also being written in the Tibetan capital character, as they early adapted their alphabet to express properly every Sanskrit word), copied from the Stangyur Do division, 90 volume, from the 223d leaf to the 377th, consisting of 60 sheets of common Cashmerian paper, having writing but on one side, and having on every page 32 lines. This vocabulary, arranged after certain matters or subjects under general heads, contains many thousand words of every description; several distinctions and divisions highly interesting in order to understand better the whole system and principles of the Buddhistic doctrine.

13. "As there is frequent mention made both in the 'Kahgyur' and 'Stangyur' of the five sciences of the greater class as: sgra-rigpa, gtantziks-rigpa, bzo-rigpa, sman-rigpa, and nangdon-rigpa, corresponding to our philology or

grammar, sabda in Sanskrit; philosophy or logic, hetu in
Sanskrit; technology, silpa in Sanskrit; medicine, vaidya
in Sanskrit, and divinity; the five small ones of the
lesser class, as ṣnyannak, ṣdebsbyor, nonthol, dasgar and
skar-rtsis (rhetoric, poesy, lexicography, dance music,
and astronomy). The same person, at my request, wrote
me a short account on grammar, and on the five sciences
mentioned in the last place. On about five sheets the
history of medicine, and the contents of its eight branches,
arranged in chapters after the system of the most celebrated physicians, also in two sheets an account on astronomy, to find the places of the sun, moon, and planets,
and to calculate eclipses. I have also in about ten sheets
an account of the whole religious system of the Buddhists,
written, at my request, in fine capital characters by a
Lama of great reputation, a relative and friend of the
Lama whose pupil I was. For an account respecting
learning in general, and logic in particular, I have the
answer of a celebrated Rab-hbyams-pa (doctor of philosophy), who was twenty-five years at Lassa, and now is
sixty-five years old.

14. "Although in modern times, in Tibetan countries,
there are several works on different branches of science,
but the bases of them all are the 'Kahgyur' and 'Stangyur' (Commandment's version, and Instruction's version,
on account of their being a version or translation from the
Sanskrit); they correspond in signification to Bed and
Shastra in Sanskrit. The first contains the doctrine and
moral precepts of Shakya, in accordance as after his death
his principal disciples arranged them. The second, written
by ancient Indians and a few Chinese learned men or
Pundits, is filled with treatises containing commentaries
on the first, many original works on religious rites, ceremonies, arts, and sciences.

15. "The 'Kahgyur' family, in manuscript exemplars
(copies), were divided according to the size of paper, characters employed in copying, into more or less, but generally

in 100 volumes. They form now in printed exemplars 90 volumes, with an additional one, containing, on 124 leaves, a prolix and historical account on several subjects, not reducible under one general head. I have now in my possession an exact copy, word for word, of the last 42 leaves, specifying the contents of the above-mentioned 90 volumes, with all their divisions and subdivisions, mentioning the names of the translators, the number of chapters and leaves in every volume, written in capital characters by a good writer, on common Kashmirian paper, bearing ink but on one side, in 30 sheets. It is impossible for me to give now a detailed account of the contents. I shall mention, therefore, the principal parts.

16. " According to this Register, the ' Dulva' (education, Vinaya in Sanskrit), in 13 volumes, in a very easy and agreeable style, gives interesting historical accounts on wars, particularly between the kings of Magadha and Anga', in Paks-yul (arya in Sanskrit, the highland) ; and for moral instruction relates many hundred fables, apologues, and parables. The *She's-rab-kyi-p'ha-rol-tu-p'hyin pa*, by contraction 'Shér-p'hyin' (evergoing or everlasting wisdom ; Prajna' pàramità in Sanskrit), written on moral subjects, contains, in 12 volumes, many excellent moral precepts.

17. " The ' Do-de,' or merely ' Do' (rule, treatise, &c. ; sútra in Sanskrit), in 30 vols., contains much from natural philosophy, divinity, and astronomy. I have with me two specimens of this class on thirty pages, elegantly copied by the Lama himself. The first is taken from the 30th volume of the ' Do,' signed with the A, the last letter of the Tibetan alphabet, beginning on the 364th leaf. This is against the holding so scrupulously on castes. When, on a certain occasion, the King of Kosala and a chief Brahmin, who frequented the meetings of Shakya, in a great assembly had expressed their disapproval, that his (Shakya's) nephew, Kungavo, although of royal family, should marry the daughter of a common man. Shakya tells a story how, anciently in India, such and such a

chief of the Sudra caste, by his learning and address, obtained the beautiful daughter of a Brahmin of high rank, for his well-educated son. This story, in the above-mentioned volume, consists of sixty leaves, and gives interesting accounts of the four castes, their origin, and a summary report on the arts and sciences. The second specimen is taken from the 2d volume of the 'Do,' signed by 'Kh,' beginning on the 120th leaf, and is against the covering of the face of women. The principal, newly-married wife of Shakya, 'Satsuma,' being solicited by her maid-servants to keep her face covered while sitting with others, expresses her sentiments against the veil in a few elegant verses, with which her father-in-law was so well pleased, that he bestowed on her a great quantity of precious stones of all sorts.

18. "The 'Gyud-de,' or 'Gyud' (line, canon, original work, &c.; Tantra in Sanskrit), in 21 vols., treats on different subjects,—natural philosophy, medicine, astronomy, astrology, charms, secret praises (snyags) to imaginary spirits, prayers, &c. For a specimen of this class I have a correct copy of that same piece which, in 1722, in the last century, excited the curiosity of the learned in Europe. It is taken from the ninth volume, signed by T., beginning on the 336th leaf.—*Vide* P. Giorgi, Alphab. Tibet, p. 665.

19. "I will not go further in specifying the other divisions of works or treatises in the remaining twenty-two volumes. It is enough to state: they contain, collectively, ample stores on the political state and genius of the ancient Indians, from the Sita (Sihon, Jaxartes), on this side of the great snowy mountains, downwards to Ceylon.

20. "There is frequent mention made, almost in every volume of the 'Kahgyur' and 'Stangyur,' of an opposite religious sect, styled in Tibetan 'Mo-stegs-chan,' Tirthika in Sanskrit, of which there are many different branches. Judging from the proper meaning in the Tibetan, and according to their principles, they were Determinists or Fatalists, and the Buddhists Indeterminists or Libertinists,

which distinction we find also among the ancient Greek and Roman philosophers. We know very well at present that the Mohammedans are generally addicted to the doctrine of Fatalism. The Buddhists declare we have free-will in our actions, and, consequently, we can be punished or rewarded for our bad or good deeds. Hence the Hell and the Paradise, the place of punishment and reward after death, and the good and bad metempsychosis, with their several distinctions in their religious system. They are all ignorant of our principles and religion, and think we are all of the same principles as the Mohammedans (*vide* P. Giorgi, Alph. Tib., p. 501, the letter of the Pro Lama, at Lassa, while the Dalai Lama, Bezah-zarboba, was exiled in China, written 1730, to P. Horatius, to be transmitted to Rome to the Pope).

21. "The 'Stangyur' (in 224 vols., 76,409 leaves, of about two feet long, on each side seven lines of middle-sized characters) contains the works of several ancient pundits in Asia, Kashmir, Sindhu, Ujain, Bengal, Nepal, and other countries. According to the register (which in 144 leaves makes the last volume), one volume, signed by the letter *K*, contains many praises and hymns to several divinities and saints.

22. "The 'Gyud Class,' in 36 volumes, contains more than 2600 treatises on several subjects, such as natural philosophy, astronomy, religious rites, ceremonies, prayers, charms, superstitious sentences, &c.

23. "The 'Do' Class, in 136 volumes, contains science after certain divisions. Ninety-four volumes are filled up with theological subjects, dogmatic, polemic, or controversial and moral. The following 21 volumes treat on philosophy, theoretical and practical, on logic, dialectic, metaphysics, and ethics. It is very probable that, whatever exercised the speculative mind of the ancient philosophers in Greece and Rome, respecting the origin and end of the world, or of the human soul: we meet with all those or like subtleties in these 115 volumes last mentioned.

D

24. " The next two volumes contain grammar, rhetoric, poesy, and synonymy, afterwards five volumes, medicine. In the next volume there are several treatises on different arts—on alchemy, the mode of preparing quicksilver, ether, &c. The rest, mostly written by ancient Tibetan scholars, contain treatises on grammar, collections of vocabularies in Sanskrit and Tibetan, of which I have now with me a copy of the largest mentioned above.

25. " As I have copied specimens for the style and contents of the 'Kahgyur,' I have taken also from the 'Stangyur' some pattern-pieces. The first is on divinity, and gives an explanation of the ten moral precepts. The second is taken from technology, and enumerates what must be the proportion in feet, inches, lines of a statue representing Buddha or Shakya. The third, from medicine, is written on temperaments, viz., sanguine, choleric, and phlegmatic, &c. The fourth is from philosophy, on the elements of right knowledge. The fifth, from ethics (*niti shastra*), a collection of apophthegms, prudential and moral. From grammar, a treatise on twenty Sanskrit particles, which, if compounded with nouns and verbs, change their signification in several manners. Every particle is illustrated by examples in Tibetan. The twenty Sanskrit particles are the following:—*Pră, pará, á, sam, anu, apa, nir, antar, vi, ava, ni, adhi, api, ati, su, ut, abhi, prati, pari, upa.* It was written by a celebrated ancient pundit or professor, Chandra Komi, in Bengal, from whom, according to historical accounts contained in the 'Stangyur,' the modern city of Chandernagore (near Calcutta) obtained its name. From this learned man there are in the 'Stangyur' principally, many excellent treatises on grammar. All these specimens here enumerated fill thirty-two pages, written in large capital characters. The volumes and pages are quoted.

26. " The whole contents of the 'Kahgyur' and 'Stangyur,' with the pattern pieces copied by the Lama and by another good writer, make a volume of 277 pages, in

folio, on kashmirian common paper, bound in leather at Kashmir, which Mr. Moorcroft had the kindness to give me on my return to Tibet. This and all other papers on Tibetan literature now in my hands belong to Mr. Moorcroft (consequently to the British Government), to whose liberality I am infinitely obliged.

27. " But since the Governor-General in Council favoured me with pecuniary aid, I beg leave to communicate my wish and plan for the future. The Tibetan literature merits, without doubt, to be fully explored. In return of my acknowledgment for the received liberal assistance, if Government pleases to permit me to be under the protection of the commanding officer at Sabathoo, and to devote myself again to the Tibetan, I hope that if I could join either the same Lama, to whose intelligence I owe now my insight into this class of Asiatic literature, or be able to procure another intelligent person, I shall be able to finish what I have commenced in the course of one year; and then

28. " I shall have the honour to present to the Government in English (*a.*) a large theoretical and practical grammar of the Tibetan language, on the five principal parts of the grammar, viz., *Orthography* (very difficult in the Tibetan, but sufficiently regulated by the best grammarians, in their collections of many words for the same purpose), *Orthoepy* (variable according to different provinces—can be fixed for the European students), *Etymology* (very simple and copious), *Syntax*, and *Prosody* (will not take much room). Specifying in etymology every part of speech, giving perfect patterns of declensions for personal, possessive, demonstrative, interrogative, relative, and reciprocal pronouns ; for numbers, cardinal, ordinal, and adverbial ; for adjectives and nouns of every kind ; patterns of conjugations for verbs, neuter, active, intransitive, transitive, passive, causal, &c. ; a complete catalogue of adverbs, prepositions, conjunctions, and interjections, and the proper use of them in the syntax. (*b.*) A *vocabulary* of more than 30,000 words in Tibetan and

English, introducing all technical terms used in arts and sciences, leaving alone every conjecture respecting the relation of Tibetan words to any other language. (c.) A short account on the Tibetan literature. (d.) A succinct history of Tibet, in Tibetan language, taken from the works of native historians, word for word, accompanied by a short geography and chronology in Tibetan. (e.) Selected specimens of every kind in Tibetan.

29. "If there is no objection, I beg you will do me the favour to obtain the Government's leave for me, to proceed with my literary labours to Calcutta, as soon as I have completed them.

30. "In support of the possibility to accomplish my engagement, I beg leave to state that I am acquainted with several ancient and modern European and Asiatic languages, and that my mother-tongue, the Hungarian idiom, is nearly related, not in words, but in structure, with the Turkish, Indian, Chinese, Mogul, and Tibetan languages. In every language of Europe, except the Hungarian, Turkish, and those of Finnish origin, there are prepositions like in the languages of Hebrew or Arabic origin, but in our tongue, like in the Indian, Chinese, and Tibetan, we have postpositions, and for the formation of different cases in declension, we have affixes with which to form from the same root several sorts of verbs. *Our idiom* [1] *is not inferior either to the Sanskrit or Arabic,* and I beg leave to confess that I am not merely a linguist—I have learnt several languages to learn polite literature, to enter into the cabinet of curiosity of remote ages, to acquire useful knowledge, and to live in every age and with every celebrated nation, as I do now with the British.

31. "It is recorded in Tibetan books that the ruin of the ancient Buddhists in the kingdom of Magadha, happened by the Turks, who, taking the city of Otantrapur, destroyed their colleges, killed many priests, and that those who escaped from the common peril fled southwards

[1] The Hungarian.

to India. I cannot now say in what year. There is frequent
mention made of Magadha in Asia, the scene (according to
what is related) of the most illustrious actions and the home
of the most celebrated learned men. I have not yet had
sufficient time to search after curiosities : I must first learn
the language. I have read but few volumes as yet from
the 'Kahgyur' and 'Stangyur'; but if we consider the words
of a prophecy by Shakya recorded in the ' Kahgyur' (probably introduced thither in modern ages from historical
evidences), that 'his religion or doctrine shall advance from
north to south, from south towards the north, and from
north to north,' as it verily happened, since historians
mention the Buddhists in Asia, Kashmir, Sindh, Malwa,
Ujain, Singhala, Kalingah, Malabar, Ceylon, Bengal, Burmah,
Bhutan, Tibet, and the Mogul countries in recent times :
we have every reason to suppose that this Asia [eminence,
the high country, which is a Sanskrit word, and its literal
translation in Tibetan is Pakspa; this also is a title of honour
for persons of high dignity, spiritual and secular, in the
same manner as we use the words ' highness,' ' eminence,'
' excellency '] is the same as the Asia of Ptolemy and of
other ancient geographers and historians, and is an appellative name for high countries in general, and comprehends
all the ancient Scythia on this side of the Imaus, consequently includes the Transoxiana, Khorassan, and Bactria.
In the same manner India or Hindia (from hin, hon, hinta
= lowness, or Hindes, low countries) must have been a
common or appellative name for many countries ; which
appellation the ancients extended so far as Arabia and
Egypt, and mentioned sometimes three Indias.

32. "This opinion is confirmed by the splendid accounts of almost all the historians of antiquity who had
mentioned these countries ; and among other Asiatic
authors by two Syrian historians, Abulferagius and Abulfida, in their ' Dynasties and Annals,' and consequently
must have been the same central country, whence, according to Sir William Jones's opinion, the Chinese, Tartars,

Indians, Persians, Syrians, Arabians, Egyptians, Greeks, Romans, Gauls, Goths, Germans, and the Sclavonians derived their civilisation or culture in their arts and sciences. There is also, according to Niebuhr, existing in the inland countries of Arabia, an ancient tradition, that they were civilised by a people which descended from the environs of Samarcund.

33. " In the eastern and north-western parts of Europe there are many vestiges of the ancient Buddhism and of Sanskrit words among all the peoples, who but of late (after the time of Charlemagne) were converted to the Christian faith by means of the sword. But the most numerous monuments thereof are Sanskrit words used by Greek and Roman writers in their accounts relating to ancient Thrace (Rumelia), Macedonia, and the countries on both sides of the Danube, Servia, Pannonia, and Dacia.

34. " I beg leave to give a few instances of my assertion. Pannonia is a literal translation of the Sanskrit word ' sarbiya,' now applied to a province on the south side of the Danube, of which Belgrade is the capital, formerly belonging to Hungary, now[1] under Turkish dominion, Dacia, or, after Greek orthography, Dakia (the modern Lower Hungary, Transylvania, Moldavia, Wallachia, Bessarabia), was probably an appellative name for those countries, on account of their being abundant in grapes, from the Sanskrit word ' dakh ' or ' dak,'[2] signifying ' the grape,' in the form of the adjective ' dakhia,' or ' dakia,' ' the graped.' This is confirmed by other historical facts. Ancient geographers and historians mention the Agathyrsi (in the same countries probably I enumerated above). Thyrsus is Bacchus' rod with the winded vines, and was an emblem of wine. The great river Dnieper, in the south-western part of modern Russia, is called by the ancients Borysthenes. This is a Hungarian name signifying ' the wine—godded ' (the river being taken for the country), from ' bor,' ' wine,' and ' isten,' ' god,' with the adjective affix ' es,' equivalent to the English ' ed.'

[1] 1825.   [2] Drákshâ.

35. "Among the many names, in different languages, designating wandering people, as, *e.g.*, Scytha (probably from the Sclavonian: Skitati, 'to wander'), Heber, or Eber, Aavor, Bunger (all from the Hebrew or Arabic, Vandal, &c., there is also a Sanskrit word, 'Geta,' signifying walking, going, wandering, the English 'to go,' the German 'gehen,' are derived probably from the same source). The Getæ are mentioned and described by ancient writers in Central Asia, the modern Chinese Tartary, near the Oxus and the Caspian Sea, the Massagetæ, farther on the north-western shores of the Black Sea, in Thrace (now Rumelia), on both sides of the Danube. Hence Ovid, in his banishment at Tomi, near the Black Sea, in modern Bulgaria, says, 'Jam didici getice sarmaticeque loqui!' 'I have already learnt to speak the Getic and the Sarmatic (Sclavonian) languages.' The modern Indians do not use the word 'geta' as a participle noun; they have changed it into 'jata;' but they form the preterite of the same verb, 'giya,' regularly from 'jata' (the jat tribes in India). Among the attributes of the Supreme Being, or his representative, the Buddha, the first name is 'Bhagvan' (overcomer, a Sanskrit word), the second 'Tatha - gata,' walking on the same road, *i.e.*, the 'Just.' Both these names also highly confirm every adopted opinion respecting Buddhism and the Sanskrit words in Europe. From the frequent mention of the Bhagvan (God) by the Buddhists, I think bigoted Christians, by way of contempt, called them Pagans, and the second word, 'Tathagata,' confirms the proper signification of 'geta,' mentioned above.[1]

36. "We know very little of the Parthians, the rivals

[1] Deductions based upon the etymology and similarity in the pronunciation of certain words, are not safe grounds upon which to rest scientific conclusions. Csoma has frequently shown his distrust of such. Yet such an objection need not preclude our noting down any striking examples which we may have fallen in with.

What may have been the faith of the Magyar ancestors is not yet decided; this subject demands yet further investigation, especially in the direction in which Csoma laboured.

Csoma says, with reference to the study of Tibetan, and especially of the Sanskrit, that his countrymen will find in it a fund of informa-

of the Romans for empire through more than four hundred
years. But since Justin, the Roman historian, calls them
the banished Scythians (*exules Scytharum*), and since, on
public monuments and coins, there are many evidences of
their being friends, admirers, and patrons of the Greeks,
we may take them to be the same leading people as the
Getæ in Europe and in Asia. Historians mention several
princes of Parthian dynasty in Asia Minor (Mithridates, in
the Greek empire, at Constantinople, in Macedonia; *vide*
Gibbon's History). After the conquest of Macedonia by
the Romans, it is probable that the Parthian chiefs retired
towards the Danube to their relatives, and from animosity
and the great hatred they conceived against the Romans,
never afterwards ceased to infest the Roman empire with
all their auxiliaries. Hence Virgil in the Eclogue: 'Aut
Ararim parthus bibet aut Germania Tigrim.' If we suppose that Alexander himself was of Parthian extraction,
we can easily explain his successes in conquering Asia,
and the subsisting for so long a time of the empire of the
Greeks in Bœotia.

37. "We must not wonder that in the ancient Greek
and Roman authors we find but slender accounts respecting
Pannonia, Dacia, and the other countries on the Danube.
Carthage was before the sight of Rome, yet very little is
known now of its internal state. The Getæ probably
descended successively from Asia (forced by Asiatic revo-

tion respecting their national origin,
manners, customs, and idiom.

Even among the early data of the
ancient history of the Hungarians,
there are words and names which
seem to point unmistakably to their
Buddhistic origin. *Bihar* is an important county in Lower Hungary.
Buda, the old capital of Hungary,
sounds the same as the name which
is still worshipped by hundreds of
millions of the human race. Why
should it be a far-fetched conclusion
to assume that on the neighbouring
hills, rising on the banks of the
Danube, there stood in ancient times
a temple of Buddha,— perhaps a
Lama monastery? Below it, on the
opposite bank, stretching into the distant plain, was built Pest. "Pest,"
"past," is a Persian word, and expresses the topographical relation
which exists between the ancient
town of Buda and the new town of
Pest. Whether this suggestion is
likely to attract the attention of
those, who are more competent to
judge may be questioned, but the
coincidence is very striking, and it
is perhaps not out of place to put it
on record here.

lutions) towards Assyria and Egypt, on one side, in a very remote age, called by these people, from their passing the great rivers Tigris and Euphrates, ' Heber' (an appellative name for wandering people), whence, about the time of Moses, several principal persons, forced to leave Phœnicia and Egypt, fled to the islands of Archipelago, Rhodes, Crete, &c.—hence the Pelasgi,—and on the other side, by Persia, Asia Minor, and so on to Thrace, Macedonia, and Thessaly. The modern language of Thessaly, and of some districts in Macedonia, blended with many Latin words, is the same as that of the Wallachians in Lower Hungary, Transylvania, Moldavia, Wallachia, and contains many Sanskrit words. It is totally different from the Hungarian idiom both in words and structure. There is a peculiarity of that language in the use of definite articles. For instance, ' Domnu, Dominus' in Latin, 'a lord' in English; with the affixed definite article *ul* we have 'domnul,' 'the lord' in English. The feminine is ' domna,' ' domina ' in Latin ; ' a lady,' or ' the lady,' in English.

38. " In the Hungarian language the definite article *a* (or *az* before words beginning with a vowel, like the Hebrew *ha*, Arabic *el*, English *the*) is invariably put before every case and number. The Greek, German, French, Italian, Spanish, &c., languages also have definite articles put before nouns, but they vary according to the different genders, cases, and numbers. The Latin, Sclavonic, and Turkish languages have no distinct signs for the expression of a definitive or emphatic locution, like the *the* in English. There are also in the Tibetan, Sanskrit, Indian, Syrian, Wallachian, and Swedish languages certain signs denoting distinction in gender, marking a definitive and emphatic locution, but all these languages have the peculiarity of such particles being affixed to the nouns. Such affixes in the Tibetan are for masculines, *pa, po, va, vo;* for feminine, *ma, mo, e.g.,* philingpa, European man ; philingma, a European woman ; rgyelpo, the prince, king ; rgyelmo, the princess, the queen ; lavo, the god ; lamo,

the goddess ; zlaba, the moon ; nyima, the sun ; contrary, nya-rgyas, full moon. In Sanskrit, deo, a god ; deva, the god ; devi, the goddess ; raj, a prince, king ; raja, the king; gang, a river ; ganga, the river. The sign for such an affix in the Syrian is the same as in the Sanskrit; for the Wallachian I refer to the above-mentioned example; for the Swedish I cannot now cite an example. As in the Indian, Persian, Sanskrit, the word *sived* or *sifed* signifies white, fair. I may conjecture that the Swedes have taken their name from those Scythian people who spoke the Sanskrit language (the Getæ) when they mixed with them in Asia Minor and in the south-eastern parts of Europe, and passed many centuries together, like the Gauls, Germans, and Saxons ; and it was in that time and in those regions that they all adopted many Sanskrit words, and that peculiarity mentioned above respecting the definitive article affix, like the Wallachians and Syrians, who have taken all these peculiarities in their language from those Scythians with whom they lived long since and formed a people under one government.

39. "The ancient Greek and Sclavonic languages, by their structure, particularly by the use of many particles, and of duals, both in the declensions of nouns and in the conjugations of verbs, show sufficiently that they were formed after the ancient Sanskrit. Those Scythians (Getæ) whose idiom was the Sanskrit, were few in number, like the Europeans in modern times in America and Asia; but as they were learned, well disciplined, possessing wealth, and being expert in warfaring with elephants, chariots (retha in Sanskrit, reda in Latin), and on horseback, with a few people displayed wonderful actions, in the same manner as the first Europeans in America and Asia with their artillery. I return now to Buddha.

40. "In the same manner as Europeans, Christians formed the word *Pagan* from Bhágván (the contemptuous name to design a Buddhist) ; so also did the Asiatics, principally the Mohammedans. They call both the Buddhists and

47. "In Derghe, the capital of Kham-yul, or Potchenpo, Great Tibet, about forty days' journey eastward from Lassa, there is another recent and more correct edition of the 'Kahgyur,' which, I am informed, is highly esteemed. Besides these two great works, there are many other printed volumes written by Tibetan learned men.

48. "There are in the 'Stangyur,' on about 18 leaves, passports for such pious men who desire to visit Kalapsa in Shambhála. The mentioning of a great desert of twenty days' journey, and of white sandy plains on both sides of the Sita (Sihon, Yaxartes), render it very probable that the Buddhist Jerusalem (I call it so), in the most ancient times, must have been beyond the Yaxartes, and probably in the country of the Yugurs.

49. "Kun-dgah Snying-po, the author of the above-mentioned 'rGyel rabs gsal-vahi mélong' (sec. 43), who wrote in the monastery of Sa-skya (two days' journey westwards from Teshi lhunpo, a very celebrated place for all sorts of manuscripts), about 800 years ago, says: 'We have received from the East, from China (Gya-nak, the black plain), medicine, astronomy, and astrology; from the South, from India (Gya-kan, the white plain), orthodox religion; from the West, from Nepaul and Sok-yul, goods and victuals (Sok-po is the common name in Tibet for Moguls, Kalkas, Kalmucks, &c.); from the North (from the countries of the Hors and Yugurs), books of laws and of workmanship. All those people in Central Asia who speak the Turkish language are called in Tibet the Hor; and Gengiz Khan, according to this and other authors, was of this race.

50. "From the same author, there is another historical work, entitled 'Depter Ningpo' (ancient memoir). I was not able to procure it, but I am informed it is a very interesting work, particularly for the history of Gengiz Khan. His apophthegms, from another work I am acquainted with, are very judicious and elegant.

51. "In the Tibetan books the name of the Yugurs is

written Yoogoor, and their country sometimes is called
Yoogera. I could not learn further any other interesting
things on the Yoogoors, except that in the 'Stangyur's' register is mentioned a small treatise translated from the Yoogoor
language, containing a short account on the wandering
from one country to another of an original statue representing Shakya, and which is now kept at Lassa, brought
thither from China by Kongcho, the wife of Srongtsan
Gambo.

52. " The most ancient Buddha on record, I believe,
was the same as Zoroaster, who, according to an ancient
author, lived in about the same age with Ninus, the great
king of Assyria. In support of this opinion the following
æras, being the times in which Shakya is supposed to have
lived, speak for themselves. The first four æras are, according to the opinions of the most learned men in Tibet and
Nepal, in Srongtsan Gambo's time, in the seventh century
after Christ. The tenth æra or opinion is that which in
modern times has most authority at Lassa.

53. " In the present year of the Christian æra (1825)
the Tibetans count the nineteenth year (*shingmocha*) of
the fourteenth cycle of sixty years, which commenced
with the new moon in February last. But this mode of
counting years is of very recent date, commenced about
eight hundred years since, and probably was adopted from
the Chinese. As with respect to more ancient times,
there is a great uncertainty in chronology: Padma Karpo,
a celebrated Lama in the Bhutan country of Tibet, in the
twenty-sixth year of the tenth cycle of sixty years, in
1592 after Christ, collected a short disquisition (now
extant, in nicely printed copies of thirty-one leaves each),
containing the different opinions of learned men in
ancient times of Tibet, Nepal, and Kashmere, on the æra
of Shakya or Buddha, the great prophet of the Buddhists.
These opinions or æras were found to be twelve in number,
to which he added his own.

54. " According to these thirteen opinions, the numbers

of years which elapsed from the death of Shakya till the
author's time, in which he wrote, viz., 1592 A.D., and then
the total number of years from Shakya till the present
year, 1825 after Christ, would be as follows:—

THE NUMBERS

Of Opinion.	Of years till 1592.	Till 1825 after Christ.
1st	4012	4245
2d	3738	3971
3d	3725	3958
4th	3729	3962
5th	2900	3133
6th	2342	2575
7th	2243	2476
8th	2136	2369
9th	2470	2703
10th	2427	2660
11th	2166	2399
12th	2474	2707
13th	2650	2883

55. "Thus I have endeavoured, to the best of my
abilities, to give a summary report of the contents of the
Tibetan books and papers in my possession as Government required from me. Both the Sanskrit and the
Tibetan literature open a wide field before me, for future
speculation on the history of mankind. I possess the
same ardour as I felt at the beginning, when I planned
and determined to come to the East. Should these first
rough drafts of my labours, arguments, and sentiments
have the Government's approbation, I shall be happy if I
can serve them with my ulterior literary researches."

Notwithstanding the change of circumstances and the
great progress which has been effected in Oriental literature, and especially in the studies to which Csoma devoted
his energies, the above paper, written though it be in
imperfect English, will still command respectful consideration at the hands of those who take an interest in

E

what Csoma has done. This is his first important essay on Tibetan learning, then so little known; many eminent scholars have since followed in the same direction; Rajendrolála Mitra, one of the greatest living Orientalists, declares "that no European has studied Tibetan with greater success than Csoma did;"[1] while Dr. Malan remarks, "Csoma laid down the foundation, and others merely built upon it."[2]

[1] Nepalese Buddhist Literature.   Calcutta, 1882.   Preface, p. xiii.
[2] "Journal Royal Asiatic Society," vol. xvi., p. 493.

whom I have the honour to know, and to whom I express, on this occasion also, my humble respects and acknowledgments. Continue, my dear gentlemen, your benevolence to a stranger, whose chief care is to merit your favour and to extol your kindness."

This communication was transmitted by Captain Kennedy to the Supreme Government, and is to be found among the records of the Foreign Office in Calcutta.

The next letter from Csoma is in the possession of the Asiatic Society of Bengal. It was forwarded, as usual, by Captain Kennedy, who wrote in very kind terms on this occasion to Dr. Wilson, and also to the Assistant-Political Agent at Umbála, concerning his protégé, pleading his cause, and requesting substantial support for him.

Csoma's letter to the Secretary of the Society is dated the 21st of August 1826. He gives an important, though not a satisfactory account of his studies. After acknowledging Dr. Wilson's communication of the 10th of August 1825, and mentioning some details about himself, he continues thus :—

" I received the pamphlets, which contained some interesting articles on the subject on which I am employed But since they came too late to me, namely, on the 26th of June, and the man who brought them was very idle and vagrant, I trusted not to send a letter by him. I beg leave that I delayed so long to write to you.

" I was not successful after my return to this place as I imagined on leaving Sabathú that I should be, the Lama being very negligent in assisting me as I desired.

" He passed but a few months with me, and I could find and employ no other person able for my purpose. I am still uncertain what will be the issue of my works, or how far I can bring them, according to my promises. Should I fail, for the present, in fulfilling in all respects my engagement, you shall have, I assure you, if not the whole, at least the grammar, and such views on the language and literature of Tibet, that will be sufficient to induce future inquirers to engage in this branch of Asiatic literature.

" I am very much obliged to you for the review of my letters, the remarks made upon them, and the hints given me. Whatever I found on the Tibetan language in the *Quarterly* was very incorrect. I will not now enumerate the defects. I hope I shall be able to fix a standard for this curious language, founded on indubitable authorities.

" I beg leave for tardiness and brevity in writing. After my return I shall be happy if I can serve you with all my acquirements," &c., &c.

Csoma returned from Pukdal to Sabathú in January 1827, loaded with literary treasures, but greatly dissatisfied with the result of the journey. The negligence of his instructor, the Lama, was a cause of keen disappointment to him, and we may well understand that this unlooked-for misfortune intensified the mortification of his sensitive and enthusiastic spirit.

CHAPTER V.

Embarrassing position—Csoma petitions Government to be allowed
to visit Calcutta, or to go to Tibet for three more years to
complete his studies.

CSOMA'S arrival at Sabathú from Pukdal was notified by
Captain Kennedy on the 17th January 1827, when he
wrote to Dr. Wilson, stating that he was shown by Csoma
" an immense mass of manuscripts and many printed
volumes, and that he appeared to have attained a thorough
familiarity with the language and literature of Tibet. He
bids me say," continues Captain Kennedy, " that it will
afford him pleasure to correspond with you upon any literary subject you may please to propound to him. He is
in no immediate need of money, having about one hundred
and fifty rupees left out of the five hundred which the
Government advanced to him upwards of two years ago.
He declines any attention that I would be most happy to
show him, and he lives in the most retired manner. Out
of nine Tibetan words which you sent to him, printed at
Serampore, he says there are five errors. I shall introduce
him to Mr. Stirling when the Governor-General arrives."

Immediately after returning to Sabathú, Csoma felt it
his duty to inform Captain Kennedy, for the information
of Government, of the disappointing result of his second
visit to Tibet. This he did in a report, of which the original, bearing the date of the 18th January 1827, is still
extant, in the possession of the Asiatic Society of Bengal.
After expressing his acknowledgments for many kindnesses

received at Captain Kennedy's hands, he writes as follows :—

"Since my former reports [1] addressed to you I have developed the contents of the Tibetan library works, and have specified some papers in my possession, and also given a scheme of a grammar, a vocabulary, and other works which I am about to prepare. Now, I will not expatiate again on Tibetan literature ; I think it sufficient to state, that I was disappointed in my intentions by the indolence and negligence of that Lama to whom I returned. I could not finish my planned works as I had proposed and promised. I have lost my time and cost. But I have brought now with me many small printed columns of good authority treating on grammar, chronology, astronomy, and on moral subjects. I have sufficient materials for a grammar, and being acquainted with the grammatical structure of the language, now I am able to prepare the elementary work, so large as they will require.

"The dictionary is too large : it is yet in pure Tibetan, written by a good hand in fine capital characters of small size, arranged alphabetically. I had not yet leisure to add the signification of each word in English. I can translate the greatest part without mistake, but for the explanation of many words I must get the assistance of an intelligent Tibetan. I have also extracts of chronology, geography, and literary history, written by the Lama according to my direction.

"From Dr. Wilson's letter and the *Quarterly* [2] sent to me I observe, there is nothing yet known of the Tibetan language and literature, and they seem also to be not much interested for them. It is certain that the Tibetan books mentioned in my former reports have been taken in the seventh century after Christ from India, especially from Nepal, Central India, Kashmir, and other countries.

---

[1] See the two letters above, dated 28th January and 5th May 1825, Chapters ii. and iii.
[2] *Oriental Quarterly Magazine*, 1825.

They contain both materially and formally (*sic*) more than the literature of any country in Asia.

"I will not make any application to Government, as Dr. Wilson advises me. I am already under heavy obligations to Government and to some gentlemen. I never meant to take money, under whatever form, for the editing of my works. I will prepare them to the best of my ability, and afterwards I wish to convince some qualified Oriental scholars of the authenticity and correctness of my communications. And I shall be happy to deliver to your Government all my papers on Tibetan literature, for the received assistance from his lordship in Council and from other gentlemen. My honour is dearer to me than the making, as they say, of my fortune.

"I have resolved not to return again to any part of Tibet, until I have delivered to the Government my present materials. I humbly beseech you to have the kindness to take me under your protection and patronage this year, and be pledge or security before Government, if it be necessary, for my conduct. I shall endeavour to be worthy of your patronage.

"I wish to live a retired life till October next, either at this place or in the neighbourhood, wherever you please to permit me to reside."

The tone of this epistle is vividly suggestive of Csoma's position; he was disappointed in his instructor and unable to find another in the Monastery of Pukdal, to render him the requisite assistance. "I have lost my time and money," was his complaint, although he did all he could, and had collected Tibetan books in large numbers, with which, after an absence of eighteen months, he returned to Sabathú at the beginning of 1827. He made a truthful report to Captain Kennedy, and through him to the Asiatic Society. His best and first friend, Mr. Moorcroft, was already in his grave; the circumstances had altered since; Csoma found that the Calcutta savants knew little of the Tibetan language and literature; and he, moreover, suspected that they did not take any particular interest in these subjects.

This was not an encouraging position for a zealous investigator, and though he could not blame himself in being unable to fulfil engagements which he so earnestly strove to accomplish, he felt, nevertheless, that he could make no further claim for support from Government, and therefore declined asking for it. He was most desirous, however, to make over to the authorities his literary collections and the grammar, which he had already completed, as a slight acknowledgment for the generous help he received at "His Lordship's and other private English gentlemen's hands."

The correspondence which passed between the parties concerned, does credit to all, as indeed does almost every letter which this memoir contains, bearing testimony to the liberality of Government on the one hand, or to the merits and deep gratitude of its object on the other. On the 3d of April, that is, two months and a half after his last letter, Captain Kennedy wrote to inquire of Dr. Wilson the result of his communication as to the fate of the Tibetan scholar, his protégé, and says :—

" Csoma is very anxious to hear from you. I have just introduced him to Lord Amherst. He proposes to remain here and compile his grammar and dictionary until next October. I rather suspect that Mr. Csoma's finances are at a low ebb, and how we shall be able to approach the Government for a further grant to him I am not very certain. Perhaps a letter from the Asiatic Society would be the most proper channel to solicit a further sanction of a few hundred rupees for him."

It is evident that a good deal of correspondence had passed between the Government officers, the Asiatic Society, and Dr. Gerard, as to what steps should be taken with respect to the further prosecution of Csoma's labours ; doubtless the question was seriously discussed as to the advisability of remaining content with what had been already attained, before sanctioning further expenditure of money, which a third journey into Tibet must necessarily entail upon the public treasury.

We find that his friend Dr. Gerard wrote to Csoma asking for copies of reports he had already furnished to Government. With reference to these, Csoma wrote to Captain Kennedy on the 5th of May 1827, as follows:—

1. "Dr. Gerard desired to obtain from me a copy of my former letters and communications to you, for the purpose of showing them to Mr. Mackenzie. I am a very bad writer; I could not copy them in a more proper manner. I thought it my duty to send them direct into your hands. If it may be your pleasure, I beg you to permit Dr. Gerard to show them.

2. "I was much perplexed by that gentleman's letter to me. In my answer to the stated subjects, I would not enter into the wide field of speculation as I was directed. My objects of research are a comprehensive grammar, vocabulary, and an account upon Tibetan books and learning. The grammar and literary history I can give whenever I shall be desired to furnish them, and will accompany them with a short geography and a succinct chronological history of Tibet, in Tibetan and English. But, as there is yet nothing fixed with respect to Tibetan orthography, I fear if I should send my papers, without going myself to Calcutta, they could not make proper use of them there, and it would give again rise to many mistakes, which, as I observe in every publication on the Tibetan language, are now also too much multiplied. The completion of the vocabulary or dictionary, since I missed my aim on my second return to Ladak, must be the fruit of some years' industry.

3. "If, then, there is no objection, I beg you will do me the favour to obtain for me the Government's permission to go to Calcutta next November, for the purpose of communicating my papers; or, if Government would yet delay my visiting Calcutta, as I observe from Dr. Wilson's

letter to you : to give me leave for three years to go to Upper Besarh, where the language is Tibetan, and to direct the Rajah of Besarh, that I should have leave to read such of the Tibetan volumes deposited in the Monastery at Kanam, in Bali Ram's possession, as I should find interesting for my purpose; and if Government will please to approve my further application to the Tibetan, and accept afterwards the results and fruits of my labours, I beg that you will have the kindness to obtain some assistance for my necessary expenses.

4. "If neither of my wishes can meet with Government's approbation, as uncertainty and fluctuation is the most cruel and oppressive thing for a feeling heart, I beg you to favour me with the Government's resolutions when obtained."

This was doubtless the most critical point in Csoma's literary career. He saw that time was going by, and his work still unfinished, and withal he felt quite powerless to complete his labours, without further help and encouragement. Everybody will sympathise when he reads at the end of his letter forebodings full of uncertainty and apprehension.

CHAPTER VI.

Government orders on Csoma's last application—Dr. Gerard's visit
to Kanum, and his letter to Mr. Fraser.

ON the 14th of June 1827 Mr. Stirling, Government Secretary, wrote to Captain Kennedy, commanding at Sabathú,
to inform him that " the Governor-General was pleased to
allow Csoma de Körös leave to proceed to Upper Besarh
for a period of three years, for the purpose and on conditions specified in his letter of the 5th of May, and that his
lordship had given authority to pay that gentleman fifty
rupees a month for his support, and perhaps enable him to
purchase Tibetan manuscripts." The same was notified in
the Government Gazette of the 10th of September following, with the remark that "these objects are the more
desirable, as we understand Mr. de Körös considers the
recent labours of Klaproth and Rémusat, with regard to the
language and literature of Tibet, as altogether erroneous."
" Monsieur Rémusat, indeed," proceeds the article, " admits
the imperfections of his materials, but Klaproth pronounces *ex cathedrâ*, and treats the notion of any successful study of Tibetan, by the English in India, with ineffable
contempt."

We know not exactly the date on which Csoma left
Sabathú, when he set out on his *third journey* into Tibet,
for we find him always most reticent in everything that
concèrned merely his own person. The permission of
Government to spend three more years in Upper Besarh,
doubtless lessened the heavy load from his anxious mind.

He travelled presumably *viâ* Simla to Kotgarh, and thence
along the valley of the Sutlej to the Monastery of Kanum.
At this place he was visited by his devoted friend, Dr.
Gerard, whose graphic pen has placed on record a most
interesting episode in Csoma's life.

Dr. Gerard, of the Bengal Medical Service, was travelling in the Himalayan countries, for the purpose of introducing vaccination there, with the humane object of putting
a stop to the ravages of smallpox, which usually caused
such devastation among the scantily peopled districts of
the highlands.   In this beneficent errand he was efficiently
seconded by the presence of the Hungarian traveller at
Kanum, and of his teacher, the learned Lama, to whose
kindly influence Dr. Gerard pays a warm tribute.   Dr.
Gerard addressed his interesting report to Mr. W. Fraser,
Agent to the Governor-General, and Revenue Commissioner
of Delhi.   Chiefly upon the few extracts of this report, is
based what is at present known, of the details of Csoma's
industry and wonderful perseverance in the Buddhist
monasteries, which, as we know, are situated in most inhospitable regions.   The Government Gazette of the 9th
of July 1829, gives some interesting extracts from Gerard's
paper, but the document is of such importance to the
memory of the subject of this biography, that we do not
hesitate to give a place for it here *in extenso*.   It alludes also
to the hardships and privations Csoma suffered at the
Monastery of Yangla, in Zanskar, in 1827, " privations
such as have been seldom endured ; " and gives some other
details of Dr. Gerard's own journey, which are worthy of
being rescued from oblivion.   A copy of the document has
been obtained from the Asiatic Society of Bengal, and
bears date, Sabathú, 21st January 1829 :—

" Having lately returned from a tour through Kunawar, where I saw Mr. Csoma, in the midst of his studies,
I imagine I shall not be tiring you by some account of
his requirements, and the progress he has made with his

literary works. He has lost none of his ardour in that secluded region, and the deeper he penetrates into those mines of learning by which he is surrounded, he finds himself impelled to further research; but I have to regret the circumstances which afforded me so short a time to profit by his conversation. Besides this interesting interview, my present journey has likewise been remarkable for some new discoveries, which have in a degree proved a consoling recompense for the sacrifices it entailed and my disappointment in the chief object that urged me to visit a country I had so frequently traversed. I have returned to Sabathú amply gratified, only to look towards the period when I may myself meet with better success; in the meantime, I should hope that my notice of Mr. Csoma's labours would be satisfactory to those who have already interested themselves in his behalf, and that any facts connected with his researches, or that have come to my own view in the course of my travels, would be sufficiently strong to awaken curiosity towards a field of such varied resources, and ultimately to details alike interesting and beneficial. If the physical character of those mighty regions is likely to receive illustration by specimens of organic remains, productions, &c., I should not consider myself unremunerated for the exertions I have made for an object which may still prove but an illusory advantage; and though I have been extremely anxious to make another journey, under the prospects which the Chinese have tantalised me to rely upon, in an invitation next season to Lake Mansarowur, I shall be unwilling to attempt it except I receive some little encouragement in the prosecution of objects which, if not of actual public benefit, are at least of public interest.

"The presence of Mr. Csoma in Kunawar and his learned associate the Lama opens a field to my view, which no exertions on my part could give me a hope of approaching. The example and influence of such a man as the Lama, who is so much respected in those regions

F

for his learning and wisdom, could not fail to advance my object of utility, especially vaccination, as he himself offered to try the experiment, could it have been effected under favourable circumstances; and should the Chinese invite me to their country, Mr. Csoma's literary pursuits will eventually derive a more extended solicitude, through the medium of a friendship established upon philanthropy.

"In this tour I have made a very curious collection of fossil shells (*Ichthyolites*), ammonites, and other petrifactions, which are chiefly valuable from the vast elevation at which they occurred, and from having myself found them *in situ*. I observed nothing very remarkable upon the nether side, except the cholera at Chepaul, in Joobul, at a height of almost 8000 feet, in spite of those theorists who would have restricted it to a lower limit, and a deodar $29\frac{1}{2}$ feet in girth, and this is surely a prodigy in nature peculiar to those mountains. I never beheld such a sight as this enormous trunk, springing up like a mound to the height of almost 200 feet. The barometer afforded me the only practicable means of ascertaining this, and I imagine there are no others in such situations except to cut the tree down. On the northern frontiers of Kunawar I obtained an elevation of 20,000 feet without closing snow, and beheld, if not China itself, its frontier,—a scene of desolation and grandeur beyond my power to describe, for here language altogether fails. The country continued peaked, arid, and free from snow, yet every point had an altitude above my own level. The thermometer stood at 27°, but I was scorched by the sun's rays.

"I now turn to the Hungarian, who is far from the least remarkable of the many objects which have passed before me in this journey, and on whose account chiefly I trouble you with so long a letter. I found him at the village of *Kanum*, in his small but romantic hamlet, surrounded by books, and in the best health. He had not forgotten his reception at Sabathú, and was eager to manifest a feeling springing from gratitude. A year and more had passed since we met, and he seemed glad and proud to show me the fruits of his labours. He has been most persevering and successful, and were not his mind entirely absorbed in his studies, he would find a strong check to his exertions in the climate, situated as he is and has been for four months. The cold is very intense, and all last winter he sat at his desk wrapped up in woollens from head to foot, and from morning to night, without an interval of recreation or warmth, except that of his frugal meals, which are one universal routine of greasy tea; but the winters at Kanum dwindle to insignificance compared with the severity of those at the monastery of Yangla,[1] where Mr. Csoma passed a whole year. At that spot he, the Lama, and an attendant, were circumscribed in an apartment nine feet square for three or four months; they durst not stir out, the ground being covered with snow, and the temperature below the zero of the scale. There he sat, enveloped in a sheep-skin cloak, with his arms folded, and in this situation he read from morning till evening without fire, or light after dusk, the ground to sleep upon, and the bare walls of the building for protection against the rigours of the climate.

" The cold was so intense as to make it a task of severity to extricate the hands from their fleecy resort to turn over the pages. Some idea may be formed of the climate of Zanskar from the fact, that on the day of the summer solstice, a fall of snow covered the ground; and so early as the 10th September following, when the crops were yet uncut, the soil was again sheeted in snow; such is the horrid aspect of the country and its eternal winter.

" I have mentioned the above as a proof of the assiduity

[1] In the district of Zanskar, in the province of Ladak.

of Mr. Csoma, who collected and arranged 40,000 words
of the Tibetan language in a situation that would have
driven most men to despair.   He has already nearly
completed the Dictionary, and the Vocabulary is far
advanced, and both, as well as I may venture to judge,
exhibit singular industry and research.   He told me with
vivacity that he has acquired a sufficient knowledge of
Tibetan, to enable him to accomplish his objects, even
should he be deprived of the Lama's services by sickness
or other causes.   He (the Lama) has, however, engaged
to remain for two years longer, and from his great erudition, being acquainted with the refined and court languages, and learned in history: his resources will long
prove an acquisition to Mr. Csoma.   He exhibits a
singular union of learning, modesty, and greasy habits ;
and Mr. Csoma in this last respect vies with his learned
companion, which is not very strange in such a country.
The Lama is a man of vast acquirements, strangely dis-
guised under modest confidence of superiority, the mildest
and most unassuming address, and a countenance seldom
disturbed by a smile.   His learning has not made him
bigoted or self-sufficient, but it is singularly contrasted
with his person and appearance, which are humble and
dignified and greasy.   Mr. Csoma himself appears like
one of the sages of antiquity, living in the most frugal
manner, and taking no interest in any object around him,
except his literary avocations, which, however, embrace
the religions of the countries around him.   He showed
me his labours with lively satisfaction.   He has read
through 44 volumes of one of the Tibetan works, and
he finds unceasing interest in their contents.   He seems
highly pleased with the prospects of unfolding to the
world those vast mines of literary riches, and I should
say that he is flattered by his own ability to illustrate
the objects which daily come to his view, but I am almost
afraid to risk making known, from mere recollection, the
attainments he has already arrived at, and the discoveries

he has made, because he is so scrupulously tenacious of correctness in everything relating to and said of him, and carries his high feeling and independence to a degree which may be the custom of his country, but I am inclined to consider a fault in one so situated. In his conversation and expressions he is frequently disconsolate, and betrays it in involuntary sentiment, as if he thought himself forlorn and neglected. He can form no idea of the spirit in which Government will receive his works, and almost fears they may not be considered with that indulgence which is due to his research. Yet he told me, with melancholy emphasis, that on his delivering up the Grammar and Dictionary of the Tibetan language, and other illustrations of the literature of that country, he would be the happiest man on earth, AND COULD DIE WITH PLEASURE ON REDEEMING HIS PLEDGE. He showed me with great animation a printed work upon poesy, in which he pointed out the original of a translation from the Mahabharut, written in a number of the *Oriental Quarterly ;* a great part of that work (the Sanskrit edition) is supposed to be lost, and the discovery of Mr. Csoma in the Tibetan books leads to the conclusion, that the whole of the Mahabharut may yet be preserved in the monasteries of that country, which seem to have afforded an asylum to literature at a very early period, even before its retrogression in India. In a small pocket abridgment of (I think Robertson's) 'India,' Mr. Csoma showed me an extract of a *poem from the Sanskrit, at the same time holding in his hands the original passage in the Tibetan.*[1] The systems of philosophy contained in those immense compilations he says are very numerous, and he thinks will astonish the learned in Europe ; some of them are sublime in conception. I was naturally anxious to know the contents of the books of medicine, of which there are five volumes, and characters of 400 diseases

---

[1] For a further explanation of this incident, see the author's Tibetan Grammar, at page 168.

he had collected and arranged. They treat copiously on physiology; and, in fact, there is no knowing yet what they do not contain. In his brief memoir to Government,[1] the five volumes upon medicine were alluded to, but in Mr. Wilson's observations on that paper they are not noticed, at which *Mr. Csoma seems disappointed,* and has strangely concluded that his assertion was discredited, but consoles himself with the prospect of disclosing many facts even much more unexpected. The Lama has informed him that at Teshi Lhunpo the *anatomy* of the human body is represented in wooden cuts or prints (for I forget which) in so many different attitudes. He also observes, that the art of lithography has long prevailed in that city and at Lassa, where learning has flourished from a very remote period.

"Mr. Csoma's objects embrace a wide expanse, of which he justly considers a grammar and dictionary of the language they relate to, as the first desideratum, and none of the specimens of words which he has occasionally gleaned from books, or those sent to him by Mr. Wilson, are correct in orthography. The works in which Mr. Csoma is now engaged will only form a prelude to their further extension and copiousness, and they cannot, I should imagine, fail to excite interest towards that end; but, poor man, his means are limited, and far from adequate to accomplish the vast objects which his mind surveys. The Lama receives twenty-five rupees a month, a servant costs him four, his house-rent one, and writing materials consume a proportion which leaves him less than twenty rupees to provide the necessaries of life, which in that remote and secluded region are very expensive, and must frequently be supplied from Sabathú, or from a distance of two hundred miles. He lives in the most economical manner; his resources would compel him to this if his inclination did not. He enjoys the best of health, perhaps in consequence; for though resid-

[1] See letter to Captain Kennedy, at page 46.

ing at a spot abounding with grapes, apricots, and many
other fruits, he assured me he had this season abstained
from everything of the sort from a prudent conviction
that they could not make him happier, and might injure
him. His chief and almost only meal is tea, in the Tartar
fashion, which is indeed more like soup, the butter and
salt mixed in its preparation leaving no flavour of tea.
It is a repast at once greasy and nourishing, and being
easily made, is very convenient in such a country.

"Mr. Csoma's hamlet is at the extreme upper limit of
the village of Kanum, at an absolute elevation of 9500
feet. Around him are the romantic abodes of monks,
whose religious ceremonies, their pious incantations, &c.,
have a singular affinity to Romish customs. Below is
the monastery, containing the Encyclopædia, but it is
also converted into what seems a more substantial purpose with the people, for on my return to Kanum in the
beginning of November I found it filled with grapes, and
about thirty whole sheep hung up for winter consumption,
yet poor Mr. Csoma can hardly afford to taste even a
piece of one. The climate here, though warm in summer,
is singularly dry, and to this circumstance more than
temperature, is owing the preservation of animal food for
months. There are several convents at this village, but
the exactions are far from rigorous, and Mr. Csoma told
me, with an air of derision, that many of the nuns
became mothers, and in fact enter the convents if
they cannot get married or do better; their choice
is therefore a prudential measure when they are liable
to fare worse: there is much sense though no merit in
this. Mr. Csoma showed me some improvements he had
made to his cottage; one was a fireplace, which has
cost him twelve rupees, and here I could not help feeling with sympathy the value of such a sum to a man,
whose whole earthly happiness consists in being merely
able to live and devote himself to mankind, with no
other reward than a just appreciation and honest fame,

while I was at the same time daily and no doubt fool-
ishly expending more than enough to give comfort and
effect to a mind so noble; feeling, as I did, how little he
wanted for himself and how little I valued that which
to him provided food for body and mind. *Two rustic
benches and a couple of ruder chairs* are all the furniture
in his small abode; but the place looks comfortable and
the volumes of the Tibetan works, the 'Kahgyur' and
'Stangyur,' his manuscripts, and papers are neatly piled
up around him.   Had Mr. Csoma greater pecuniary
resources, he would invite learned men from Teshi
Lhunpo, Lassa, and with their assistance study the
Mongol language, which he considers the key to Chinese
literature.   There are many valuable works in the
libraries of those ancient cities which are likely never
to become an acquisition to our knowledge but through
the labours of such a genius as Mr. Csoma. *His great
aim and unceasing anxiety is to get access to Mongolia* and
make himself acquainted with the language and people
of that strange and very ancient country.   The study
of dialects to him is no labour, grounded as he is in a
perfect knowledge of classical literature and more or less
familiar with the structure of every spoken language; but
he wants books to revive his early impressions.   With a
knowledge of the Mongols, their literature, history, and
customs, his hopes of new discoveries would never cease
to occupy his mind, and on the completion of his present
studies he will direct his views to those higher objects.

"Though residing within the British dominions in a
country where the inhabitants are morally good, nevertheless Mr. Csoma has to combat against several irksome
restraints.   The bigotry of the Lamas attached to the
monastery, arising from their ignorance of their own
faith and of the contents of their beautifully printed
works, is a source of much disquietude; while the
Wuzeers of the Besarh frontier (Hindoos), under whose
care the building is placed, having themselves little

interest in an institution which emanates from a region where the cow is killed and eaten, but still keeping up the mummery and superstitious reverence of regard, and protecting and in some degree respecting the house of learning, are very intolerant. Mr. Csoma, it is true, has access to the works in the monastery, but this is not without some suspicious vigilance on the part of both Lamas and Hindoos, who allow but two or three volumes to leave the monastery at a time, while his labours require simultaneous resolution, and wound that self-esteem and independent feeling with which he used so frequently to provoke us at Sabathú. His motives are no doubt the best, but they are too refined for society, and certainly would not be always tolerated with patience, especially amongst strangers. He still refuses every offer of assistance, and will not accept of the most trifling article, though in a situation which ought not to admit of such ceremonious policy. I imagined that the late English papers would afford him amusement, but after a few days, he desired me not to send them, adding, that he would not throw himself open to the imputation of suspicion by attending to anything but that which he had pledged himself to prosecute; he then with great emphasis revived his old and strange ideas of his having been taken for a spy, treated at Sabathú as a fool, caressed and ridiculed at the same time, adding, with much self-complacency, that the world would soon see what he was. The same singular feeling regulates his conduct on every occasion. He is jealous of the least suspicion, even of his habits of life. I asked him if he ever used the spirits made from the grape (which are nearly as good as Scotch whisky). He told me that on one occasion of sickness he had procured a little, but afterwards, conceiving that the people of the country might give him the repute of drinking instead of studying, he resolved never again to touch spirits.

"On leaving Kanum, I thought I might venture to ask his acceptance of a cloak which was well adapted for so cold a climate. I sent him also some rice and sugar, but he returned the whole, and out of his scanty resources sent me sixteen rupees to purchase a few articles at Sabathú, which I have despatched since my arrival. All this is no doubt commendable, but I cannot think it very wise. Yet though thus extremely tenacious of his own independence, Mr. Csoma would accept of assistance only from a public source, because he seems confident of his ability to return a remunerating advantage; but to private individuals he says he has nothing to give. The only things he would receive from me on his first arrival at Sabathú were a few books to read, and the first he asked for, was the Bible, as best calculated to revive his English, which he had studied grammatically on getting here. This he read through in eight days, and on his journey from Zanskar he accepted of a Latin Dictionary, and on my late tour I left with him a Greek Lexicon. These last are useful to his present studies. He is greatly in want of books of reference, and particularly anxious to see some of the numbers of the *Oriental Quarterly Magazine* relating to his avocations, two having been sent to him by Mr. Wilson, which from their inaccuracies and references to other numbers excited his curiosity to see more. He would be glad to see some authors on ancient Geography, such as Quintus Curtius, Ptolemy, Diodorus Siculus, and Pliny. Mr. Csoma's researches are not merely confined to the compilation of the Grammar and Dictionary of the Tibetan language; they embrace many objects of remote ages, illustrative of ancient geography and history, to which the old authors would contribute identity and explanation. He has collected from the printed works and manuscripts in the possession of the Lama much curious information on the geographical and physical features of Tibet. Those records

treat fully, and, I should say, sensibly, of the route and
sources of rivers, remarkable mountains, mines, statistics,
religions, creeds and institutions, chronology and historical
events.   For instance, Lake Mansarowur has always been
considered by Eastern geographers as the central source
of the great rivers of India, Brahmapootra, Gogra, Sutlej,
and Indus, and the highest table-level there, because the
waters are thrown off in every direction from that point;
but our over-scrupulous exactitude, in literally deriving
those rivers from the same lake because the Hindoos had
assigned a common origin to them, has led us to tax
their ancient traditions with vagueness, incorrectness, and
falsehood.   Mansarowur being the reputed or even veri-
table source of these rivers, was a mere figurative position: it was also celebrated on account of Kylas, the throne
of Mahadeo, which spires up from that lofty base in the
form of a cone, sheeted in snow, and is, without a doubt,
the highest point of the earth's surface.   The Hindoos
knew as well as we did, that two rivers in so rugged a
country could not flow out of the same lake in opposite
directions, but there is no question about the proximate
conjunction of the whole four.   We have yet to learn the
Tibetan accounts, and as they promise to be free of much
of the theological tincture of the Hindoos, we have still
before us an unexplored field of interesting prospects.

"Mr. Csoma is anxious that some British officer who
has studied Sanskrit, should make himself also acquainted
with Tibetan, as he says they would give reciprocal light
to each other, and to a just estimation of the value of the
latter language.   He himself, though ardent in his researches, is at the same time careful and cautious in his
deductions, though these may appear extravagant to others
who have no access to the sources of his knowledge, and
on this account he is reserved and diffident in communicating all he has acquired; but he only wants encouragement to give full effect to his varied and comprehensive
resources.   He is deeply sensible of the liberality of

Government towards him; but at the same time feels his own ability to make a suitable return. For my own part, I should say that the works he is now engaged in (if justly appreciated) will far exceed in actual value and ulterior importance the support he has received from our Government for their accomplishment, though without it he might certainly still have remained in obscurity; and with such men as Mr. Wilson, Mr. M'Kenzie, and Mr. Stirling—all of whom are acquainted with his situation and objects,—I can anticipate nothing but a reward worthy of the individual, and he looks to the future with no small degree of concern. He wants but the means of subsistence, and has only to speak for himself to gain sympathy and respect; but *he is poor, humbly clad,* and reserved, unless stimulated to animation by some temporary interest; and to see him, as I have seen him, wrapped in sheepskin, and measuring his wants by his means, one would little suppose him to be the man destined under good fortune to perform the great works he has now in progress. Nothing pleases him so much as to appear interested in his conversation; but he has evidently not been accustomed to the society of the world, and from not knowing the idiom of the English language, he often puts a misconstruction upon words, and breaks forth into singular and dignified irritation at times; he is full of vivacity, but this is often interrupted by the anxiety most natural to him, and he lapses into gloom without a visible cause. When he spoke of his want of books, he remarked that these were few and easily supplied, but that they had not been considered. He particularly dwelt upon the resources of the Asiatic Society—forgetting, however, that he had never solicited their aid. He is too diffident to appeal in his own behalf, and too independent to seek the means through the hands of others. When I offered to make known his situation and the progress he had made with his literary works, he thanked me, and perhaps felt more

than he wished to express, though in doing so I but do
justice to merit in one so situate; and being myself almost
the only person who has visited his sequestered retreat,
and knowing what is expected from him, any observations
may be satisfactory; and I can only add that, if means
could be devised to increase his small allowance even to
100 rupees a month, it would be liberality well conferred, and must eventually be well repaid.   Mr. Csoma
has no selfish gratification; the tribute of honest fame
is his only ambition.   There are no doubt many in India
who would afford him the aid he requires; he peremp-
torily refuses to accept of anything, but from a public and
recognised source.   I cannot myself venture to seek the
aid of the Asiatic Society in behalf of so bright an object
of their patronage, but I should hope that the merits of
so highly-gifted and modest an individual will not be
long unnoticed.   Mr. Csoma will give a most satisfactory
explanation of his views, but he would like to be addressed by some one either on the part of the Asiatic
Society or Government.   He would be flattered and
stimulated by such a recognition.   The Society, in sup-
porting such a man, would receive their fullest reward
in his contributions of literary knowledge of the highest
order, and belonging to countries which are yet only
known to us as vast terra incognita both in regard to
physical configuration, mankind, and learning, and Mr.
Csoma would in his turn derive his best gratification from
his alliance with an institution so highly established.

"As I was residing in the Monastery at Kanum, I
took an opportunity of getting access to the Tibetan
Encyclopædia, by stepping in behind the officiating Lama
when he came to worship.   On discovering me he made
some civil remonstrance, and then allowed me to stand
behind the door when he slowly opened the folding
leaves of the library, and in the interval I stepped up
and looked over his shoulders.   The works, being distinct,
are arranged in separate places.   These resemble large

chests or cisterns, standing on end, and partitioned into cells, each containing a volume, which is carefully wrapped within many folds, laced with cord, and bound tightly between boards of cypress or cedar. The 'Kahgyur' is a work of morality, and is, in fact, the Bible, and consists, I believe, of 104 folio volumes, each containing from 500 to 700 pages, all beautifully printed from wooden types. The 'Stangyur' is more copious, comprising 240 volumes, and treats upon arts and science. Five volumes are devoted to medicine; the others comprehend astronomy, astrology, rhetoric, poesy, philosophy, history, and a vast variety of subjects. Some of the volumes were opened before me, and I gazed with a sort of reverential feeling upon such gigantic compilations yet unfolded to the world, and thought of the humble individual in the hamlet who was occupied in illustrating their unexplored contents. It is rather singular that those works should be found planted in a Hindoo village, or, at least, established amongst people who are not alienated from Hindoo tenets, though tinctured with Buddhist principles; but poor Moorcroft mentions, in his tour to Mansarowur, having seen a greater number of Hindoo images in the Tartar village of Dala, than he ever recollected meeting with before in India, at any one spot. The contrast is, however, great, though there is both identity and unity in their divinity and chief duties, for Mr. Csoma affirms that the Tibetan faith, both in precept and practice, approaches nearer to the Christian religion than that of any Asiatic nation whatever. The Tibetan works appear to have been very widely disseminated throughout that country, and we may safely ascribe this multiplicity of books to the facility which the art of printing afforded. We find fragments and manuscripts of great antiquity scattered about and deposited in situations which are now almost deserted by man. At the village of Skuno, which lay in my route, and is planted upon the eastern frontier of Kunawur, near the confines of

China, at a height of 12,000 feet, is a *labrung* or monastery, a melancholy record of better times. Here the
traveller beholds files of printed papers full of learning,
bound up in cypress boards, as if shut for the last time.
I had a Chinese interpreter with me, who dipped into
one of the books and read some passages relating to
science. I could not but gaze with wonder and reverence upon those relics of learning now no longer useful,
but as dead records : nobody turns over the fine pages of
those ancient and extraordinary works, upon which time
has made but little change, and in so cold and arid a
climate will remain when the temple itself falls to ruin,
and this is going on gradually ; but two hundred years
have effected little decay. The type of the printing is
very beautiful, and looks fresh ; bound as they are closely
together, in an atmosphere without insects or moisture,
in a climate rude even in summer, they seem calculated
to defy time itself. In former days those books were
read and people attended here at prayers, but now there
is nothing left of what has once been. The masters are
gone for ever, but the temple and books stand still, like
the pyramids, pointing to times which have no other
record. I was much tempted to commit sacrilege here,
and steal away some of the scientific volumes, but I had
not a good opportunity.

"The edition of the 'Kahgyur' and 'Stangyur' at
Kanum was sent from Teshi Lhunpo only about nine
years ago ; the printing bears a date of ninety years, yet
the ink and type look as perfect and fresh as ever. No
insects attack them, though the climate here is varying
in summer. The book-cases being made of cedar are
indestructible. The fact of printing in Tibet, however
curious, can no longer be questioned, for I myself have
brought down a specimen of it from Sungnam. The
types are not movable, but cut in wooden frames, which
must be productive of great labour and bulkiness, if used
to any extent ; but I suspected that at Teshi Lhunpo

and Lassa the types are alphabetical, and like our own
are movable.   Should this not be the case, the only
other substitute instead of frames would be lithography,
which is known to prevail there; but Mr. Csoma says
that the art of printing dates a little posterior to the era
which discovered it in Europe.   There are no images in
the temple at Kanum, and worship seems to be performed out of pure respect for the house of learning.
Kanum is the only spot of Kunawur which possesses
those works entire.

"We find indeed detached volumes and piles of papers
in many of the other villages, as Sungnam, Skuno, and
Nissung; and in Piti, in Ladak, where those works are
sheltered, beautiful paintings and casts as large as life
adorn the monasteries, leaving us wondering at the origin
and antiquity of such remains in regions wild in aspect
and sterile in production.   Additional interest is thrown
over those mighty scenes of the Himalayas in the curious
fact, which has recently come to my knowledge, of
the discovery in an obscure spot of Kunawur of a
relic of the Romish missionaries' work on Tibet, the
Speculum Veritatis, bearing a date of 1678.   This
curious record was picked up by the Rev. Mr. W., whom
I met with in my travels, and then little thought
that so precious a fragment would have found its way
into his hands, judging from an observation on first
meeting him on the northern face of the Himalaya.   The
fragment of literature acquired by Mr. W. (which I suspect
is part of Andrada's mission) has been sent to Mr. Csoma
for elucidation, and I expect soon to hear of its contents.

"In all this, I have only been able to trace a margin
of a new and gigantic map; we must look to the
central plateau of Tartary for that knowledge which we
have seen indicated elsewhere, and a grander field as
regards natural aspect and configuration could not be
selected, an aspect barren, it is true, but interesting from
the grandeur of its barrenness, and concealing under its

rugged and forbidding features, resources the most varied
and estimable to science, literature, and art. To speak of
those positive advantages in respect of climate and production even within our territory: such is the aridity of
the interior of Kunawar that the roots of the *rheum
palmatum*, which I dug up from amidst patches of snow
on the slope of the pass in the Himalayan chain in the
end of June, were already dry and pulverisable the following month, and moist opium received from Kotgarh
in July became brittle and fit to be powdered in August,
while in Calcutta this is impracticable in the driest season
without the aid of adventitious heat.

"It was now the end of September, and the climate
was highly agreeable, the grapes being already ripe.
Here, at an elevation of nine thousand feet, the vine finds
a temperature congenial to its perfect maturity ; but it is
to the summer heat of those spots that its successful
culture is indebted, since in winter reigns a keen and
protracted frost, and the snow falls from four to five feet
deep, lying in the fields till April. The vines are left
unprotected, and remain buried under their congealed
clothing. Fruits of various kinds, as apples, apricots,
and nectarines, come to high perfection in a climate
free from periodical rains and exposed to intense solar
radiation. Thus a region which produces the finest
grapes if in insolated exposure, or lying on the Indian
aspect of Himalaya, will hardly yield a crop of grain,
owing to the want of a stronger ephemeral heat. For the
same reason grain succeeds in the valley of the Sutlej,
and in spots within the Chinese dominions, at eleva-
tions which, on the southern side of the Himalayas, are
loaded with ice; but the winters of the interior, on the
other hand, teem with rigours which we can form but
little idea of. It is true, the sky is mostly clear, and the
sun's rays at the loftiest spots are sufficient to keep the
people, or rather one side of them, warm in the dead of
winter. During my stay at Kanum the extremes of the

G

thermometer were 33° to 77°; but when I returned, only one month later, I found them 30° and 52°, and snow had fallen. So sudden is the vicissitude in an atmosphere deriving its heat from solar radiation. I left a thermometer with Mr. Csoma, being desirous of ascertaining the winter climate of the spot which rears the vine so abundantly. But Mr. Csoma has little or no interest in anything beyond his literary studies, and I was often provoked at his indifference to objects calculated to illustrate the physical character of the countries he resides in and add to the value of his own pursuits.

" He has promised to keep a register of the temperature for me.

" On the 30th of September I took leave of the Hungarian and his intelligent companion the Lama."

Csoma's aversion to occupy himself with anything outside the range of his studies has been noticed already; but to please his friend Dr. Gerard he was induced to make meteorological observations, and *did* furnish valuable records from Kanum, extending over a period of two years. These came ultimately into General Cunningham's hands, and were embodied by him into his own work on " Ladak," at page 184.

CHAPTER VII.

Csoma completes his Tibetan studies at Kanum ; Correspondence
with Dr. Wilson, Captain Kennedy, and Mr. B. H. Hodgson.

THE perusal of Dr. Gerard's almost forgotten letter gives
a vivid picture of the strange surroundings in the midst
of which Csoma was placed whilst studying at the
Buddhist Monastery among the Himalayan Mountains.
In the truthfulness of the description, Gerard's pen
surpasses almost the fancies of imagination. The devoted student spent four winter seasons exposed to the
rigorous climates of Yangla and Kanum in the pursuit,
not of imaginary theories, as has been so often stated
of him, but in the fulfilment of engagements which he
undertook for the Government.

"He is frequently disconsolate, and betrays it in involuntary sentiment, as if he thought himself forlorn and
neglected. . . . He told me with melancholy emphasis,"
continues Dr. Gerard, " that on his delivering up the
Grammar and Dictionary to the Government, he would
be the happiest man on earth, and could die with pleasure
on redeeming his pledge."

Dr. Gerard has given expression in another place of
the deep interest he felt for Csoma's studies and in
his personal concerns. On the 22d of January he wrote
a private letter also to Mr. Fraser ; a fragment only of it
is extant, in the Library of the Asiatic Society in Calcutta. Even this fragment, however, is worth preserv-
ing, as it relates to Moorcroft's papers, and shows the
attempts made and the anxiety displayed by the Government to recover them after his death, and also bears

witness to the confidence felt in the ability and in the spirit of enterprise of the Hungarian traveller, when there were thoughts of entrusting him with the mission to Andkhoi in Bokhara, where Moorcroft died.

This is the fragment, dated Sabathú, 22d of January 1829 :—

"MY DEAR FRASER,—Since my return from Kunawar I often thought that I might be doing a service to the Hungarian traveller by just making known a few facts connected with his pursuits and situation in that sequestered region. I am anxious enough to believe that I shall not be imposing a tax on your patience, and I am sure I shall not be deceived in anticipating your views and estimation of an object so deserving of encouragement. It is natural in me to interest myself in Mr. Csoma's welfare, since I was the first who received him at Sabathú, and I am now the last who has seen him amongst his researches, and on this account I perhaps have the best knowledge of his situation and the objects that can be obtained.

" In sending you the accompanying remarks,[1] I have a conviction that your own high and liberal mind may suggest some means calculated to bring Mr. Csoma into notice, for where merit is the appeal, I need not stay to consider the effect with you. I have a strong idea that Sir Charles Metcalfe would not be an unmoved spectator of zeal and talent so remarkable as that which characterises the individual who is now devoting himself to researches so interesting amidst the rigours of climate and the restraints of poverty. Sir Charles took sufficient interest in him from Moorcroft's fate, when he forwarded my application to go to Ladak, for the purpose of requesting the Hungarian to undertake the trip for the recovery of his papers, to excite me to rely upon one so generous. And I am an " —— The fragment ends here.

What splendid testimony is this to the confidence

[1] See preceding chapter.

which was reposed in the unselfishness and ready self-sacrifice of the Hungarian scholar, who at that time was engaged in his studies at the Monastery of Pukdal! Moorcroft's papers had been secured, before Csoma was made aware of the important project regarding himself.

William Moorcroft, the ill-fated traveller whose name is so intimately connected with the Hungarian philologist, was director of the Government studs in India. Attached to the cavalry, he arrived in Bengal in 1808, and was soon afterwards selected for employment as Government Agent in Western Asia; during his journey he suffered much hardship, and was more than once in danger of his life. In 1819 he started on a fresh expedition, accompanied by his relative, George Trebeck, and visited the Panjáb, Kashmir, Tibet, and Bokhara. Having faced many obstacles and escaped imminent perils, he was seized with fever and died on the 27th August 1825. His tomb is at Andkhoi in Bokhara, to which place he went for the purpose of buying horses for Government. Moorcroft's diary was arranged and edited in two volumes by Dr. H. H. Wilson, under the title, "Travels in the Himalayan Provinces, by William Moorcroft and George Trebeck, in 1819–1825. London, 1841." At page 338 of vol. i. is described the first meeting between Moorcroft and the Hungarian traveller in the valley of Dras in Ladak.

Gerard's friendly pleading for Csoma was not without effect. We find extracts from his letter cited in the *Government Gazette* of 9th July 1829, with the following prefatory remarks :—

"The extracts read from Dr. Gerard's paper respecting the labours of Mr. Csoma de Körös were of a most interesting nature, not only as giving a vivid idea of the admirable, we may say heroic devotion, of that singularly disinterested and enterprising person to the cause of literature, in spite of difficulties that would confound a less determined spirit, but as referring to depositories of learning, which for ages have been confined to a peculiar people, of whose language and institutions but little is known to Europeans, but which, through the fortunate instrumentality of Mr. Csoma de Körös and his learned associate the Lama, it is hoped, will not long remain a fountain sealed to the literary world."

In the same article occurs a paragraph which shows the ultimate aim of Csoma as to his researches:

" In the libraries of the ancient cities of Teshi Lhunpo and Lassa there are said to be many valuable works, which the world is likely to become acquainted with only through the instrumentality of such a genius as Mr. Csoma. He is very anxious to get to the country of the Mongols, and make every possible research into the history and institutions of that ancient people."

The Council of the Asiatic Society of Bengal resolved to grant Csoma a monthly allowance, equal to that he was receiving already from Government. This step was due to the exertions of Sir Charles Metcalfe, Mr. Simon Fraser, Mr. Calder, Mr. Mackenzie, and Captain Stacy, all of whom strongly urged that Csoma should be more liberally provided for while studying at Kanum. Captain Stacy, in a letter dated 3d May 1829, to the address of Dr. Wilson, says: " Csoma expends very little upon himself; he dresses in the coarse blanket of the country, and eats with the natives."

There is no doubt, therefore, that Csoma had to suffer many privations, but he never uttered a word of complaint on that account; what affected him deeply, however, was the thought of his being neglected and forgotten in the far-off monastery. We know, however, that such was not the case. A stranger and foreigner could never wish to find warmer friends than Csoma found in Captain Kennedy and Dr. Gerard. The former was always a faithful exponent of his wishes before Government and private friends, and Dr. Gerard's letters testify to the

sincere interest he took in him. Dr. Wilson, on behalf
of the Asiatic Society, wrote on the 15th July 1829,
informing Csoma of the Society's resolution as to the
increase of his stipend, part of which was at once forwarded to him through Captain Kennedy. Dr. Wilson
added, "I have been also instructed to procure for you such
books as you may think serviceable to your inquiries."

Csoma's character showed traits of a quiet melancholy and desponding tendency. The following original
letter, the paper of which is already much damaged by
age, shows with what anxieties his mind was beset; but,
when his isolated position is considered, and the other
depressing circumstances under which he lived, nobody
will feel surprise at them.

This letter of Csoma's to the secretary of the Asiatic
Society, is dated 21st August 1829 [1] from Kanum, and
reads as follows :—

"I beg leave to acknowledge the receipt of your letter,
together with a draft, dated Calcutta, 15th July 1829,
which reached me this day. I feel much obliged to the
Asiatic Society for the interest they have been pleased
to take with respect to my literary inquiries in Tibet,
and for the kind resolution they came to in granting me
50 rupees a month for my support. But since I found
their resolution to be of very indefinite character, which
leaves me for the future as uncertain as I ever was, since
my first study of the Tibetan, and since I cannot employ
with advantage the offered money during the short period
I have still to stay here: I beg leave for declining to
accept the offered allowance and of returning the draft.

"In 1823, in April, when I was in Kashmir, in the
beginning of my engagement with the late Mr. Moorcroft,
being destitute of books, Mr. Moorcroft, on my behalf,
had requested you to send me certain necessary works.

[1] The original is in the possession of the Hungarian Academy of
Sciences in Budapest—a generous
gift, with two other original letters
of Csoma's, from the Council of the
Asiatic Society of Bengal in 1883.

I have never received any. I was neglected for six years. Now, under such circumstances and prospects, I shall want no books. If not prevented by some unforeseen event, next year I shall be ready with my papers. Then, if you please, you shall see what I have done and what I could yet do.

"If the Asiatic Society will then earnestly be desirous to get further information respecting Tibetan literature both in India and Tibet, I shall be happy to enter into an engagement with them or with the Government on proper terms."

Reasons were especially given for his refusing to accept the Society's proffered aid, but it was nevertheless considered by Csoma's well-wishers a mistake to push his spirit of independence so far. This disapproval may be guessed at from Captain Kennedy's letter also, addressed to Dr. Wilson. It should be borne in mind, however, on the other hand, that Csoma was not aware of the steps taken on his behalf, and the endeavour made by his friends to improve his position was entirely unknown to him at Kanum. No doubt Csoma need not have held so tenaciously to his ideas of independence; such policy was of no advantage to either of the parties concerned.

Captain Kennedy, on forwarding Csoma's last letter of refusal, writes to the secretary of the Asiatic Society on the 3d of September 1829:

"I am disposed to think that, on a better acquaintance with Mr. Csoma, you will find him a most eccentric character. He is enthusiastic in the object of forming a grammar and lexicon of the Tibetan language, and appears anxious to avoid the society and attentions of Europeans, chiefly, in my opinion, to retain the *incognito* he lives in at the Monastery of Kanum in Upper Besarh. He is a man of most sanguine, hasty, and suspicious disposition. I have left no act undone to accommodate and to meet his wishes, and I think that he feels grateful to me; but on some occasions he has received my advances, to be obliging, with a meanness not to be accounted for. There can be no doubt but that he is a man of eminent talents, possessing a most retentive memory, and apparently much versed on subjects of general literature. He considers himself acting under a solemn pledge to Government to furnish the grammar and lexicon by the end of the ensuing year, at which period he proposes to proceed to Calcutta to superintend their publication. His wants are few, and I am informed his expenses on diet, &c., are of the most moderate description, in fact, not more than of one of the inhabitants of the village in which he resides.

" Should you wish to have any further communications with Mr. Csoma, I shall be most happy to be the medium of it; and I beg you will command my best services whenever there may be occasion for them."

Csoma's studies among the Buddhist monks were now drawing towards completion. On the 26th March 1830, Csoma applied for permission from Government to remain at Kanum till after the rainy season should cease. Captain Kennedy notified this request to the Resident at Delhi on the 9th of June, asking at the same time for a grant to Csoma of a sum, by way of travelling expenses, to enable him to visit Calcutta, and to take his Tibetan books and manuscripts with him. Captain Kennedy observes, in the course of his letter :

" I deem it my duty to mention that Mr. Csoma's conduct has been exemplary during the three years he has resided within the protected British territory, and, as I have reason to believe, he has achieved the object he had in view by visiting these states, of forming a grammar and lexicon of the Tibetan language. I beg to submit for your consideration, and eventually for that of Government, the propriety of advancing this learned and enterprising individual a small sum of money to enable him to reach Calcutta, the amount of which I do not apprehend would exceed 500 rupees."

This was sanctioned on the recommendation of the Resident at Delhi, dated 14th June 1829.

Two more original letters in Csoma's handwriting are extant, written by him at Kanum, and addressed to Mr. B. H. Hodgson, resident at Katmandú, in answer to certain questions which that gentleman addressed to Csoma. These documents also are now in the possession of the Hungarian Academy of Sciences. They were generously presented by Mr. Hodgson in 1882, with a request for them to be preserved among the relics of the late Tibetan scholar, in the archives at Budapest. These letters refer to questions of much scientific interest at the period when they were written, and throw light upon the history of Buddhistic literature, when Hodgson and Csoma were fellow-labourers in the same field of Oriental learning. They have not been published before, and deserve, therefore, to find a place in this biography.

The first letter is dated 30th December 1829, and reads thus:

"SIR,—I beg to acknowledge the receipt of the volume you have favoured me with, which reached me on the 21st instant. I feel much obliged for the kindness you have done me, in making me acquainted with the names and contents of so many valuable works you have brought to public notice, and with many other things respecting Buddhism in Nepal. Since you desired me that I should make any remarks on the twelfth article of the volume, I beg you will kindly accept of some observations I take the liberty to make on the subject. And I beg to have me excused for my not having been more particular, as perhaps you had expected from me; my circumstances have not permitted me to do otherwise.

2. "(With reference to p. 410, &c.) Tibetan words, if written properly, are very distinct for the eye, but very confused for the ear, as they are generally uttered.

In the whole of Tibet there is but one mode of writing, with respect to orthography; there are several ways of pronunciation, according to the several distant provinces. Hence that great discrepancy in the catalogues of Tibetan words furnished by several Europeans. There are to be found in Tibet several examples of alphabets used anciently in India. The late Mr. Moorcroft had sent to Calcutta a copy of the same set that have been exhibited in the plates. The Lantsa letters and their skeletons (that have been likewise represented on the same plate) are used sometimes by the Tibetans now too for inscriptions. They generally use their own characters, either the capital or the small. Their literature in general is contained in books written in any of these two. When one is acquainted with the principles of the Tibetan language, he can read easily both.

3. "Many of the works enumerated, pp. 424, 427, 431, are to be found also in the Tibetan translations. Since I shall give the names or titles of all the several works contained both in the Kah-gyur and the Stan-gyur divisions of the Tibetan collection, I thought not necessary to specify those now I have found in the mentioned pages. The Lalita Vistára, as has been observed on page 424, is in Tibet also one of the chief authorities for the life and history of the Shakya. Likewise, in Tibet, too, the Buddha Scriptures are of the same twelve kinds as have been described on p. 426, the twelve Tibetan names being exactly translated from Sanskrit.

4. "In general the whole information given of Buddhism, of the character of Buddhistic works, and the lists of the Tathagatas, is mostly in the same tenor or spirit as it is taken in Tibet. During my reading of the Tibetan volumes, I have met frequently with these and other fancied Buddhas, Bodhisatwas, &c. At the beginning of some lectures, it is sometimes too tedious

to read over all the names of such supposed hearers.
And it is especially at this occasion, that the author of
the Sútras terribly mixes divine and human things together.   The Buddhas, Bodhisatwas, and many other
pretended divinities, good and evil spirits, are, in general,
fancied or metaphysical beings, which in the Buddhistic
Pantheon have been multiplied to an incredible number.
It is impossible, therefore, and unnecessary too, to
labour to describe them with any precision.   Their
names, epithets, or attributes being taken sometimes
in a general, sometimes in a particular sense, many
times as symbolical names, or as so many models of
virtue, vice, mercy, wisdom, power, &c.   Since the
Buddhistic works consist not merely of wild metaphysical speculations, but contain several volumes of
practical topics also, we should be acquainted with the
whole, and judge accordingly.   When Europeans shall
have been acquainted with the practical part of the
Buddhistic doctrine, with the language of Tibet, and
with the several useful popular works it contains, then
I think they will excuse them in some degree for
the extravagance in the dogmatical part of their
religion.

5. " (With respect to p. 434.)   According to the
testimony of several Tibetan writers, the Tibetans
have derived their religion and literature in general
from India, commencing about the middle of the
seventh century after Christ, and have formed their
alphabet in imitation of the Devanagari letters.   Several
Tibetan scholars resided for many years in India, and
became well acquainted with the Sanskrit literature of
the Buddhists of that country.   Learned pandits were
invited many times to Tibet to assist the Tibetans in
the translation of the Sanskrit works.   Many translations have been made in concert, and according to
certain plans.   By these means they have wonderfully
improved and enriched the Tibetan language.   They

have formed, with a few exceptions, words for the expression of everything that occurred in Sanskrit. Now the Tibetan language, if well understood, may be consulted with advantage for the explanation of many technical terms in the whole complicated system of the Buddhistic doctrine, there being extant several collections of Sanskrit and Tibetan words and phrases for this purpose.

6. "(With respect to the 422d page.) The doctrine taught by .Shakya, according to many Tibetan authorities, was collected at three different times after his death. It was first collected immediately after his decease, by three of his principal disciples, whose names are mentioned. The second collection was made one hundred and ten years after the death of 'Shakya, in the time of the King Ashoka or Asoka. The third in the time of Kaniska, the king, four hundred years after the death of Shakya, when the followers of Buddha had separated themselves into eighteen different classes or sects. After that time, it is probable the Buddhistic doctrine in India itself has undergone several modifications, and the more so in the countries into which it was afterwards propagated. It was commenced to be introduced into Tibet in the seventh century after Christ, was very flourishing in the ninth, it was greatly persecuted and almost suppressed in the beginning of the tenth, it was again firmly re-established in the eleventh century. What progress it made afterwards in Tibet and in the Mongol countries, there are many historical documents thereof extant in the Tibetan books.

7. "Thus I have endeavoured to express my sentiments, with respect to some pages of the twelfth article of the volume, without touching the topics of higher speculation.

"I beg you will kindly excuse me for any defect. I shall do all in my power, in my further studies, to merit the continuance of your favour. I have the honour to remain, with much respect," &c.

The second letter, dated 29th April 1830, is an answer to Mr. Hodgson's strictures on subjects contained in Csoma's preceding communication. We find in what follows another proof of the writer's diffidence and modesty, which Mr. Torrens so forcibly points out as "the surprising trait of Csoma's character." In this letter Csoma postpones his full reply to a more favourable opportunity, because, he adds, "I know. not how to write Sanskrit and Tibetan words in Roman characters," and that he was "unacquainted with the Sanskrit," nor had he the "command of the English language."

"SIR,—I beg leave to acknowledge the receipt of the pamphlet, together with your letter of the 15th of February last, which reached this place on the 14th instant. I am much obliged for your kindness.

2. "I have seen with much satisfaction the great coincidence of the Buddhistic faith in Nepal with that of Tibet. The figures on the Plates I., II., IV., the list of the Buddha Scriptures on p. 4, &c., and the whole sketch of Buddhism, exhibit a wonderful agreement, with a few exceptions. Since I am unacquainted with Sanskrit, neither know I how to write the Sanskrit and Tibetan in Roman characters to be intelligible, nor have I the command of the English language, I beg you will kindly excuse me for my not having entered upon particulars on the subject. I shall find opportunity, perhaps, hereafter to supply the defect of my present communication.

3. "I beg you will pardon me; I have never said that the Tibetans have only one alphabet of their own. If you will inspect the second paragraph of my former letter to you, you will find that I have stated there, 'In the whole of Tibet there is but one mode of writing, with respect to orthography, &c.' But since you seem to have been offended at my expression, I beg now to state:

out of the four alphabets printed opposite page 418 of the volume formerly sent to me, the three first are Tibetan, called capital, small, and running hand; the fourth, or Lantsa (Lanja), is of India, but used sometimes in Tibet too for inscriptions in Sanskrit. And the infinite variety of letters given opposite to page 420 of the volume referred to are not Tibetan, neither are used by Tibetans, but belong to different parts of India, whence they were brought to Tibet in ancient times.

4. "The six predecessors of Shakya, occasionally mentioned in the Tibetan volumes too, I think are imaginary Buddhas, like those one thousand others (among whom Shakya also is described with his predecessors) that are to appear hereafter, and that are particularly in the Bhadra Kalpika, the first volume of the Door Sútra class of the ' Kah-gyur.'

5. "Buddhism was unknown in Tibet till the seventh century of our era. It was derived from India. The Buddhistic doctrine is contained now in Tibet in many hundred volumes. It is no easy task to ascertain how many books or treatises were borrowed from Sanskrit, and how many are original. It would require a perfect knowledge both of the Sanskrit and the Tibetan languages. The volumes of the 'Kahgyur' are generally attributed to Shakya; those of the 'Stan-gyur' to some fancied Bodhisatwas and to several Indian pandits. Besides these, there are many composed in Tibet in imitation of the former. I beg you will kindly excuse me for my defect in answering to the desired points."

CHAPTER VIII.

Csoma arrives in Calcutta—Resolution of Government of India as
to the publication of his works—Was elected Honorary Member
of Asiatic Society.

CSOMA'S long-cherished desire of visiting Calcutta was at
last realised in April 1831. He remained at Kanum
till the commencement of the previous cold weather.
After arrival at Sabathú, the Government having supplied
him with funds for the journey, he was enabled to take
with him, to the Presidency, the manuscripts and books
which he had so eagerly collected. On 5th of May
he reported himself to Mr. Swinton, the Secretary to
Government, and placed all the literary treasures in his
possession at the disposal of the authorities.

Dr. Wilson at the same time reminded the members
of the Council of the Asiatic Society, in a memo., dated
21st May 1831, that they were under a promise to
Csoma to grant him 50 rupees a month from the 15th
of April 1830 to date, which sum, however, he refused
to accept. But the Government sanctioned 100 rupees a
month, on condition that Csoma would prepare a *catalogue raisonné* of the Tibetan works Mr. Hodgson had
forwarded from Nepal.

A letter from Dr. Wilson to the Secretary of Government refers to the arrangements which had been made
with regard to Csoma. It bears the date 15th July
1831, and states that the Society were willing to avail
themselves of Csoma's services for two years, on the

salary which the Government had already sanctioned to him.

Eighteen months after the date of the above, Dr. Wilson wrote another letter, announcing to Government the completion of Csoma's works for the press, and suggesting, at the same time, how they should be dealt with.

On the 26th of December 1832, Dr. Wilson writes that, besides the Dictionary and the Grammar, a translation of a Tibetan vocabulary, containing "a summary of the Buddha system,"[1] was ready for publication and at the disposal of Government, "to whom the author considered his works to belong, in return for the patronage it had been pleased to afford him. Should it be the pleasure of Government to defray the cost of publication, which has been estimated at from 3000 to 4000 rupees, Mr. Csoma will be happy to conduct them through the press in Calcutta; or he is willing, should the Government think proper, to send them, through me, to England, where, perhaps, the Honourable Court of Directors or some literary association may undertake their publication."

Dr. Wilson was preparing to leave India, and he was ready to take charge of the manuscripts, with a view to their being published in Europe.

The following was the resolution of the Government as to the publication of the Grammar and Dictionary, and this finally decided the hitherto pending question. The order was, that the works should be printed in Calcutta at the expense of Government, which had certainly the very great advantage of the author's immediate supervision whilst issuing from the press.

The Government Secretary's letter to Dr. Wilson is dated the 27th of December; it alludes to circumstances of some interest, and pays a deserved tribute to his remarkable merits as a man of science, on the eve of his departure for Europe.

[1] See Appendix XVI.

H

"The Vice-President in Council is disposed to think it most desirable that the Tibetan Grammar and Dictionary prepared by A. Csoma de Körös should be published in Calcutta, at the cost of the Government, India being the most appropriate place for the publication, and the Government being the only party likely to incur the expense.

"I am instructed to observe," continues Mr. Swinton, "that the Government is sensible of the advantage which would be derived from your taking charge of these works and superintending their publication in England, if it were proposed to transmit them for that purpose; and recognises in your offer the same disinterested zeal which has ever distinguished your devotion to the advancement of literature.

"The Vice-President in Council has perused with much gratification the report of the meritorious labours of Mr. Csoma."

In January 1833, Dr. Wilson, having spent many years in the study of Oriental literature, left Calcutta for England, to devote the remainder of his days to the same cause, as Professor of Sanskrit in the University of Oxford. Other and more worthy pens have done justice to the brilliant talents and meritorious accomplishments of Horace Hayman Wilson. A grateful remembrance of him is due also from the biographer of Körösi Csoma Sándor, for the interest he took, when in Calcutta, in the Hungarian traveller, and for his kindness afterwards in publishing a biographical sketch of him in the "Journal of the Royal Asiatic Society" in 1834. The sketch, so far as it went, has hitherto served as the basis of all notices of Csoma's earlier life.

Dr. Wilson was succeeded by Mr. James Prinsep as Secretary to the Asiatic Society of Bengal, who considered it as one of his most important duties to urge that Csoma's works should be pushed through the press as rapidly as possible. Mr. Prinsep's letter on the subject is dated the 30th of January, and is addressed to the Secretary of the Government, giving full details as to expenses connected with the publication, and mentioning other arrangements also. Mr. Prinsep, writing in the name of the Asiatic Society, "trusts that the Government regard Csoma's labours of national interest."

"Previous to the departure of Dr. H. H. Wilson for England, that gentleman placed in my hands a copy of the letter which he addressed to the Government on the 26th ultimo, relative to the Tibetan manuscripts of Mr. Csoma de Körös, and your reply of the 27th of the same month, conveying the sentiments of the Honourable the Vice-President in Council upon the best mode of publishing them, in order that I might submit the whole to the Asiatic Society, to whom the responsibility and honour of superintending the publication of Mr. Csoma's Tibetan Grammar and Dictionary naturally devolves: upon the determination of the Government in favour of printing the work in this country, in lieu of committing it to the care of Dr. Wilson for publication in Europe.

2. "The President and Committee of Papers of the Asiatic Society now direct me to report, for the consideration of the Honourable the Vice-President in Council, that they have made the requisite inquiries as to the probable expense of printing the manuscripts in Calcutta, and they are happy to assure his Honour in Council, that the cost will be trifling compared with the importance of the work to literature, and considering the necessity of preparing an entirely new fount of type in a character as complicated, from the number and form of its compounds, as the Sanskrita itself.

3. "Mr. Pearce, of the Baptist Mission Press, states that the Grammar and Dictionary together may be comprised in one neat quarto volume of about 600 pages in typography and 32 in lithography. Supposing the work to be included within these limits, and 500 copies to be

struck off, he engages to execute it at the rate of 8 rupees per page, or about 5000 rupees for the whole, exclusive of all extra charge for the new fount of type. The expenses per copy, on superfine English paper, will thus be about 10 rupees, besides a trifle more, say one rupee, for binding.

4. " Mr. Csoma de Körös has expressed to the Society his entire readiness to undertake the superintendence and correction of the press, provided the work be commenced immediately, so as not to detain him in Calcutta much beyond the current year. On the part of the Society I beg also to tender my own services, in inspecting and correcting the English portion of the volume, and in otherwise co-operating with Mr. Csoma, to the utmost, in expediting the appearance of the volume.

5. " The Asiatic Society's funds, owing to the recent untoward pressure in commercial affairs, are not in a condition to enable it to bear the whole, or even any part, of the expense of publication, however desirous it would have been to do so under other circumstances; but the Society trusts that the Honourable the Vice-President in Council will regard the matter as one of *national interest*, and will coincide with itself in thinking that the support already given to Mr. Csoma, while prosecuting his studies, will have been misapplied, unless followed up by the immediate diffusion of the knowledge gained through his unwearied labours, and now so honourably tendered by him to the nation from whom he first received assistance, although the learned of his own and of other countries of Europe would do much to induce him to transfer its possession to them."

The only reward which Csoma ever looked for was an appreciation of his labours by his contemporaries and posterity. The esteem which he had won, even at that time, from his fellow-labourers, will be best understood when we look at the opinion of the Council of the Asiatic Society, given previous to his election as an Honorary member of that Society. That opinion is thus recorded in the Minutes of the Proceedings of the meeting held on the 30th January 1834 :—

"Mr. Alexander Csoma de Körös was proposed as an Honorary Member by Mr. Trevelyan, seconded by Mr. Prinsep.

"The nomination was referred to the Committee of Papers.

"*Remarks by Mr. Prinsep.*—The Committee of Papers are aware of Mr. Csoma's qualifications as a Tibetan, Sanskrit, and general linguist, and I need say nothing in recommending him to the honour proposed to be conferred on him further, unless it be to remind the members that he has spent the last two years in preparing catalogues, translations, and superintending the printing of his Dictionary, without accepting any remuneration from the Society or the Government.

"*By Rev. Dr. W. H. Mill.*—I heartily concur in this nomination, as strictly due to the extraordinary merits of M. De Körös.

"*By Dr. A. Wallich.*—I am most happy in concurring entirely with the sentiments expressed by the Secretary and by Dr. Mill.

(Signed) "C. T. METCALFE, B.S. Sen, R. W. FORBES, C. E. TREVELYAN, J. TYTLER, JOHN FRANKS, C. CROZIER."

It is unnecessary to add that Csoma was unanimously elected Honorary member of the Society, on the 6th of February 1834.

The individual opinions of his fellow-labourers recorded here testify to the sincere appreciation entertained of his merits, and doubtless Csoma felt great satisfaction at the honour thus conferred on him. He probably thought of the lines which he once wrote for his friend, Szabó de Borgata, when a fellow-student at Göttingen :

"A viro laudato laudari pulchrum est," &c.

Beyond this solitary honour Csoma declined all others

which the Societies of Europe and Asia sought to confer
on him.   He cannot, however, deny himself the title, so
says a writer, " of an indefatigable student, a profound
linguist, and of a man who devoted his life to the cause
of learning, regardless of any of its popular and attractive rewards, and anxious only for the approbation of
posterity." [1]

[1] See " Journal of Asiatic Society of Bengal," 1834, p. 655.

CHAPTER IX.

The Tibetan Grammar and Dictionary are published at Government expense—Mr. Prinsep's letter to Government—Prince Esterházy to Mr. Prinsep—Mr. Döbrentei of Pest to the same.

CSOMA'S principal effort was now directed towards the issuing of his Grammar and Dictionary from the press. This was finally accomplished in January 1834, and the fact was notified to Mr. Macnaughtan, the Secretary to Government, on the 5th of that month by Mr. Prinsep giving a detailed account of all the circumstances connected with these works. In that letter is found a summary of the pecuniary aid which the author had received from the Indian Government for the previous fourteen years, that is, since the 14th of October 1820, when, on his arrival at Teheran, Csoma applied to Major, afterwards Sir Henry Willock, for help and protection. This the recipient gratefully acknowledges in the Preface to the Tibetan Dictionary. The flattering distinction which Csoma had just obtained from the Asiatic Society by being elected an Honorary member, was doubtless highly gratifying to such highly sensitive feelings as his; but his systematic silence and reserve in regard to everything that concerned himself deprive us of the opportunity of being partakers of such pleasures as occasionally cheered his toilsome career. We miss also many details of events and incidents such as always constitute an attractive charm in a biographical sketch like the present.

The above-mentioned letter of Mr. Prinsep's, announcing to Government the completion of Csoma's works, reflects honour, not only on the achievements of the indefatigable scholar, but also on the authorities for their long-continued generosity. It likewise does credit to Mr. Prinsep himself from the graphic description his report contains of the various details and of the difficulties that had to be overcome.

"I have the honour to report," says Mr. Prinsep, "that the work sanctioned by Government has been completed, and beg to forward a copy for the inspection, and I trust approbation, of the Governor-General.

"The original estimate supposed that both the Dictionary and the Grammar might occupy 600 pages, which Mr. Pearce of the Baptist Mission Press undertook to print at 8 rupees per page, casting a new fount of type for the purpose.

"It will be seen by the bill that the actual expense of printing has fallen within that sum, the number of pages being 588, and the cost ₨4985, As.4. There is, however, a separate charge for lithographing 40 pages of alphabetical matter, which it was found indispensable to execute in this manner, to furnish a proper model of the Tibetan characters, which were not very well formed in the Serampore fount, whence the types were cast for the body of the work. Mr. Tassin (as will be seen by his note) has charged 32 rupees per page for drawing and printing, which, for 500 copies of each, appears very reasonable, the cost of striking off being one half of the amount.

"The whole cost of the two volumes, therefore, including stitching and covering the copies, has been ₨6412, As.4, for which, if it meet with the sanction of his Lordship in Council, I have to request an assignment on the Treasury.

"From the delay of constructing new type, and the repeated corrections which were required to ensure accuracy in the Tibetan portion of the text, the time occupied in passing the work through the press has been prolonged to two years, in lieu of one, as stipulated by the author. Mr. Csoma has, however, with unwearied patience and application, devoted himself to the revision of the proofs through this lengthened period, and he is now rewarded with the satisfaction of seeing his labours ushered to the world in so creditable a manner, only through the liberal patronage of Government. He has expressed his acknowledgments publicly, in the preface to both volumes, but his extreme modesty will neither permit him to address his patrons in his own name, nor will it permit me, while writing on his behalf, to indulge in any eulogium on his learning and accuracy. He is contented to leave the merits of his Dictionary and Grammar to be appreciated by the learned and by posterity.

" I must, however, venture to break the silence he would enjoin, for the purpose of representing the pecuniary situation of Mr. Csoma, and the claims which he has hitherto allowed to lie dormant.

" The Right Honourable the Governor-General in Council was pleased to authorise an allowance of 50 rupees a month to the Hungarian student in June 1827 for the prosecution of his Tibetan researches. On his arrival in Calcutta this allowance was increased[1] to 100 rupees, with an anticipation of its continuance at that rate for two years, after which a report was to be made of the progress of his labours.

" With exception, however, of the first two months (July and August), Mr. Csoma has never drawn any part of this allowance, and he has continued to live upon the slender savings he had previously to that date lodged with the treasurer of the Asiatic Society, which are now in consequence nearly exhausted.

" It may, perhaps, be known to Government that Prince Esterházy and some Hungarian Nobles remitted a donation of £142 through the Secretary of the Austrian

[1] 22d July 1831.

Legation in London, the Baron Nieumann, to Mr. Csoma in 1832. This money was unfortunately lodged by my predecessor in Messrs. Alexander & Co.'s house,[1] and was consequently lost by their failure. Mr. Csoma has frequently alluded to this loss, with an apparent impression that the honour of the British nation is concerned in replacing this sum, intrusted as it was to its care by a foreign power for a specific object : not that he himself had contemplated applying for it to his own support, this he had from the first refused, but that he desired to expend it in purchasing Sanskrit manuscripts for the learned institutions of his country, and otherwise prosecuting the researches he would now pursue relatively to the connection of the Hungarian with the ancient languages of India.

" It would therefore be more agreeable to Mr. Csoma to receive a part of the remuneration to which he is now entitled in the shape of a compensation for the loss sustained by the failure of his agents. Of any further receipt of money he expresses indifference, and he protests that he will remit whatever sum may be granted him direct to Hungary to found scholarships, &c. Still I imagine the Government will not allow the peculiar sentiments of the meritorious scholar to interfere with his just expectations, although the form of donation may be varied to make it more acceptable to him. I beg leave, therefore, to recommend that the former rate of salary, 50 rupees a month, should be made good up to the 31st December 1834,—

	Rupees.
Being 3 years 4 months at 50 rupees	2000
And that the sum lost by the failure be replaced, viz. .	1400
Making a total of	3400

which is little more than would have been granted by the 100 rupees salary for two years and a reduction afterwards to 50 rupees.

" I venture humbly to make these suggestions, leaving

---

[1] It was remitted through them, and never drawn out of their hands.

the Government to determine as to their propriety, and as to the continuance of its patronage to Mr. Csoma during the travels he now projects into Tirhut, Nepal, and Ladak for the further prosecution of his studies, particularly in the Sanskrit literature of the ninth and tenth centuries. The very moderate scale of his habits and wants cannot be placed in a more conspicuous point of view, than by summing up the money upon which he has lived during the last fourteen years. The marginal statement[1] shows that in this period he has received 4226 rupees, of which he has expended 4000 rupees, being little more than 20 rupees per *mensem* for food, travelling, clothes, and wages of servants and pandits, while in Tibet.

"The Dictionary and Grammar now submitted form but a small part of the works Mr. Csoma has executed while in Calcutta. A catalogue and analysis of the voluminous manuscripts received from Mr. B. H. Hodgson of Nepal, and a valuable and most extensive polyglot vocabulary[2] (of which M. Rémusat attempted a small portion in Paris from Chinese works), and several minor translations are deposited with the Asiatic Society. The vocabulary would merit well to be printed, but the expense would be considerable, and the author is averse to the further detention, which its publication would entail on him at the present moment.

"It remains for me to request the orders of Government as to the distribution of the five hundred copies of the Grammar and Dictionary.

"The author solicits for himself one hundred copies that he may send them to the Universities of Austria, Italy, and Germany.

		Rupees.
[1] From Mr. Wilcock	. . . .	300
From Dr. Moorcroft	. . . . . .	300
From Government, 14th June 1827 to 30th June 1830 .	.	2926
Two months at 100 rupees per month .	. . . .	200
For travelling expenses.	. . . . . .	500
	Total	4226

[2] See Appendix XVI.

"The Asiatic Society will in the same way, if permitted, undertake to distribute to the learned societies of England, France, and other countries with which it is in literary communication; it would, of course, make known that the presentation was made on the part of the Government of India, under whose auspices the works have appeared.

"A portion may be sent to the Society's booksellers in Calcutta and London for sale, and perhaps the Government may desire to forward fifty copies or more to the Honourable the Court of Directors.

"Copies may also be properly deposited in the libraries of the colleges in the several Presidencies of the Indian Government.

"For all the details of these arrangements, I beg leave, on the part of the Asiatic Society, to tender my services, happy in having already been able to assist in the publication of a work which I feel confident will do honour to the author, and the Government of India as his patrons."

The epitaph engraved on the tombstone at Darjeeling, referring to these works, truly says that "these are his best and real monuments."

Jäschke, whose dictionary is based on Csoma's, acknowledges that it is the work of an "original investigator, and the fruit of almost unparalleled determination and patience."

The Dictionary was ready some months before the Grammar. It contains 345 quarto pages; the Grammar is smaller, of 204 pages, with 40 pages of lithography.

In the preface to the first-named book Mr. Csoma states the scope of his work, with the plan he was induced to follow in its preparation, and explains his views as to the remarkable similarity of linguistic structure he had discovered between the Indian, including the Sanskrit languages, and his mother tongue, the Hungarian. This we find mentioned already in his letter to Captain Kennedy in 1825. It is presumed that Csoma's suggestion will hardly find favour with many philologists, because the scientific theories of the present day have established distinctive lines of demarcation between the Arian and Turanian group of languages, the Hungarian being assigned to the latter; yet Csoma gave reasons for maintaining such opinion, and adduces examples for its support.[1]

"The Tibetan Dictionary now presented to the world," says Mr. Csoma, "is indebted for its appearance to the liberality of the two successive Governors-General, Lord Amherst and Lord William Cavendish Bentinck." It is with profound respect that he offers his performance as a small tribute of grateful acknowledgment for favours conferred upon him, not only by Government, but by the liberal assistance and kindness of several English gentlemen whose names are already familiar to the readers of these memoirs. Besides the names of his English friends and others already mentioned, he does not forget two humble citizens who had been kind to him, namely, a merchant at Aleppo, a native of Bohemia, Ignatz Pohle, and Joseph Schaefer of Tyrol, a blacksmith at Alexandria, in Egypt.

"He begs to inform the public that he has not been sent by any Government to gather political information, neither can he be counted of the number of those wealthy European gentlemen who travel at their own expense for their pleasure or curiosity, but is only a poor student, who was very desirous to see the different countries of Asia, as the scene of so many memorable transactions of former ages, to observe the manners of several people, and to learn their languages."

"Though the study of the Tibetan language," proceeds Csoma, "did not form part of my original plan, but was only suggested after I had been by Providence led into Tibet, and had enjoyed an opportunity, through Mr.

[1] See Appendix XVII.

Moorcroft's liberal assistance, of learning of what sort and origin the Tibetan literature was, I cheerfully engaged in the study of it, hoping that it might serve me as a vehicle to my immediate purpose, namely, my researches respecting the origin and language of the Hungarians. The result of my investigation is that the literature of Tibet is entirely of Indian origin, the immense volumes, on different branches of science, being exact and faithful translations from Sanskrit works. Many of these works have again been translated from Tibetan into Mongol, Mantchu, and Chinese languages, so that by this means the Tibetan became in Chinese Tartary the language of the learned, as the Latin is in Europe.

"After thus being familiarised with the language and general contents of the Buddhistic works of Tibet, the author thought himself happy in having found an easy access to the whole Sanskrit literature. To his own nation he felt a pride in announcing that the study of Sanskrit would be more satisfactory to it than to any other people in Europe.

"The Hungarians," he declares, "would find a fund of information from the study of the Sanskrit respecting their origin, manners, customs, and language, since the structure of the Sanskrit, and also of other Indian dialects, is most analogous. As an example of this close analogy, in Hungarian postpositions are used instead of prepositions; by a simple syllabic addition to the verbal root, and without any auxiliary verb, the several kinds of verbs, namely, the active, passive, causal, desiderative, frequentative, and reciprocal, are formed in the same manner as in Sanskrit."

The author further informs us that the Grammar and Dictionary had been compiled from authentic sources, with the assistance of an intelligent Lama of Zanskar, who resided with Csoma at the Monastery of Kanum from 1827 to 1830. His name is mentioned on the title-page as: Bandé Sangs-RGyas PHun-Tsogs.

At first, the author had naturally to contend with many difficulties, as, beyond the "Alphabetum Tibetanum" of Father Giorgi, he had no elementary works to assist him, and his teacher the Lama, "at whose feet," as Pavie says, "the pupil of Blumenbach, and a graduate of the University of Göttingen, learned how to spell Tibetan like a child," knew no other tongue but his own.

Sanskrit terms seldom occur in Tibetan books, Csoma tells us, with the exception of a few proper names of men, places, precious stones, flowers, and plants ; but the technical terms in the arts and sciences found in Sanskrit have been rendered by their precise syllabic equivalents in Tibetan, according to a system framed expressly for the purpose, by the pandits who engaged in the transla- tion of the sacred works of the Buddhists into Tibetan, as may be seen in several vocabularies of Sanskrit and Tibetan terms,[1] of which a large one has been translated into English, and presented to the Asiatic Society by Csoma ; the same, he afterwards found, had been previ- ously made known to the learned of Europe by Monsieur Abel Rémusat, as stated above.

The Grammar was the second of Csoma's great works, published a few months after the Dictionary. Some of the remarks prefacing it will be read with interest.

"Tibet being the headquarters of Buddhism in the present age, the elementary works herewith published," says Csoma, "may serve as a key to unlock the immense volumes, faithful translations of the Sanskrit text, which are still to be found in that country, on the manners, customs, opinions, knowledge, ignorance, superstitions, hopes and fears of great part of Asia, especially India, in former ages.

"It is not uninteresting to observe the coincidence of time with respect to the great exertions made by several princes on behalf of the literature of the three

---

[1] See Appendix XVI.

great religions, Christianity, Islamism, and Buddhism, in the Latin, in the Arabic, and in the Sanskrit languages, the epoch being the eighth and ninth centuries of our era— in Germany and France by Charlemagne; at Baghdad by the Khalifs Al-Mansur, Harun al-Rashid and Al Mamun; in India by the kings of Magadha; in Tibet by Khrisrong, De'hu tsan, Khri De'srong tsan, and Ralpachen; in China by the Emperors of the Thang dynasty.   But whilst learning has continually decreased among the Buddhists and Mohammedans, it has developed immensely in countries professing the religion of Christ, and the two rival religions are studied in their original languages by the learned of Europe.

"The students of Tibetan have been most rare, if they existed at all.   Isolated among inaccessible mountains, the convents of Tibet have remained unregarded and almost unvisited by the scholar and traveller; nor was it until within these few years conjectured, that in the undisturbed shelter of this region, in a climate proof against decay and the destructive influences of the tropical plains, were to be found, in complete preservation the volumes of the Buddhist faith in their original Sanskrit, as well as in faithful translations, which might be sought for in vain on the continent of India.

"I hope that my sojourn in this inhospitable country, for the express purpose of mastering its language and examining its literary stores, will not have been time unprofitably spent, and that the Grammar and Dictionary may attest the sincerity of my endeavours to attain the object I have determined to prosecute.

"The structure of the Tibetan language is very simple.   There is only one general form for all sorts of declinable words.   In the verbs there is no variation in respect to person or number.   The orthography is uniform throughout Tibet, but the pronunciation differs, especially with reference to the compound consonants.

" My selection of the English language," remarks Csoma, " as the medium of the introduction of my labours, will sufficiently evince to the learned of Europe at large the obligations I consider myself under to the English nation."

We have two more letters which reflect on the events of this epoch in Csoma's life—one from Prince Eszterházy, the Austrian Ambassador at the Court of St. James's, and the other from Mr. Döbrentei, secretary to the Hungarian Literary Society at Pest; both are addressed to Mr. Prinsep, expressive of acknowledgments for the kindness and protection shown to their distinguished countryman.

The Prince's letter is dated the 4th of August 1835, and will be read with interest. One more act of generosity of the Indian Government towards Csoma de Körös is acknowledged here by the Ambassador, and it is but justice that the same should be recorded.

The Prince writes :—

" SIR,—In reply to the letter you addressed to me of the 25th January last, I have the honour to acknowledge the receipt of the two boxes, containing each twenty-five copies of the Tibetan Dictionary and Grammar, prepared for publication by the Hungarian traveller, Mr. Alexander Csoma de Körös, and printed at the expense of the British Indian Government under the auspices of the Asiatic Society.

" These fifty copies being destined by Mr. Körösi to be presented to the different public institutions of His Imperial Majesty's dominions, I lose no time in assuring you that the learned author's intentions shall be faithfully fulfilled.

" The enclosed letters and the Oriental works you have sent to the Aulic Councillor von Hammer have also been forwarded to their destination.

" I have not failed to inform my Government of the

I

liberality with which the Indian Government has replaced the sum of 300 ducats transmitted through this Embassy to Mr. Csoma de Körös, which had been lost by the failure of Messrs. Alexander & Co.; and anticipating its intentions, I seize with great pleasure this opportunity to express to you, and through you to the Indian Government, as well as to the Asiatic Society, the high sense I entertain of the kind protection afforded to my learned countryman in His Britannic Majesty's dominions in India.

"Allow me to offer my sincerest thanks for such generous conduct.—I have the honour to be, sir, your most obedient servant,

(Sgd.)   "ESZTERHÁZY."

Mr. Döbrentei's letter to Mr. Prinsep is dated the 30th of September 1835, and, like the preceding, is extant among the papers in the Library of the Asiatic Society in Calcutta. Döbrentei states that Mr. Prinsep's letter excited the greatest attention when its contents were made known to the meeting of the Literary Society at Pest, because there was no reliable news of Csoma since he wrote from Teheran to his friends at Nagy Enyed in 1820. Mr. Döbrentei expresses gratitude for the protection his countryman enjoyed in India, and mentions the willingness on the part of Hungarians to send pecuniary aid to him if required.

CHAPTER X.

Csoma asks for a passport in November 1835, enabling him to travel in Hindustan — Leaves Calcutta — His last letters to Mr. Prinsep—Return to Calcutta in 1837.

WE have noticed already that four and a half years had passed since his arrival in Calcutta, before the result of Csoma's literary labours could be brought to completion and published. This done, he made fresh plans for the further prosecution of his studies.

In answer to letters of Prince Eszterházy and of Mr. Döbrentei, he wrote in Latin, having made a spontaneous promise to Government, through Mr. Prinsep, to correspond with Europe in that language only ; and in order to avoid every suspicion (remembering what had happened at Sabathú in 1825, which he had never forgotten), he sent all his letters open, to be forwarded by the secretary of the Asiatic Society to their destination.

On the 30th of September 1835 Mr. Döbrentei wrote to Csoma as follows: " Be so good as to inform us, in all sincerity, whether it is your wish that a public subscription be opened on your behalf. This would at least give an opportunity to the Hungarian nation to provide in a suitable manner for one of her sons, who, for the sake of her ancient history, is sacrificing himself on such a thorny path."

Judging from Csoma's ideas and general conduct in such matters, there can be no doubt that he declined to sanction Döbrentei's proposal.

On the 30th of November Csoma wrote to Mr. James Prinsep, asking for a passport from Government. His letter (now in the possession of the Hungarian Academy of Sciences), so characteristic of the man, runs as follows :—

"At my first arrival in British India, though furnished with an introductory letter from the late Mr. W. Moorcroft, I was received with some suspicion by the authorities in the Upper Provinces. But afterwards, having given in writing, accordingly as Government desired from me, the history of my past proceedings and a sketch of my future plans, I was not only absolved by Government from every suspicion I was under, and allowed to go to whatever place I liked for the prosecution of my studies, but Government generously granted me also pecuniary aid for the same purpose. Thus, during the course of several years, I have enjoyed a favourable opportunity of improving in knowledge, especially in the philological part, for my purpose.

2. "I beg leave, sir, to offer and express herewith, through you, my respectful thanks to the Government and to the Asiatic Society, for their patronage, protection, and liberality in granting me every means for my study at their library. But since I have not yet reached my aim, for which I came to the East, I beg you will obtain for me the permission of Government to remain yet for three years in India, for the purpose of improving myself in Sanskrit and in the different dialects; and, if Government will not object, to furnish me with a passport in duplicate, one in English and one in Persian, that I may visit the north-western parts of India. For my own part, I promise that my conduct will not offend the Government in whatever respect, and that I shall not have any correspondence to Europe, but only through you, and that in Latin, which I will send to you, without being closed, whenever I want to write to my own country.—I remain, with much respect, Sir, your most obliged humble servant,   A. CSOMA.

"CALCUTTA, 30th November 1835."

Mr. Prinsep, ás on so many former occasions, took this opportunity, unsolicited, to plead Csoma's cause, in a letter addressed to Mr. Macnaughten, the secretary to Government. From this we learn, also, that of the money which was received on Csoma's behalf from Hungary, he would retain nothing for himself, but it had to be sent back, at his request, to found scholarships with, and also for the benefit of his relatives in Transylvania.

" SIR,—I have been requested," writes Mr. Prinsep, " by Mr. Alexander Csoma de Körös to report for the information of the Honourable the Governor-General of India in Council, that he is desirous of terminating his residence in Calcutta, and of proceeding to the interior, for the purpose of further prosecuting his studies in the Oriental languages. He begs me, accordingly, to solicit permission for his continuing for three more years within the British Indian territories, and, further, to request that he may be furnished with two passports, to be produced when occasion may require—one in the English language, in which he would wish to be designated by the simple title of ' Mr. Alexander Csoma, a Hungarian philosopher, native of Transylvania,' and one in the Persian language, describing him as ' Molla Eskander Csoma az Mulk-i Rúm.'

2. " It is Mr. Csoma's present intention, after having pursued his researches into the dialects of Mithila, &c., to return to the Presidency, and then to prepare the results of his studies for the press.

3. " As he does not consider himself for the last year to have been labouring in any way for the British Government, Mr. Csoma has prevented me from making any application for pecuniary assistance. I cannot, however, forbear from bringing to the notice of the Honourable the Governor-General that the means at the disposal of this indefatigable and unpresuming student are by no means equal to meet the expense of a journey of three years, even on his very moderate scale of expenditure.

4. "I hold in my hands a balance of five hundred rupees at his disposal. The money granted by Government on the 12th January 1835, as arrears of the salary of 50 rupees per *mensem*, due to Mr. Csoma while employed on the Tibetan Grammar and Dictionary, and as compensation for loss of the boon from the Hungarian nobleman, was for the greater part remitted home by myself, at his express desire, for the benefit of his relations in Hungary and of the Hungarian Literary Society jointly, nor could I persuade him that justice to himself required him to retain at least enough to meet his own wants and comfort.

5. "I would respectfully submit, that however unwilling Mr. Csoma may be to place himself under obligations, where, as he asserts, he has done no service, the nature and bent of his studies into the antiquities of India would amply justify the liberality of Government towards so meritorious an individual. Many of his publications on Buddha literature, in the pages of the Asiatic Society's Journal, are of the highest interest. A portion of his Analysis of the Tibetan works (for which, at the time, he was promised a salary of 200 rupees a month for two years) has just been printed in the Asiatic Researches, and I have the honour to enclose a copy of the article, from which the Government may appreciate the labour it must have cost him to go through the 100 volumes of the 'Kahgyur' in the same careful manner.

6. "Under these considerations, I trust it will not be deemed presumptuous in me to recommend that the allowance of 50 rupees per *mensem* may be continued to Mr. Csoma as long as he may remain prosecuting studies from which the Government or the learned of our country may derive benefit, and that I may be permitted to draw it on honour on his account from the expiration of the last payment, or the 31st December 1834.

7. "It will be understood that his services will be at all times available to examine and report on Tibetan

works, of which the Resident at Nepal has recently despatched a large supply for presentation to the Honourable the Court of Directors. The Court will doubtless be well pleased that these should be examined in this way by almost the only scholar capable of reading and explaining their contents."

Csoma's passport, issued by Government, is of interest in his biography; the text was in English and Persian, and was worded thus :—

"Mr. Alexander Csoma de Körös, a Hungarian philologer, native of Transylvania, having obtained the permission of the Honourable the Governor-General of India in Council, to prosecute his studies in Oriental languages in Hindustan for three years, I am directed by his Honour in Council to desire all officers of the British Government, whether civil or military, and to request all chiefs of Hindustan in alliance and amity with the British Government, to afford such protection to Mr. Csoma as may be necessary to facilitate the object of his researches.

" By command of the Honourable the Governor-General of India in Council.

" Fort William, The 14th December 1835."	Wafer Seal.	(Sgd.) W. H. MACNAUGHTEN, *Sec. to Government of India.*

Having provided himself with the necessaries for the voyage, Csoma did not delay his departure from Calcutta; he travelled by boat, and we hear of him at Maldah, which place he reached on the 20th January 1836: we learn this from a letter to Mr. Prinsep, in possession of the Asiatic Society of Calcutta.

"SIR,—I beg leave to acquaint you that I have

safely reached this place yesterday in the morning. The cold north wind has somewhat retarded our progress, but in other respects I have suffered nothing of which I should complain. These men have been honest and active enough during the whole time, since we left Calcutta, and I feel much obliged for the kindness and good service done to me by you, and by those whom you had employed to procure me this boat with such men.

"According to the agreement made with the Manji, which I have enclosed here, I had paid him 8 rupees in Calcutta, besides one for oil and Masul or duty, and of the remaining 6, I have given him here again 3 rupees, and I beg, sir, you will order the other 3 rupees also to be paid him, and to be put on my account. Besides the above specified 12 rupees, · I have given yet to these five men in common, 3 rupees as a reward for the service done me by them.

"To-morrow I shall leave this place, having hired again a small boat for 8 rupees to carry me up to Kissenganj. When I shall have fixed myself at any place in the upper part of this country, for a certain time, and have visited the Sikkim Raja, I shall be happy to acquaint you with what I shall have learned. My earnest desire is to merit the continuation of your favour."

Early in March we find Csoma at Julpigori, where he met a sympathising friend in Major Lloyd, commanding the frontier station. This gentleman offered him every attention and hospitality, but they were declined by Mr. Csoma, on the ground that his staying with Government officers of high position would deprive him of the intercourse with natives, whose familiarity it was his chief endeavour to cultivate. There is only one more autograph letter still extant from Csoma, and this he wrote to Mr. Prinsep on the 7th of March 1836 from Julpigori. The original is in the possession of the Academy of Sciences at Budapest:—

"Sir,—I beg leave to acknowledge that the packet containing some papers, which by the Asiatic Society's direction you had addressed to me, on the 8th of February last, safely reached me on the 19th of the same month, having been forwarded to me by Major Lloyd's kindness. I would have immediately acknowledged the receipt of those papers, but as I was yet at that time very unsettled, respecting my remaining here or moving from this place, I have delayed till now to write to you. I beg you will excuse me for my tardiness.

"I feel greatly obliged to you for the kind communication of a copy of His Excellency Prince Eszterházy's reply to your letter of the 5th January last year. I am glad to know that the 50 copies of my Tib. Grammar and Dictionary have safely reached London, and that they have been also forwarded to their farther destination. I was also happy to see how His Excellency has expressed his thanks, through you, to the British Indian Government and to the Asiatic Society, for their kind protection and liberality to me.

"While I gratefully acknowledge the favours thus conferred on me through this kind communication, I am sorry that, for my own part, I can send nothing to you, not having been able, as yet, to learn anything interesting. Together with your note, I have received also the two facsimiles of inscriptions, but I am unable to give any satisfactory explanation of them. Though I admit the one to be in the Tib. character and language, I dare not say anything about its contents.

"According to your direction, I take now the liberty of addressing my letter to you through W. H. Macnaughten, Esq., chief secretary to Government, knowing that it will be afterwards sent to you. Though I feel much obliged for

the favours thus conferred on me by this kind arrange-
ment with Mr. Macnaughten respecting my future communications to you, I am sorry that I shall not be able
to send any interesting information, since I shall perhaps not visit Sikkim, Nepaul, and the other hilly tracts,
being informed that the travelling in those parts would
be dangerous, difficult, very expensive, and of little advantage to my purpose; but after remaining in these parts
for a certain period, to study the Bengalee and Sanskrit,
afterwards I shall go by water to Patna, whenever,
successively, I shall visit again by water the upper
provinces, devoting my whole time to the study of the
Sanskrit language and to the acquirement of the principal
dialects.

" Since I intend to prosecute only my philological researches, and will abstain from every statistical, political,
or even geographical inquiry, if I shall write but seldom
to you, and at that time also shortly, I beg you will
excuse me.   I hope, if I survive, and can again safely
return to Calcutta, I shall be able to communicate to you
the results of my studies and Indian tours.   I shall want
but little for my expenses, and I hope that the five
hundred sicca rupees, left in your hand at my leaving
Calcutta, will be sufficient during the time I intend to
make my peregrination in India.   Should I fail in
making any useful progress in my studies worthy of the
Government's patronage, the Asiatic Society may always
dispose of that money for literary purposes which you
successively receive from Government on my behalf.

"Should you wish to communicate to me any papers,
I beg you will address them to the care of Major Lloyd
at Titalya, who will have the kindness to forward them
to me.   Pray not to send me the numbers of the 'Asiatic
Society's Journal' or any other book until I shall write
to you, or shall go to Patna; but I shall be much obliged
if you will favour me with any letters received from my
own country."

. As Csoma wrote, so probably he acted. His object being exclusively literary researches, he seldom wrote letters to anybody, and to this fact is attributable the circumstance that, after the last-mentioned date, we meet with but few records of Csoma's doings, which otherwise would have enriched the narrative of his life.

Major Lloyd writes about him as follows:—

. "At the beginning of 1836, when Csoma quitted his apartments he had in the Asiatic Society's house, he wished to study Bengalee, and I sent him to Julpigori, where he remained about three months; but being dissatisfied there, he returned to Titalya, I think, in March. He would not remain in my house, as he thought his eating and living with me would cause him to be deprived of the familiarity and society of natives, with whom it was his wish to be colloquially intimate; I therefore got him a common native hut, and made it as comfortable as I could for him, but still he seemed to me to be miserably off. I also got him a servant, to whom he paid three or four rupees a month, and his living did not cost him more than four more. He did not quit Titalya, I think, till the end of November 1837, and all the time he was there he was absorbed in the study of the Sanskrit, Mahratta, and Bengali languages. I think it was in November that he left, purposing to go to Calcutta. At one time he was intending to travel through the mountains to Katmandú, . . . but he seemed to have a great dread of trusting himself into Tibet, for I repeatedly urged him to try to reach Lassa through Sikkim, but he always said such an attempt could only be made at the risk of his life. I was therefore surprised at his coming here (in 1842) apparently with that intention."

After a sojourn of nearly two years in the east of Bengal, in the neighbourhood of Sikkim, Csoma returned to Calcutta, as surmised by Major Lloyd.

Towards the latter part of 1837, Dr. Malan succeeded Mr. James Prinsep as secretary of the Asiatic

Society, and he then found our scholar in Calcutta. In 1838, Captain Pemberton invited him to join the Government mission to Bhútan, but the offer was not accepted, because there was no prospect of reaching Tibet by that route; Csoma therefore continued to live in the Asiatic Society's rooms in his capacity as librarian. Whilst at Titalya (in 1837) a correspondence passed between himself and Mr. Hodgson; this gentleman invited Csoma to Katmandu, but when the latter found that he could not pass into Tibet viâ Nepal, the proposed visit was abandoned.

From the end of 1837 till the early part of 1842, Csoma remained in Calcutta, arranging the Tibetan works of the Asiatic Society, as its librarian. He published several scientific treatises and articles, and was engaged by Dr. Yates and other missionaries in the translation of the Liturgy, the Psalms, and the Prayer-book into Tibetan. M. Pavie writes thus:[1] "I saw him often during my stay in Calcutta, absorbed in phantastic thoughts, smiling at the course of his own ideas, taciturn like the Brahmins, who, bending over their writing-desks, are employed in copying texts of Sanskrit. His room had the appearance of a cell, which he never left except for short walks in the corridors of the building. What a pity it is," continues Pavie, "that a scientific mind like his was so little given to writing except on his special study; but under the influence of ideas of a peculiar kind he accomplished that laborious and useful task which constitutes his glory."

A member of the Hungarian Academy of Sciences, Mr. Emil Thewrewk de Ponor, made an interesting communication to a Budapest journal, the "Nemzet," on the 31st of March 1883, according to which it would appear that Josef Szabó de Borgáta, a fellow-student at Göttingen, and afterwards professor of the Lycæum of Sopron, was the first who induced Csoma to undertake a

[1] "Revue des Deux Mondes," vol. xix.

journey to the East. This Professor Szabó was still alive, and in his ninety-fourth year in 1883.

Mr. Thewrewk refers further to a letter of a Hungarian artist, Mr. Schoefft, from Pest, who *lived in India* and knew Csoma well. The letter was written in March 1842. An extract of it is appended:—

" I was on very friendly terms with Csoma during my stay in Calcutta, where I found to my satisfaction that the people of that city had much clearer ideas about Hungary than before, for which, doubtless, we are indebted to Csoma. Nevertheless, the truth must be told, that I never saw a more strange man than him. He lives like a hermit among his Tibetan and other works, in the house of the Asiatic Society, which he seldom leaves. Of an evening he takes slight exercise in the grounds, and then he causes himself to be locked up in his apartment; it therefore invariably happened that when, during my evening rides, I called on him, it was necessary for me always to wait a while till the servants produced the keys to unlock the door of his apartment. He was cheerful; often merry, his spirits rose very considerably when we took the opportunity of talking about Hungary. Altogether, I found him very talkative, and if he once started on this strain there was no getting to the end of it. Often, when speaking of our native land, or discussing the subject concerning the origin of the Hungarians, our pleasant conversation was protracted till after 10 o'clock. I began to suspect, however, that he would never see his native land again, being then already advanced in age, and yet he proposed remaining for ten years longer in the country, to enable him to glean whatever he could find in the old writings, and such a secluded, one would almost call it a prison life, might soon undermine the powers of any constitution and leave but a mere shadow of an existence."

Besides the aged Professor Szabó, there is yet another living witness who knew Csoma face to face, namely, the

Rev. S. C. Malan, D.D., Oxford, now Rector of Broad-windsor, Dorset.   He was connected with the Bishops' College of Calcutta, and during his short stay there, as secretary of the Asiatic Society of Bengal, was on inti-mate terms with the subject of this memoir.

Dr. Malan says[1] as to Körösi, "I never think of him without interest and gratitude.   I had heard of him and seen his Tibetan Grammar and Dictionary before leaving England.

"One of my early visits was to the Asiatic Society's house, Calcutta, where Csoma lived as under-librarian. I found him a man of middle stature, much weather-beaten from his travels, but kind, amiable, and willing to impart all he knew. . . .

"I happened to be the only person who was troubling himself about Tibetan; he and I became very good friends during the whole, alas! too short, stay in India. And when we parted he gave me the whole of his Tibetan books, some thirty volumes.   I value such relics highly, and still use the same volume which I used to turn over with him."

These volumes, forty in number, are now the property of the Royal Hungarian Academy of Sciences, through the kindness of Dr. Malan, the donor.[2]

There is a more recent letter from Dr. Malan to the writer, giving his opinion about a likeness of Csoma, and which is quoted at the end.

[1] Ralston's "Tibetan Tales."   London : Trübner and Co.   1882.
[2] See "Journal of the Royal Asiatic Society," 1884, vol. xvi. p. 492 *et seq.*

CHAPTER XI.

Csoma's stay in Calcutta from 1837 to 1842—Last arrangements—
. Leaves Calcutta for the last time—Sets out on his journey to
Lassa—Death at Darjeeling—Dr. Campbell's report—His grave
and tombstone.

IN April 1842, Csoma reached the fifty-eighth year of
his age; but his ardour in his favourite studies and his
power of hard work continued the same as in earlier
days. In the early spring of that year he was planning
to resume his researches and to labour for ten years longer
in the East before returning to his native land. The
contemplation of these plans induced him to start once
more towards Tibet on a journey to Lassa.

His first knowledge of the Tibetan tongue was
acquired in Ladak in the west; he now purposed visiting the north-easterly parts of Tibet proper. During
the latter years he displayed great eagerness in the study
of the Mahratta, Bengali, and Sanskrit languages.

On the 9th of February a letter, addressed by Csoma
to the Secretary of the Asiatic Society, Mr. Torrens, may
well be regarded as his testamentary disposition :—

" SIR,—Since I am about to leave Calcutta for a certain
period to make a tour in Central Asia, if possible, I beg
you will receive and keep this memorandum after you
have communicated it to the Society.

" I respectfully acknowledge that I have received
many benefits from the Asiatic Society, although I have
declined always to accept the allowance of 50 rupees
which they generously granted me in 1829, 1831, and
1841, since the Government allowance to me during
several years was sufficient for my support.

" I intend again to return to Calcutta and to acquaint the Society with the results of my travels. But in case of my death on my intended journey, since I sincerely wish the prosperity and pray for the long continuance of this noble establishment, I beg to leave my Government securities, as also the books and other things now taken with me, *at the disposal of the Asiatic Society*, delivering herewith to you my last account of the 31st January 1842, with the Government agent, who is my attorney, and with whom the Pro Notes are kept, and who will favour me once a year with interest on those papers.

" Since I purposely decline any correspondence with those in Europe, I beg you will kindly excuse me, if any letter or packet should be sent to me, to do with it as you think best." [1]

The secretary was requested to reply to Mr. Csoma, expressing the Society's willingness to accept the trusteeship of his funds for his benefit, assuring him of its earnest desire to forward his views in India in every possible way, and to render him any assistance, as well as of its willingness to receive any further directions as to his funds, and expressing its best wishes for his welfare and safe return from his enterprising expedition into Bhútan and Tartary. It was also determined that a copy of Mr. Csoma's letter should be transmitted to the Government Agent.

It will always remain a matter of regret that Csoma's determined wish was not secured in a legal manner, for the benefit of the Asiatic Society, to which he desired to bequeath all he possessed, as a token of gratitude for the benefits he received. It could hardly be expected that Csoma should be versed in legal technicalities, but these doubtless he would have been ready to attend to had he received any suggestion on the subject.

The exact date is not recorded on which Csoma left the Presidency, nor do we know the details of his journey towards Sikkim. Most probably he travelled as he

---

[1] See "Proceedings of the Asiatic Society of Bengal," 4th March 1842.

was wont, in a native boat up the river Hugly to reach the opposite shore of the Ganges, and afterwards by land, and through the Terai, in the direction of the Darjeeling range of hills. In the vicinity of Titaliya, in the district of Rungpore, the level begins to rise, and the malarious sub-Himalayan belt of dense jungle has to be crossed before ascending the hills.

The Terai of the present day cannot bear comparison to what it was in Csoma's time. To a great extent it is now laid out in carefully cultivated tea-gardens; the danger which formerly beset every traveller through that district has almost disappeared. Not many years ago the crossing of the Terai for a European was accompanied by great risk to health, and had to be performed as expeditiously as was practicable in the day-time, whilst the sun was up; and to spend a night there was certain to be followed by dangerous paroxysms of fever.

Csoma reached Darjeeling on the 24th of March. He travelled slowly and inexpensively, probably on foot. There is every reason to suspect that a night was spent by him in the Terai. Campbell says that on the 6th of April he was ill with fever, which in six days terminated fatally.

Dr. Archibald Campbell, the Superintendent and Government Agent, was the chief officer at that station. He knew Csoma by reputation for many years, and personally since they met at Captain Kennedy's house at Simla. Every attention, therefore, that was possible was bestowed upon the patient.

The report of Csoma's death is addressed to Mr. Bushby, secretary to Government.

Dr. Campbell wrote as follows : [1]—

"It is with much regret that I report the death at this place, on the 11th instant (April 1842), of Csoma de Körös, the Hungarian traveller and Tibetan scholar. He fell a victim to fever, contracted on his journey hitherto,

---

[1] See "Journal Asiatic Society of Bengal," vol. xi.

for the cure of which he would not be persuaded to take
any medicines until it was too late to be of any avail.

"M. de Körös arrived here on the 24th ult. (March
1842), and communicated to me his desire of proceeding
to the residence of the Sikkim Raja, and thence to Lassa,
for the purpose of procuring access to stores of Tibetan
literature, which he had been taught to believe, from his
reading in Ladak and Kanum, were still extant in the
capital of Eastern Tibet (Lassa), and might have thence
found their way into Sikkim.

" As the eldest son of the Sikkim Raja is by the usage
of the family a Lama, and as the present *Tubgani Lama*
is a learned priest, and said to be in possession of an
extensive library, I had some hopes that by making the
Raja acquainted with M. de Körös' unobtrusive character
and known avoidance of political and religious subjects
in his intercourse with the people of the countries he has
visited, I might have contributed to procuring him permission to proceed into Tibet, and to this end I sent the
Raja's Vakeel to visit M. de Körös, that he might satisfy
himself as to the extent to which he had prosecuted his
studies into the language and literature of Tibet, as well
as of the objects he had in view in desiring to visit the
Tubgani Lama and the city of Lassa. The Vakeel, who
is a man of intelligence and some learning, was altogether
amazed at finding a Feringhee a complete master of the
colloquial language of Tibet, and so much his own superior in acquaintance with the religion and literature of
that country. I endeavoured to answer his numerous
questions about M. de Körös by detailing the particulars
of his early life and later travels in Asia, with which I
was acquainted; by stating his devotion to the prosecution of his lingual and literary studies; my certain knowledge that in permitting him to visit Sikkim and Lassa
the Raja would have nothing to apprehend from ignorance of the usages and religion of the people, nor an
indiscreet zeal in the attainment of his objects; that he

was not at all connected with the service of our Government, or any other power in India, but that the Governor-General had granted him his permission to travel through India, and that any facilities afforded him by the Raja would be noted approvingly by his lordship and myself.

"The Vakeel at my desire addressed the Rajah, explaining fully my wishes, and M. de Körös resolved to remain here, pending a reply from Sikkim. He was full of hope as to the favourable result of the reference, and in the most enthusiastic manner would dilate on the delight he expected to derive from coming in contact with some of the learned men of the East (Lassa), as the Lamas of Ladak and Kanum, with whom alone he had previous communion, were confessedly inferior in learning to those of Eastern Tibet. He was modest and almost silent on the benefits which might accrue to general knowledge from the results of his contemplated journey; but '*what would Hodgson, Turnour, and some of the philosophers of Europe not give to be in my place when I get to Lassa ?*' was a frequent exclamation of his during the conversations I had with him previous to his illness. He had arranged, in the event of his getting permission to proceed, to leave with me all his books, papers, and bank-notes to the amount of 300 rupees, to be cared for on his behalf; and a complete copy of the 'Journal of the Asiatic Society,' which he had received from the Society, he said he should ask me to keep, in the event of his never returning. How soon were all his enthusiastic anticipations clouded, and his journeyings stopped for ever!

"On the 6th instant I called on him, and found him feverish, with foul tongue, dry skin, and headache. I urged him to take some medicine, but in vain. He said he had suffered often from fever and other ailments, from which he had recovered without physic; that rhubarb was the only thing of the sort he had ever used, except tartar emetic. The former had been recommended to him by Moorcroft, and the latter by a Persian doctor.

He took out of his box a small bit of decayed rhubarb and a phial of tartar emetic, and said, with apparent distrust in their virtues, 'As you wish it, I will take some to-morrow, if I am not better; it is too late to-day, the sun is going down.' I sent him some weak soup, and returned to see him on the 7th. He was then much better, got off his pallet, entered into conversation, chatted animatedly with me for an hour on his favourite subjects of thought and inquiry. For the first time since I had seen him, he this day showed how sensitive he was to the applause of the world as a reward to his labours and privations. He went over the whole of his travels in Tibet with fluent rapidity; and in noticing each stage of the results of his studies, he mentioned the distinguished notice that had been accorded in Europe and India to the facts and doctrines brought to light by him. He seemed especially gratified with an editorial article by Prof. Wilson in the supplement to the 'Government Gazette' of 9th July 1829, which he produced, and bid me read; it related to the extreme hardships he had undergone while at the monastery of Zanskar, where, with the thermometer below zero, for more than four months he was precluded by the severity of the weather from stirring out of a room nine feet square; yet in this situation he read from morning till evening without a fire, the ground forming his bed, and the walls of the building his protection against the rigours of the climate, and still he collected and arranged forty thousand words of the language of Tibet, and nearly completed his Dictionary and Grammar.[1] Passing from this subject, he said, in a playful mood, 'I will show you something very curious,' and he produced another number of Wilson's paper of September 10, 1827, and pointing to one editorial paragraph, desired me to read it first, and then hear the explanation.[2] It runs thus (after

---

[1] See page 80 *et seq., ante.*
[2] See Government Gazette of that date.

noticing some communications to the Asiatic Society from Mr Hodgson): 'In connection with the literature and religion of Tibet, and indeed of the whole of the Bhoti countries, we are happy to learn that the patronage of the Government has enabled the Hungarian traveller, Csoma de Körös, to proceed to Upper Besarh to prosecute his Tibetan studies for three years, in which period he engages to prepare a comprehensive Grammar and Vocabulary of the language, with an account of the history and literature of the country.

" 'These objects are the more desirable, as we understand M. de Körös considers the recent labours of Klaproth and Rémusat, with regard to the language and literature of Tibet, as altogether erroneous. Monsieur Rémusat, indeed, admits the imperfectness of his materials, but Klaproth, as usual, pronounces *ex cathedrâ*, and treats the notion of any successful study of Tibetan by the English in India with ineffable contempt.' 'Now, I do not recollect,' said M. de Körös, 'that I gave my opinion of Klaproth as it is given here, but, oh! Wilson was very, very,' and he shook his head significantly, 'against Klaproth, and he took this opportunity to pull him down, and favour Rémusat. It is very curious;' and he laughed heartily. Not being of the initiated in the curiosities of Tibetan literature, I did not fully appreciate the jest, but others probably will; and I was greatly interested with the keen enjoyment produced in the mind of the Ascetic by this subject.

" At the same visit he produced Hodgson's 'Illustrations of the Literature and Religion of the Buddhists,' and asked me if I had seen it. On being told that I had a copy, and had been familiar with its contents in progress of collection, although unversed in the subject, he said, 'He sent me this copy; it is a wonderful combination of knowledge on a new subject, with the deepest philosophical speculations, and will astonish the people of Europe. There are, however, some mistakes in it.' I

think he then said: 'In your paper on the *Limboos* you
asked if the appellation "Hung," distinctive of families
of that tribe, had any reference to the original "Huns,"
the objects of my search in Asia.   It is a curious similarity, but your "Hungs" are a small tribe, and the
people who passed from Asia, as the progenitors of the
Hungarians, were a great nation.'   I replied, that as the
original country of the Limboo 'Hungs' was undoubtedly
north of the Himalaya, and as he believed the same to
be the case as regarded the 'Huns,' it was at all events
possible that the 'Hungs' of this neighbourhood might
have been an offshoot from the same nation.   'Yes, yes,'
he rejoined, 'it is very possible; but I do not think it is
the case.'   And then, as if preferring to luxuriate in remote speculations on his beloved subjects rather than in
attempting to put an end to them by a discovery at
hand, he gave a rapid summary of the manner in which
he believed his native land was possessed by the original
'Huns,' and his reasons for tracing them to Central or
Eastern Asia.   This was all done in the most enthusiastic
strain; *but the texture of the story was too complicated for
me to take connected note of it.*   I gathered, however, from
his conversation of this day, and of the previous ones
since our acquaintance, that all his hopes of attaining the
object of the long and laborious search were centered in
the discovery of the country of the 'Yoogars.'   This land
he believed to be to the east and north of Lassa and
the province of Kham, and on the western confines of
China.   To reach it was the goal of his most ardent
wishes, and there he fully expected to find the tribes he
had hitherto sought in vain.   The foundation of his hopes,
to any one not deeply imbued with enthusiasm, or accustomed to put faith in philological affinities, will probably appear vague and insecure.   It was as follows, in
so far as I could gather from his repeated conversations:—In the dialects of Europe—the Sclavonic, Celtic,
Saxon, and German—I believe the people who gave their

name to the country now called Hungary, were styled
'Hunger' or 'Ungur,' 'Oongar' or 'Yoongar,' and in
Arabic, Turkish, and Persian works there are notices of a
nation in Central Asia resembling in many respects the
people who came from the East into Hungary. In these
languages they are styled 'Oogur,' 'Woogur,' 'Voogur,'
or 'Yoogur,' according to the pronunciation of the Persian letter; and from the same works it might be inferred,
he said, that the country of the 'Yoogurs' was situated
as above noted. There were collateral reasons which led
him to this conclusion, but he did not lay much stress on
them, and they have escaped my memory. It has since
occurred to me, that at the time of the conversations now
detailed, M. de Körös had some presentiment that death
was near him, for on no former occasion was he so com-
municative, nor did he express opinions as if he was very
anxious they should be remembered. On this day he
certainly did so, and I feel it due to his memory to record
them, even in this imperfect manner. *To give his opinions*
point, it would require a knowledge of the subjects on which
he discoursed, to which I cannot pretend; yet such as they
are, they may, as the last words of an extraordinary man,
be prized by those who honoured him for his acquirements, and admired him for his unwearied exertions in
the cause of literature, languages, and history.

"Although so much better on the 7th than on the
previous day, I dreaded that a return of fever was
impending, and I again urged him to take medicine,
but in vain. On the 8th I did not see him, but on
the morning of the 9th, on visiting him with Dr.
Griffith, I found that fever had returned; he was
confused and slightly delirious, his countenance was
sunken, anxious, and yellow, and altogether his state
was bad and dangerous. After much trouble, we got
him to swallow some medicine, and had his temples
rubbed with blistering fluid. On the morning of the
10th he was somewhat better, but still unable to talk

connectedly or distinctly; towards evening he became comatose, and continued so until 5 A.M. of the 11th, when he expired without a groan or struggle. On the 12th, at 8 A.M., his remains were interred in the burial-ground of this station. I read the funeral service over him in the presence of almost all the gentlemen at the place.

"The effects consisted of four boxes of books and papers, *the suit of blue clothes which he always wore*, and *in which he died*, a few sheets, and one cooking-pot. His food was confined to tea, of which he was very fond, and plain boiled rice, of which he ate very little. On a mat on the floor, with a box of books on the four sides, he sat, ate, slept, and studied, never undressed at night, and rarely went out during the day. He never drank wine or spirits, or used tobacco or other stimulants.

"Annexed is a detailed list of the contents of the boxes. Among his papers were found the bank-notes for 300 rupees, to which he alluded before his death, and a memorandum regarding Government papers for 5000 rupees, which is stated in transcript of a letter to the Government, dated 8th February 1842, it was his wish to leave at his death to the Asiatic Society of Bengal for any literary purpose. Cash to the number of 224 rupees of various coinage, and a waist-belt containing 26 gold pieces (Dutch ducats, I believe), complete the money part of his effects. From this I shall deduct the funeral expenses and wages due to his Lepcha servant, and retain the remainder, along with the books and papers, until I receive the orders of Government for disposing of them. As the deceased was not a British subject, I have not made the usual adver-tisement of the possession of his effects, nor have I taken charge of them in the civil court, but in my capacity of political officer in this direction.

"From a letter of James Prinsep's among the papers, I gather that he was a native of the town of Pest, or

Pesth, in the province of Transylvania,[1] and I have found transcript of a letter addressed by him to the Austrian Ambassador in London, apparently on matters connected with his native country; I presume, therefore, that the proper mode of making his death known to his relations, if such there be, and of disposing of the money not willed by him, will be through the Austrian Ambassador at the British Court. In some documents I found his address to be Körösi Csoma Sandor."

In a footnote Mr. Henry Torrens remarks as follows : " I may add to Mr. Campbell's interesting paper such information as my memory enables me to give of the opinion held by the deceased philologist on the *origin of the Huns*, which, with singular opinions on the Buddhist faith, constituted his most favourite speculations. He, on more than one occasion entered on the subject with me at great length, detailing in particular the Sanskrit origin of existing names of places and hill-ranges in Hungary. My constant request at the close of these conversations used to be that *he would record these speculations. He invariably refused, alluding darkly to the possibility of his one day having it in his power to publish to the world something sounder than speculation.* In proportion as I pressed him on the subject, he became more reserved with me on these particular questions. He seemed to have an antipathy to his opinions being published. I remember his giving me one day a quantity of curious speculation on the derivation of geographical names in Central Asia. Some months afterwards I had occasion to annotate on a theory of the nomenclature of the Oxus, and, writing to him, recapitulated his opinion on the subject, and begged to be allowed to publish it. His answer was that ' he did not remember.'

" His exceeding diffidence on the subjects on which he might have dictated to the learned world of Europe and Asia was the most surprising trait in him. He was very

---

[1] This is evidently a mistake.

deeply read in general literature independently of his Tibetan lore, but never did such acquirements centre in one who made such modest use of them."

The contents of this report were communicated to the Asiatic Society, by whom one thousand rupees was voted for the purpose of being placed into the hands of Major Lloyd that a suitable monument be erected over the grave. The inscription was approved by the Society at their meeting in February 1845, which the Secretary, Mr. H. Torrens, introduced with the following words :—

"I beg to submit the epitaph to be placed on the tomb of our lamented friend, Csoma de Körös, as approved by the committee."

H. J.

ALEXANDER CSOMA DE KÖRÖSI,[1]
A Native of Hungary,
Who, to follow out Philological Researches,
Resorted to the East ;
And after years passed under privations,
Such as have been seldom endured,
And patient labour in the cause of Science,
Compiled a Dictionary and Grammar
Of the Tibetan Language,
His best and real monument.

On his road to H'Lassa,
To resume his labours,
He died at this place,[2]
On the 11th April 1842,
Aged 44 years.[3]

His fellow-labourers,
The Asiatic Society of Bengal,
Inscribe this tablet to his memory.

REQUIESCAT IN PACE.

---

[1] This should be, de Körös, without the terminal *i*. See page 9, *ante*.
[2] Darjeeling, in British Sikkim.
[3] This is a mistake, as he was born in April 1784.

124

d

Grammar

Dr. Archibald Campbell's report on Csoma's closing days, and his subsequent memorandum,[1] will always be read with deep interest, the contents of which have been quoted already. Dr. Campbell again mentions in it Csoma's ardent wish to reach Lassa, where, strengthened with his linguistic attainments, he formed enthusiastic hopes of realising the objects of his research. "Could he reach Lassa, he felt that Sanskrit would have quickly enabled him to master the contents of its libraries, and in them he believed was to be found all that was wanting to give him the real history of the Huns in their original condition and migrations. The power of acquiring languages was the extraordinary talent of Csoma. He had studied the following ancient and modern tongues, and was proficient in many of them: Hebrew, Arabic, Sanskrit, Pushtu, Greek, Latin, Sclavonic, German, English, Turkish, Persian, French, Russian, Tibetan, with the addition of Hindustani, Mahratta, and Bengali. His library at his death had a dictionary of each of the languages he was acquainted with, and on all were his manuscript annotations."

These remarks, recorded by a kind friend under the influence of sorrowful sympathy, have been looked upon by many, in the absence of any other information, as the chief if not the *sole* clue to the proper understanding of Csoma's whole career and aspirations. Relying on imperfect data, Csoma's aims appeared to his critics as very illusory, if not altogether erroneous. But any one, wishing to do justice to the memory and labours of this extraordinary man, and keeping in view his long scientific preparation, both in his own country and in Germany, to enable him to attain a special and well-defined object, Dr. Campbell's remarks will not be regarded in any other light than what they are, and as he doubtless wished them to be regarded, namely, a graphic description of the incidents of the last scenes of a dying man. Words which were uttered by the patient between the paroxysms

[1] "Journal Asiatic Society of Bengal," vol. xiv. p. 823.

of his fatal disease will not be taken as a legitimate basis upon which *alone* to pronounce a satisfactory judgment of a life-long career, particularly after what Dr. Campbell tells us, that "the context of the story was too complicated for me to take connected note of it."

In the oft-mentioned letters to Captain Kennedy in 1825, Csoma expressed his opinion as to the coincidence of certain geographical names and words derived from the Sanskrit, which live to this day in the countries bordering on the Lower Danube. He spoke likewise of the country of the Huns and Yugurs on the western border of China, which, if possible, he desired to visit that he might become acquainted with the Mongol people. But he nowhere insists on any special linguistic affinity between the Magyar and the Tibetan tongues, which affinity, by itself, would have induced him to devote so much precious time to this language.

In the course of his Tibetan studies, pursued, as so often mentioned, in fulfilment of a solemn engagement towards the Indian Government, Csoma discovered, as he tells us in his second letter to Captain Kennedy, paragraph 50 and 51, that among the contents of the libraries in Tibet was to be found all that was wanting to give the real history of the Huns in their original condition and migrations. "What would Hodgson, Turnour, and some of the philosophers of Europe not give to be in my place when I get to Lassa!" was a frequent exclamation of Csoma's during his fatal illness.[1]

To reach Lassa, therefore, and to examine the contents of the libraries there, was the proximate aim of the journey during which he died.

There can be little doubt as to what would have been the direction of his ulterior steps, supposing him to have safely reached Lassa, and there obtained what he hoped for. He would most likely have endeavoured to penetrate into Mongolia and the country around it.

[1] See Dr. Campbell's Report, page 147, *ante.*

No unprejudiced person, therefore, who had the opportunity of weighing all the circumstances and the actual facts, will assuredly feel justified in pronouncing a condemnation, and in showing up Csoma as one who had wandered in search of fantastic ideas, and sacrificed the labours of a long life in vain.

A few words will explain our meaning.

In a book recently published [1] we find it stated that Professor Hunfalvy, a great authority on Finnish philology, had declared that "Körösi, during his stay in Calcutta, experienced the bitterest moments of his life, being *conscious* (?) that up to that time he had fruitlessly looked for the origin of the Hungarians."

Such disappointment we find nowhere alluded to by Csoma; he spoke nowhere of any bitter sorrow at the uselessness of his labours, yet such an opinion seems to have been shaped after his death.

Another great authority, Arminius Vámbéry, in a letter to Mr. Ralston, draws the conclusion that "*Körösi was a victim* to '*unripe*' philological speculation, because he was looking for a nation *speaking the Magyar tongue*, and suffered much disappointment at not finding the looked-for relatives."

Professor Vámbéry continues—

"And this (viz, finding Magyar-speaking relatives) was impossible for Körösi to attain, because the Magyar tongue is a mixture of an Ugrian and Turko-tatar dialect. This knowledge, however," says Vámbéry, "is the result of recent (principally his own) investigations, and *poor Körösi* could have had hardly any notion of it!"

Such is the learned Professor's judgment on Csoma in 1882.

We may mention that the Ugric and the Turko-tatar theory was strongly advocated by Vámbéry in his last great philological work.

[1] Ralston's "Tibetan Tales." Trübner & Co., London, 1882. Introduction, p. 21 *et seq.*

Summing up the preceding remarks, it may be stated that—

Firstly, we have already adduced proofs to show how scrupulously careful Csoma's critical mind was not to run into philological or any other speculations. He guards himself very distinctly against such when he says, " I was much perplexed by Dr. Gerard's letter to me. In my answer I would not enter into the wide field of speculation." [1]   Henry Torrens speaks of it,[2] and Dr. Malan is very positive on the subject [3] when he says, " Csoma did not scrutinise the intricacies of hypotheses ; he had too much sense for that."

Secondly, no proof can be found anywhere among Csoma's writings of his having searched after a people in Asia " speaking the Magyar tongue."   Such a theory may have been propounded by idle literary speculators or elated enthusiasts on his behalf, as was recently done in Count Béla Széchényi's case, but a childlike chimera of the sort cannot be laid to his charge unless proof positive exists that he *enunciated* such an opinion and design, and persevered in it to the end.

Thirdly, the position of the Hungarian tongue in reference to the Finnish, the Ugric, and the Turko-tatar dialects is far from being settled yet by the philologists. Moreover, Csoma's studies and labours moved in an entirely different philological and ethnographical sphere from that to which these several dialects belong.   No critic who was not able to pay due attention to a field of research on which Csoma laboured, namely, the Indian, the Sanskrit, and the Tibetan languages, could be expected to understand and to appreciate his ideas, motives, and conclusions as they deserve, nor yet claim the right to pronounce final judgment upon his merits.   Nevertheless, an opinion stands on record that Csoma's philological views are not considered by his countrymen as " deserv-

---

[1] See chap. v., p. 77.   [2] See chap. xi., p. 153.
[3] See " Journal Royal Asiatic Society," vol. xvi., p. 493.

ing serious consideration."[1] But this is only in the Finnish and Turko-tatar direction, in which the special studies of these ʻcritics lay, being quite distinct from those of Csoma, which, by the way, have not as yet been inquired into by them. It is not fair towards a thoroughgoing student such as Csoma was to treat his labours in an off-hand manner, and to misinterpret the tendency of his thoughtful conclusions.

Csoma was filled, as every earnest investigator should be, with a never-flagging devotion to his object; but he was not a dreamer, as some of his least-informed critics seem to wish to suggest that he was. All his philological deductions were based on carefully selected data, which he always adduced.

Impelled by a noble devotion to historical and philological science, he set out unaided on his solitary journey to the East, endeavouring to penetrate into the northern parts of the Chinese Empire, especially into Mongolia and the surrounding countries, his sole object being to study, from a Hungarian point of view, several yet unsolved ethnological and historical problems, hoping that his labours generally might be found useful by *posterity*, whose appreciation he looked for as his only reward. As long as life was spared him he remained faithful to this purpose, worthy to be followed up still by any one really competent for the task.

Step by step, cautiously and with deliberation for two-and-twenty years, he directed his efforts among difficulties which would have driven a less heroic mind to despair, and yet with a *modesty* and ready self-sacrifice quite exceptional. When we consider the physical difficulties alone, we find that Csoma traversed greater distances than did any other traveller before him or since under *similar circumstances.*

The memory of Körösi's uncomplaining endurance, unselfishness, and modesty will ever remain recorded

---

[1] Ralston, *op cit.*

among the pioneers of philology, and be cherished with gratitude in his native land.

What other tribute indeed but that of admiration and reverence could be rendered to such a labourer!

Even among the people and the high ecclesiastics of Tibet the fame of the Hungarian scholar lived for many years after him. The name of "Philangi Dàsa," the European disciple, as he was affectionately called there, has been mentioned with appreciation to Dr. Leitner, who in 1866 had an interview at Pukdal with the Abbot of the Monastery in which Csoma lived. Judging from Dr. Leitner's report, we find that Csoma's sympathetic individuality left a lasting impression behind him, and when the Tibetans heard that Leitner was a fellow-countryman of Csoma's, he was received with every mark of attention, and the Abbot offered to conduct Dr. Leitner safely to Lassa, leaving, if desired, his two sons as hostages in the hands of the Government. As, however, Dr. Leitner was not prepared to accept the unlooked-for offer, the Abbot was willing to extend it to any other European who may be actuated by the same love and devotion to philological researches as Csoma had been.

This circumstance was repeatedly brought to public notice by Dr. Leitner, but no advantage has as yet been taken of an opportunity so favourable to linguistic and perhaps political objects.

In the Székler land, his native province, Csoma's memory lives in affectionate remembrance.

The Kenderessy-Csoma Scholarship, founded by him at the College of Nagy Enyed, is administered in accordance with his wishes. Csoma's relations made an endowment at the village school of Körös, at which, as a child, he learned his first lessons. The yearly proceeds of this sum are devoted partly to purchasing of books, and partly to improve the stipend of the schoolmaster. There is a third memorial also, namely, the donation made by Csoma in 1836 to the Military Institute of Kezdi-

Vásárhely. After the historical events of 1849 the funds of this Institute were amalgamated with those of the College of SzentGyörgy; towards this the Emperor-King, Francis-Joseph, contributed ten thousand florins. Csoma's money is administered in a separate account there, and the yearly proceeds are divided among the most industrious scholars, each prize-book being marked with the founder's name.

"I have no doubt," adds Baron Orbán Balázs, "that a day will come when a better future dawns upon our country, and when past omissions and neglect will be made good, and then a substantial monument will rise to the imperishable memory of Alexander Csoma de Körös."

We heartily add our Amen. May it be so!

The contents of the four boxes mentioned by Dr. Campbell, constituting Csoma's travelling library, were as follows :—

1st Box.

1. Grammar and dictionaries of Bengali, Turkish, Tibetan, Greek, Latin, French, and English languages. 7 volumes.
2. New Testament in Russian.
3. Hodgson, on Buddhism in Nepal.
4. Index of the Asiatic Society's Transactions.
5. The twentieth volume, Part I., of Asiatic Researches.
   Total 13 volumes.
   A medicine-box.

2d Box.

1. Grammars and dictionaries :—
   Wilson's Sanskrit Dictionary; Sanskrit Grammar; Bengali and English Dictionary; Bengali, Turkish, and English grammars; Sanskrit Dictionary; Greek Exercises; English, Bengali, and Manipuri Grammar and Dictionary.
2. Alphabetum Tibetanum of Giorgi.
3. Bible in English; New Testament in Sanskrit; St. Matthew's Gospel in Bengali; Genesis in English.
4. Raja Tarangini, 2 volumes; Mahavansa; eight Bengali pamphlets.
5. Journal Asiatic Society, 9 volumes; Asiatic Researches, twentieth volume, Part I.; foreign books, 6 volumes.

L

3d Box.

Tibetan Grammar ; Mahabharata, ' 4 volumes ; Raja Tarangini ; Suarita ; Naishada Charita ; four Bengali pamphlets.

4th Box.

1. Grammars and dictionaries :—

   English Grammar and Exercises ; English and French Dictionary ; English pocket-dictionary ; English and Bengali Dictionary and Exercises ; Yates' Sanskrit Grammar ; Bhutia Vocabulary ; Tibetan Grammar and Dictionary, 3 copies ; Russian Grammar ; two Latin and one Dutch Dictionaries ; Latin Selections ; Greek Grammar.

2. New Testament in Greek and Latin ; Prayer-Book in Bengali.

3. Æsop's Fables in German ; 2 volumes Cicero's Orationes ; Quintilianus ; Homer ; Horace ; Cæsar's Commentaries, Livy, Ovid, Tacitus, Virgil, Sallust, Juvenal, Xenophon, altogether 13 volumes.

4. Robertson's History of India ; Klaproth's Tibet ; Dickens' Pickwick ; Journal Royal Asiatic Society ; Prinsep's Useful Tables, 1 volume.

5. Small Atlas ; Map of Chinese Empire ; Map of Western Asia ; a memorandum book.

6. Inkstand, ruler, bundle of pencils, wafers, slate, a small glass.

N.B.—The blue dress was given to his Lepcha servant.

CHAPTER XII.

Prince Eszterházy's inquiry regarding Csoma's papers—List of some of
them—Renewal of his tombstone at Darjeeling—Placed on the
list of public monuments by the Government of India—His
portrait—Conclusion.

THROUGH the Indian Government Csoma's death was
notified to the authorities in England, and we find that
Prince Eszterházy wrote to the directors of the East India
Company thanking them for their communication of the
sad event, and inquiring at the same time whether the
Asiatic Society of Bengal would feel disposed to put the
Transylvanian authorities in possession of any papers
that may have been found among Csoma's writings relat-
ing to special researches concerning the history of the
Hungarians in ancient times.

This letter of the Ambassador was transmitted to
Calcutta, but led to no result. Csoma left no formal
will. His memorandum of the 9th of February, by which
he appointed the Asiatic Society the sole heir of all his
money, books, &c., was not admitted as a valid testamentary document. The Administrator-General, therefore,
submitted a statement on the 8th of June 1843, according to which the estate appears to have consisted of
3000 sicca and 2000 Government rupees, besides 26
Dutch ducats ; the Administrator-General adding, " I
shall be obliged by your forwarding the money to the
Government for transmission to the Honourable Court of
Directors for information of the next kin of the deceased."

On his first arrival in Calcutta, in February 1854, as
medical officer on the Bengal Establishment of the

Honourable East India Company, the writer, through the introduction of Mr. Arthur Grote of the Bengal Civil Service, obtained admission to the Administrator-General's office, where a small iron box, with the name of Alexander Csoma de Körös painted on, was placed before him, containing papers of the late Tibetan traveller. He prepared a list of its contents at that time, being fortunate enough not to have neglected the opportunity that offered, as three years later, on renewing his inquiry, he learnt that the box in question could not again be found ; its contents had been destroyed with other similar unclaimed documents. The following is the list prepared in 1854:—

1. Government Gazette, dated 10th September 1827, in which it is announced that Csoma had obtained permission from Government to reside in Upper Besarh for three years for the study of the Tibetan language and literature. See chapter vi.

2. Government Gazette of 9th July 1829, containing a report of the meeting of the Asiatic Society under the presidency of Sir Charles Grey, when a monthly allowance of 50 rupees was voted to Csoma, in consequence of Dr. Gerard's letter to Mr. Fraser.

3. Bengal Hurkaru, dated 13th November 1829, containing a report of the Asiatic Society's meeting, when Csoma's letter was read declining to accept the proffered pecuniary assistance till he arrived in Calcutta.

4. Copy of a letter (Latin) to Prince Eszterházy, forwarding 50 copies of the Tibetan Grammar and Dictionary for the learned societies of Hungary and of the Austrian Empire, dated 1st July 1835.

5. A diploma of membership of the Hungarian Scientific Society, dated 15th November 1833.

6. Copy of letter to Mr. Döbrentei, secretary to the Hungarian Society, dated 1st July 1838.

7. Two letters from Mr. Döbrentei, dated 1838. Already alluded to.

8. Mr. James Prinsep's letter, with duplicates of two cheques, one of 200, the other for 450 ducats, dated 8th and 10th of February 1836 respectively.

9. Copy of Csoma's letter to the College of Nagy Enyed, forwarding 450 ducats and founding a scholarship under the name of the Kenderessy-Csoma Scholarship.

10. Klaproth's letter in German, dated Paris, 26th August 1836, thanking him for the Tibetan works and expressing opinion on subjects of Oriental literature.
11. Mr. James Prinsep's letter enclosing Bhote alphabet, 26th June 1837.
12. Dr. Wilson's letter, in which he asks for assistance in translating the Liturgy into Tibetan, 14th September 1840.
13. Mr. Yates' letter about the Psalms in Tibetan, dated 5th October 1841.
14. Mr. Worsdale's letter about a Tibetan prayer-book.
15. A friendly letter from Mr. John Barits, dated Kolosvar, 1st May 1840.
16. Copies of two letters to Mr. Boucher of Chandernagore, dated 7th November 1841.
17. Copy of letter to Mr. M'Clintock, dated 8th February 1872.
19. Two passports from Supreme Government in Persian. The last dated 27th September 1841.
20. Three Tibetan manuscripts of 60, 30, and 26 pages respectively. The latter was marked thus : "Specimens of letters in Tibetan."
21. Dr. Campbell's letter, forwarding one from the Lama of Kanum.
22. Two pieces of paper with Tibetan characters.
23. Mr. Grenolly's letter on money matters, 7th February 1842.
24. A fragment.

Only a few more words remain to be added. Before all, an apology is due from the writer of this biography for mentioning incidents which refer to himself alone.

In the year 1856, and as long as Dr. Collins remained civil surgeon of Darjeeling, he took a kindly interest in Csoma's monument in the station cemetery; and later, when the writer was fortunate enough to be appointed by the Lieutenant-Governor, Sir William Grey, to the medical charge of the Sanatorium, it was a special delight to him to have the privilege of being able to look after his illustrious compatriot's tombstone.

In February 1883 he again visited Darjeeling during his short temporary sojourn in Bengal, and was agreeably surprised to find that the monument over Csoma's grave had been entirely rebuilt. A few seasons back the heavy rains in the hills caused a landslip on the mountain-side on which the station cemetery stands, and Csoma's monument sustained damage. This was soon restored by order of the Lieutenant-Governor, Sir Ashley Eden, and the grave is now placed on the list of those *public monuments* in India which are under the immediate care of the Public Works Department.

The writer begs to express again his sincere acknowledgments to the Council of the Asiatic Society of Bengal, and to the Under-secretary of the Foreign Department, Mr. Durand, for placing copies of several documents at his disposal, without which it would have been impossible to fill up the gaps hitherto existing in the biography of the Hungarian traveller. In the library of the Asiatic Society there were six original letters in Csoma's handwriting; three of these have been most courteously transmitted, through the late lamented Dr. M'Cann,[1] to the Royal Academy of Sciences in Hungary, to be preserved as relics in the archives at Budapest. A similar magnanimity towards the same learned body was manifested a year earlier by Mr. B. H. Hodgson, whose name so often occurs in these pages, by sending him two original letters of Csoma, which are published in chapter vii. Besides these his thanks are due to Mr. Arthur Grote, to Dr. Rajendrolála Mitra, and to his friend Dr. George King, for kind assistance. In Hungary, Mr. Paul Gyulai, Emil Thewrewk de Ponor, Bishop Szász, Madame Szabó de Borgáta, Baron Nicholas Horváth, Professor Budenz, and others furnished valuable data for the preparation of this memoir, all of whom have placed the writer under deep obligation.

Regarding the portrait which faces the title-page, the Reverend Dr. Malan wrote as follows on the 15th of October 1883:—

"I thank you for giving me the pleasure of seeing

[1] To whose courtesy an especial tribute is due here, with the expression of deep regret at his untimely death by cholera in May last.

Csoma's likeness. It reminds me very well of him, although it is younger than when I saw him; he was then weather-beaten, and looked older than this picture, but he wore no beard when I knew him.[1] I hope you will have the likeness photographed, then may I beg a copy of it, for I always remember him with gratitude and pleasure; I used to delight in his company, he was so kind and so obliging, and always willing to impart all he knew. He was altogether one of the most interesting men I ever met."

Dr. Malan is presumably the only witness still living who knew Csoma face to face so well. Mr. Hodgson was in correspondence with him, but, as far as is known, they never met.

This memoir would be incomplete without a respectful mention of the names of Mr. Hodgson, and particularly of Dr. Malan. This latter gentleman, with great generosity, recently presented Csoma's Tibetan books and MSS., as a spontaneous gift, to the Hungarian Academy of Sciences,[2] in whose library at Budapest they will in the future be carefully preserved.

---

[1] Dr. Archibald Campbell speaks of Csoma's grizzly beard.
[2] See "Journal Royal Asiatic Society," vol. xvi. p. 486.

APPENDIX.

CSOMA's writings may be divided into two categories. To the first belong his Tibetan Grammar and Dictionary, and the essays which were published in various periodicals of Calcutta. To the second belong his manuscripts.

The first class consists of the following :—

1. Analysis of the Kahgyur and Stangyur. "Bengal Asiatic Researches," vol. xx.
2. Geographical notice of Tibet. "Bengal Asiatic Society's Journal," vol. i., p. 122.
3. Translation of a Tibetan fragment. "Bengal Asiatic Society's Journal," vol. i., p. 269.
4. Note on Kala Chakra and Adhi Buddha systems. "Bengal Asiatic Society's Journal," vol. ii., p. 57.
5. Translation of a Tibetan passport, dated 1688. "Bengal Asiatic Society's Journal," vol. ii., p. 201.
6. Origin of the Shakya race, translated from Kahgyur. "Bengal Asiatic Society's Journal," vol. ii. p. 385.
7. Mode of expressing numerals in the Tibetan language. "Bengal Asiatic Society's Journal," vol. iii., p. 6.
8. Extracts from Tibetan works. "Bengal Asiatic Society's Journal," vol. iii., p. 57.
9. Grammar and Dictionary of the Tibetan language in two volumes. Calcutta, 1834.
10. Interpretation of the Tibetan inscription on a Bhotan banner taken in Assam. "Bengal Asiatic Society's Journal," vol. v., p. 264.
11. Translation of the motto on the margin of a white satin

scarf of Tibetan priests. " Bengal Asiatic Society's Journal," vol. v., p. 383.

12. Notices on the different systems of Buddhism. "Bengal Asiatic Society's Journal," vol. vii., p. 142.

13. Enumeration of historical and grammatical works which are to be found in Tibet. " Bengal Asiatic Society's Journal," vol. vii., p. 147.

14. On Buddhist Amulettes. "Bengal Asiatic Society's Journal," vol. ix., Part II., p. 905.

15. The aphorisms of Sa-Skya Pandita. " Bengal Asiatic Society's Journal," vol. xxiv., p. 141.

In the second category are—

16. A collection of Buddhist terms in Tibetan and English, and

17. A collection of Sanskrit, Hindi, and Hungarian words. A fragment.

A brief notice will be given of each in the form of appendices.

I.

ANALYSIS OF THE BKAHGYUR AND THE BSTANGYUR.

This is contained in the twentieth volume of the "Asiatic Researches," which volume consists of two parts.

The analysis of the Kahgyur is divided by Csoma into three articles—

a. The analysis of the Dulva. As. Res., Part I., p. 41-94.

b. Notices on the "Life of Shakya" from the MDo part. As. Res., Part II., pp. 285-318.

c. Analysis of Sher-chin. As. Res., Part II., pp. 393-553.

The analysis of the Stangyur. Its abstract contents, divided into two classes, RGyud and MDo. As. Res., Part II., pp. 553-585.

A. The Kahgyur.

a. The analysis of the Dulva.

The Dulva is the first division of the Kahgyur. The whole

of the Kahgyur consists of one hundred volumes, of which thirteen are allotted to the Dulva, in Sanskrit, called Vinaya or Discipline, being the introduction to the whole Buddhist Encyclopædia, containing descriptions of observances to be practised
by the votaries of Buddhism, but more especially by those
persons, whether male or female, who adopt a religious life.
These observances are of a very comprehensive description,
extending not only to moral and ceremonial duties, but to
modes of personal deportment, and to the different articles of
food and attire. The precepts are interspersed with legendary
accounts, recording the occasions on which Shakya thought it
necessary to communicate his particular instructions to his
disciples.

The Dulva comprises seven portions; some authorities
divide it into four.

The first of the seven portions, the Vinaya vastu in Sanskrit, Dul-va-zhi in Tibetan, treats of the circumstances under
which the religious profession may be adopted. It opens with
an account of the hostilities that prevailed between the kings
of Anga and Magadha, until the latter was overpowered and
made tributary to the former.

The particulars of Shakya's birth are not enumerated at
this place, but we find here an account of his two first disciples,
viz., Sariputra and Magalyana, two young philosophical Brahmans, who, being attracted by his teaching, attached themselves
to his person.

The doctrine of Shakya was patronised by the King Vim-
basara; at Rajagriha he enjoyed great fame and made numerous
converts. The mode in which his converts were received into
the order of monks, either by himself or by his disciples, is
described. Two presidents are appointed, and five classes of
teachers ordained. Questions to be discussed are given, and
a description is given of persons who are from bodily imperfections or disease inadmissible. A variety of rules on the subject
of admission is laid down.

The conduct of the person after admission is regulated,
various moral obligations are prescribed; resignation and
forbearance under maltreatment or when reviled are particularly inculcated.

Stories are related of improprieties committed by some of

the juvenile members of the community, and, in consequence, Shakya rules that none shall be admitted who are under fifteen, and that no priest be ordained under twenty years of age.   He prohibits the admission of slaves, debtors, runaways, hermaphrodites, diseased or maimed persons, of young men without consent of their parents, and of individuals who have families dependent on them.   No person is to be admitted except in a full conclave, and no one is allowed to reside among the monks without ordination; no thieves, parricides, matricides, or murderers are to be admitted.

The next subject is the performance of the great Buddhist rite, the "Confession and Expiation," which should be observed every new and full moon in a public place, and before the whole congregation of monks.   The ceremony is fully detailed.

The rest of the volume contains a number of precepts and prohibitions; some of them are of a whimsical character.

The second volume treats on matters of dress, fitness of leather or hides for shoes to be worn by the priests.   There is a treatise on such drugs as the disciples are permitted to use and to carry about them.   There is also an account of how the King of Magadha entertained Shakya for three months. Various legends are told, and in the course of them the six chief cities of India are mentioned, namely, Sravasti and Saketana in Oude, Varanasi (the Benares of to-day), Vaisali (now Allahabad), Champa (Bhagulpore), and Rajagriha (Behar, Gaya).

From Magadha Shakya went to Vaisali upon invitation of the Lichchavi inhabitants of that city, who appear to have been republicans and very wealthy.   The peregrinations of Shakya are continued, in which he made many converts, relating the events of their present and previous lives, as well as those of his own, and how he became a Bodhisatvan or a sage.   The conclusion of the second volume leaves him, with thirty-six of his principal disciples, at the lake Mansarowar, or Manassarovara, in the northern Himalayas, near the source of the Ganges and the Indus.

The third volume continues in the same strain.   At a place in Kosala, Shakya and his followers were entertained by certain people with the view of ascertaining the habits of the Buddhist monks; they were found moderate in their enjoyments and easily satisfied. Their opponents, the Brahmans, on the contrary, showed greediness and insatiability.

Special lessons are given to the priests, as in the preceding volumes. They are permitted to eat treacle, to cook for themselves in time of famine, to eat meat under certain restrictions, and to accept gifts from the laity. These lessons are interspersed with notices on medicines and on the mode of administering them; the employment of charms and incantations is inculcated.

Next are laid down rules for the proper attire to be worn by the disciples of Shakya. They are directed to wear not more than three pieces of cloth of a red colour, to use cotton garments when bathing, to be clean in their dress and in their bedding, and never to go about naked as the Brahmin fakirs do. The subject of dress is followed up by directions as to the use of mats or sheets to lie upon.

Important injunctions are given regarding the conduct to be observed towards refractory and quarrelsome brethren. They are first to be admonished in the congregation, and if still impenitent, to be expelled from the community. The mode in which confession, repentance, and absolution are to be practised is explained and illustrated by examples.

The residences and furniture of the monks are next described, and the dissensions of religious communities considered; other miscellaneous matters are discussed, and a historical account is given of the origin of the Shakya race, and of the master's birth and education.

The fourth volume continues the story of Shakya's life, and mentions the circumstances which led to his becoming an ascetic. In this book the Shakyas are called inhabitants of Kosala (a country bordering on the Kailas mountains), and are said to be descendants of the Hindú king Ikshwaku. The birthplace of Shakya is declared to be Kapila-vastu, near the Himalayas, on the banks of the river Bhagirathi.

The last pages of the book treat on the evils of causing schisms; the inveterate hostility of his nephew, Lhas-Kyim, towards himself, is mentioned.

The fifth volume commences with Pratimoksha Sútra, that

is, short precepts for securing final felicity, the sum of which is, that "vice is to be diligently avoided, virtue invariably practised, and the passions kept under entire subjection."

Then follows a code of laws for the monks. The subject is enlarged more in the sixth, seventh, and eighth volumes, which comprehend 253 rules. Each of these arises, in general, from some improper conduct of a religious person. The offence comes to Shakya's knowledge, who summons the culprit into the congregation and reproves him publicly. On his confession and penitence he is pardoned; then Shakya pronounces the law with a view of preventing a like transgression in future.

The ninth volume is of the same general tenor as the preceding four, but it is addressed to the female followers of Buddha, the priestesses or nuns, "Gélong-má," or "Bhikshuni" in Sanskrit. Many of the rules are repeated from the foregoing volumes, and almost in identical terms.

The tenth and eleventh volumes relate to matters and rules of minor importance, such as, that the monks shall not use vitrified bricks as a flesh-brush, nor fragrant ointments, nor wear rings or seal-rings made of precious metals, nor eat garlic, nor learn music and dancing. There are directions for the building of chaityas or religious edifices to deposit relics in, such as the hair, nails, &c. of Buddha, which he gave to various persons during his lifetime. There are also to be found some tales of a political and historical character, an account of the destruction of Kapila, the metropolis of the Shakyas, the murder or expulsion of its inhabitants, many of whom are said to have fled into Nepal.

The eleventh volume closes with an account of the "Nirvaná," or emancipation and death of Shakya in Kamrup, in Western Assam. Eight cities contend for his remains, which are consequently divided among them and deposited in chaityas built for that purpose.

On the death of Shakya, Kasyapa, the head of the Buddhas, directs five hundred superior monks to make a compilation of the doctrines of their master. Thus: the *Do* was compiled by Ananda, the Dul-va by Upali; the Ma-mom, Abhi-dharma, and Prájná-páramita by Kasyapa himself. He presides over the sects at Rajagriha till his death. Ananda succeeds him, as Buddha. On Ananda's death his relics are divided between the Lichchavis, the republican inhabitants of Vaisali, and the King of Magadha, and two chaityas are built for their reception, one at Vaisali (in Tibetan Yangs-pa-chen, Allahabad), and the other at Pataliputra (Patna).

One hundred years after Shakya's Nirvana, his religion is carried into Kashmir. After a further period of one hundred and ten years, in the reign of Asoka, a king of Pataliputra, a new compilation of the laws of Buddha was prepared by 700 monks at Yangs-pa-chen.

The twelfth and thirteenth volumes of the Dulva contain supplementary rules, as communicated by Shakya to Upali his disciple in answer to certain inquiries.

At the end of the analysis of this part of the Kahgyur, in the twentieth volume of the " Asiatic Researches," Part I., p. 94, Csoma placed the following note :—" I may here close my analysis of the Dulva collection; from the tenor of which it may in some measure be judged what is to be found in the remaining eighty-seven volumes of the Kahgyur. Of the whole of the voluminous compilation, I have prepared a detailed analysis with occasional translations of such passages as excited curiosity, particularly the relation of the life and death of Shakya. The whole are deposited in manuscript, among the archives of the Asiatic Society, and will at any time be available to the scholar, who may consult the first volume of the Asiatic Society's Journal, page 375, for a general view of their contents, by Professor Wilson. For further information and details of the Kahgyur, a reference may be made to the publication indicated above."

b. Notices on Shakya's life are contained in two principal Tibetan works, namely, the Gya-ch'her-rol-pa and the Non-par-byung-va.

c. Sher-ch'hin or Shes-rab-kyi-pha-rol-tu-p'hyin-pa (Prajna paramita in Sanskrit, transcendental wisdom), fills twenty-one volumes.

B. The Stangyur.

The second part of the great Tibetan encyclopædia, the *Stangyur*, consists of two principal divisions, with a third one, consisting of a collection of hymns and prayers. The whole makes 225 volumes, namely :—

The *Gyud* treats on ritual and ceremonies, and extends over eighty-seven volumes.

The *Do* treats on science and literature, and occupies 136 volumes.

The hymns and praises are contained in one volume, and there is one volume more representing the index of the whole compilation.

II.

Geographical Notice of Tibet from Native Sources.

The vast mountainous country between 73° and 98° E. long. from Greenwich, and 27° and 38° N. latitude may be assigned to Tibet, since the Tibetan language is generally understood there, from Baltistan or little Tibet to the frontier of China, although there are various dialects; but the inhabitants of those countries have the same manners, customs, and faith, viz., Buddhism; have the same religious books, written or printed in characters common to all the provinces.

The native name of Tibet is Pot or Bod: Bod-yul, the country of Tibet; Bod-pa, a native man of Tibet; Bod-mo, a Tibetan woman. The Indian name for Tibet is Bhot.

Bod-yul, *par excellence*, is Middle Tibet, namely, the provinces of U and Tsang, with the capital of Lassa and Zhikátsé. Eastern Tibet or Great Tibet is called *Kham* or *Kham-yul*, the north-western part towards Ladak is *Nári*, and the southern part Bhutan; Lhopato or simply Lho, meaning south.

The whole of Tibet is highland, and lies among snowy mountains. In Tibetan books it is called by various poetical names, in allusion to snow, ice, glaciers, cold, and high elevation. The highest plateau is in Nari; the most elevated peak is Tisé or Tésé, called in Sanskrit Kailasa, about 80° E. longitude, and 34° N. latitude. The sources of the Indus, Sutlej, Gogra, and Brahmaputra are in Nári. Tibetan writers, in describing the situation of Tibet, have likened Nari to a waterpond, the provinces U- and Tsang to four canals, and Kham-yul to a field of crops.

On the north, Tibet is bounded by the countries of the Turks and Mongols, called by Tibetans Hor and Sok.

On the east by China (Gyanak); on the south by India (Gyagar); and on the west by India, Kashmir, Afghanistan, and Turkestan.

The neighbouring hill people are called by Tibetans "Mon," their country Mon-yul; the males Mon-pa, and the females Mon-mo.

From the first range of the Himalayas on the Indian side to the plains of Tartary, they count six chains of mountains, running in the north-western and south-eastern direction, viewed from the lofty mountain Kangri in Nari.

In the spacious valley between the third and fourth range is the main road between Ladak and U-tsang. The three great divisions of Tibet described are—

1. U-tsang or Tibet proper, divided into several districts. The capital, *Lassa*, situated in the district U, is the residence of the Great Lama, the government of Tibet, and of the Amban the Chinese Ambassador. The number of the inhabitants of this part of Tibet is reckoned at 130,000 families, who are, of all the Tibetan races, the most industrious, skilful, and polite.

2. The second or Eastern Division of Tibet is Kham-yul or Great Tibet; the east is bordered by China and subdivided into many small principalities. Its inhabitants differ much from other Tibetans in their stature, features, dress, and customs, as well as in the pronunciation of Tibetan. In physique they are very robust and simple, but very passionate ; not fond of ornaments of any kind. The sect called Pon or Bon, very numerous here, still practise the ancient religion of Tibet; have a literature of their own, religious orders, monasteries, and many superstitious rites. They kill several animals for sacrifice.

3. The third great division is Nári, extending from Tsang to Ladak. The area of this is very extensive, containing many deserts, and is sparsely inhabited. The number of families, including Ladak and Beltistan, does not exceed 50,000. They dwell in tents made of haircloth, and lead a pastoral life, eschewing agriculture.

The more north-westerly part of Tibet is Belti-yul—Beltistan or little Tibet—divided among several chiefs. In the mountain defiles on the south live the predatory people known as the Dardús; they are barbarians of Afghan or Hindu origin.

M

The inhabitants for the most part are Shiah Mohammedans. Their language is a dialect of the Tibetan, but what literature there is, is Persian. The climate is warm; in the lower part snow never falls.

Lakes in Tibet are few. The principal one is Ma-pham-yu-tsho (Mansarovara), in Nari; its circumference is one and a half day's journey (*i.e.*, about thirty miles).

Medicinal and hot springs are in the provinces of U and Tsang, and to the east of the Mapham lake.

Four glaciers are enumerated, and called mountains of frozen snow, namely, the Tisé, Havo, Shámpo, and Pulé.

There are mines in Tibet, but they are not worked. Some gold-dust is gathered in Nári, Gugé, and Zanskar.

In Tibet there is a great deficiency of wood. In Beltistan and Bhutan fruit-trees are cultivated. In Khamyul some forests are found. In the western parts of Ladak and Beltistan grapes come to maturity.

The slopes of the mountains are mostly bare. In the valleys, where irrigation is practised, some cereals, such as wheat, barley, buckwheat, millet and pease, are sown. Tibet has no ricefields, but beans and lentils, turnips, cabbages, onions, &c., are cultivated.

The daily food of a Tibetan consists of gruel prepared from the meal of parched barley; meat, bread, sour-milk, curds; and tea, prepared in the Tartar fashion in a churn with butter and milk.

The origin of the Tibetan race is attributed to a fabulous union between a she-demon and an ape. Some refer their origin to India, others to China, others again to the Mongols or Turks. They admit five races among themselves, according to the countries they live in; their pronunciation differs much, but they all understand each other. Except the Mohammedans of Ladak and Beltistan, they all profess the religion of Buddha, whose records are written in the same language and character.

III.

TRANSLATION OF A TIBETAN FRAGMENT, WITH REMARKS BY DR. WILSON.

In the ninth volume of the Gyut class of the Kahgyur occurs the original of a Tibetan fragment which created in the beginning of the last century a lively sensation amongst the learned men of Europe, and the history of which furnishes an amusing instance of the vanity of literary pretensions, and of the patience and pain with which men of talent and erudition have imposed upon themselves and upon the world.

In the end of the 17th and beginning of the 18th century the Russians, in their incursions into Siberia, came upon various deserted temples and monasteries, in some of which considerable collections of books were deposited. These were in general destroyed or mutilated by the ignorant rapacity of the soldiery; but fragments of them were preserved, and found their way as curiosities into Europe.

Among these some loose leaves, supposed to have been obtained at the ruins of Ablakit, a monastery near the source of the Irtish, were presented to the Emperor Peter the Great. Literature being then at a low ebb in Russia, no attempt was made to decipher these fragments, and they were sent by the Czar to the French Academy, whose sittings he had attended when in Paris, and who deservedly enjoyed the reputation of being the most learned body in Europe. In 1720 the Abbé Bignon, on the part of the Academy, communicated to the Czar the result of their labour, apprising him that the fragments sent were portions of a work in the Tibetan language, and sending a translation of one page made by Abbé Fourmont with the help of a Latin and Tibetan Dictionary. The letter was published in the "Transactions of the Academy of St. Petersburg," and the text and translation reprinted by Bayer in his "Museum Sinicum." Müller, in 1747, criticised Fourmont's translation, and gave a new one of the first lines, prepared with the double aid of a Tangutan priest, who rendered it into Mongol, and a Mongol student, who interpreted it to Müller. It was afterwards reprinted, with corrections and additions, and a new translation, by Giorgi in his "Alphabetum Tibetanum," and was at the beginning of the present century made the subject of animadversion by M. Rémusat in his "Recherches sur les Langues Tartares."

Of the previous performances M. Rémusat thus speaks: "On avait d'abord admiré la profonde erudition qui avait permit à Fourmont de reconnaitre seulement la langue dans laquelle le volume etait écrit; on a vanté depuis celle de Giorgi, qui avait rectifié le texte et la traduction. Je ne sais, comment on peut traduire ou corriger un texte qu'on n'est pas même capable de lire. Il n'y avait rien d'admirer dans tout cela; interprètes et commentateurs, panegyristes, et critiques tous étaient presque également hors d'état, je ne dis pas d'entendre une ligne, mais d'épeler une syllable du passage sur lequel ils dissertaient."

The consequence was what might have been expected, and the attempts at translation and correction were most ludicrously erroneous. The greatest liberties possible were taken with the words, letters were omitted or inserted at pleasure, and the translation was not only unlike the original, but unlike common sense, and the Latin was quite as unintelligible as the Tangutan.

The three translations are given—namely, that of Fourmont, of Müller, and of Giorgi. Regarding the last, Dr. Wilson remarks, "This display of unprofitable erudition is in fact only a shelter for his ignorance, and Giorgi knows no more about the matter than did Fourmont, without having the merit of his blundering simplicity."

After this follows Csoma's exact translation of the whole passage with the original text in Tibetan, and its translation in Roman characters, from which those to whom this object is of interest will readily estimate for themselves the superiority of Csoma's labours if they compare them with the text and the previous translations.

IV.

NOTE ON KÁLA-CHAKRA AND ADI-BUDDHA SYSTEMS.

The peculiar religious system entitled the *Kála-Chakra* is supposed to have been derived from Shambála, a fabulous country in the North. Its capital was Kalapa, a splendid city, the residence of many illustrious kings, situated beyond the river Sita or Yaxartes, where the increase of the days from vernal equinox till the summer solstice amounts to twelve Indian hours—that is, four hours and forty-eight minutes of our reckoning.

This system was introduced into Central India in the latter half of the tenth century A.D., and afterwards, viâ Kashmir, found its way into Tibet, where, in the course of the fourteenth, fifteenth, and sixteenth centuries several works were published on it.

Padmo Carpo thus describes its introduction into Nalanda in Central India by a certain pandit called Chilu. Having designed over the door of the Vihar the ten guardians of the world, he wrote underneath the pictures thus :—

"He that does not know the chief first Buddha (Adi-Buddha) knows not the circle of time (Kala, time ; Chakra, a wheel, a circle).

"He that does not know the circle of time knows not the exact enumeration of the divine attributes.

" He that does not know the exact enumeration of the divine attributes, knows not the Supreme Intelligence.

" He that does not know the supreme intelligence knows not the Tantrika principles.

" He that does not know these, and creatures like him, are wanderers in the orb of transmigration, and are out of the path of the Supreme Conqueror.

"Therefore, Adi-Buddha must be taught by every true Lama, and every true disciple who aspires to liberation is bound to hear him."

V.

TRANSLATION OF A TIBETAN PASSPORT,
DATED A.D. 1688.

In Hyde's "Historia Veterum Persarum" is an engraving of a passport granted by the Grand Lama of Lassa to an Armenian, which at the time of its publication could not be deciphered by any European; and the learned author was nearly as much misled regarding its character and the manner of reading it, as was Monsieur Fourmont of the French Academy on another occasion. It informs us also of the insecurity in travelling in the countries to which it refers.

The translation of the curious text follows :—

"From the noble city of Lassa, the circumambulating race of religion.

"To those that are on the road as far as Arya Désa (country of Aryans, India); to clerical, laical, noble, and not noble lords or masters of men; to residents in the forts; to stewards, managers; to Mongols, Tibetans, Turks; to dwellers in tents in the desert; to envoys and ambassadors going to and fro; to keepers of bye-ways; to headmen charged to perform any business of small or great importance;—to all these it is ordered, respecting the four persons named in the passport, not to hinder, rob, or plunder them, but let them go to and fro in peace."

The document is provided with a square seal | Seal. |

VI.

THE ORIGIN OF THE SHAKYA RACE.

On a certain occasion when Shakya (Sansrgyas, bĊhom-ldan-hdas, Buddha Bhagavan) was in Nyagrodha (A'rama) grove, near Kapilavastu, many of the Shakyas who inhabited Kapilavastu being gathered together in their council-house, questioned one another, saying, "Shes-dan-tak ! (intelligent brethren) whence did the Shakya race spring ?

"What is their origin ?

"What is the cause or reason thereof ?

"What is their ancient descent as a nation ? If any one should come and ask us about these points, we could not tell him whence the Shakyas originated. Come, let us go to the Bhagaván and ask him to enlighten us on the subject, that we may abide by his advice."

Thereupon a very great number of Shakyas, inhabitants of Kapilavastu, went to the Bhagaván, and after having made their salutation by prostrating themselves at his feet, sat aside.

In addressing him they explained the cause of their errand, and begged him to enlighten them.

Bhagaván thought that, should he himself tell the story, his opponents the Tirthikas and others might say that he was telling only what was pleasing to himself. Not to give, therefore, an opportunity for such remarks, he intrusted his disciple Mongalyana to impart the required information, to which Mongalyana assented.

Shakya seeing that he was obeyed, folded up his cloak and composed himself to sleep.

Mongalyana, in order to collect his ideas on the subject, entered into deep meditation. Recovering from his ecstasy, he sat down on a carpet, surrounded by his priests, and addressed them at length.

Mongalyana's story was that, after the world was destroyed, men were born in heaven among gods ; they walked in the air, and their food consisted of pleasures only. Afterwards the earth turned into water, and there was nothing but one ocean, which covered all. On this a thin film like milk was visible, which became thicker and thicker, and thus was formed the present earth.

Then some animated beings inhabiting the heavens, having finished their lives there, were born again to taste the condition of manhood, and came to the earth. They were perfect animal beings, and lived for a long period. At that time there was no sun, no moon, and no stars, no time, no night, and no day. No distinction between male and female. They were all called animals.

Afterwards an animal, being of a covetous nature, tasted the earthly essence; the more he tasted it the more he liked it. Other animal beings did the same.

When they all had eaten a mouthful of the earthly substance, as a consequence solidity and weight entered into their bodies. The brightness of their colour vanished, and darkness set in in the world. When darkness was thus established, the sun and moon appeared, the stars, and the division into night and day.

Their food continued as before; those that had eaten little of that food acquired a fine complexion and colour; those that had eaten much, on the contrary, became of a bad colour, Then they began to reproach each other and to dispute.

On account of the sin of such vainglorious talk the earthly essence disappeared.

This was the cause of much lamentation, and there arose from the earth a fatty substance. It was enjoyable as food; but the same happened regarding its use and effect as in the former case, and owing to the sin of pride and division among themselves this substance also disappeared.

The greasy substance was then replaced by sugar-cane plantations, and these again, for similar reasons, by pure rice (salu), without ploughing or sowing the fields. If cut in the evening, the harvest ripened over night and was ready for next morning, and so it continued for a long time.

From the use of rice arose the distinction of sexes. At first the different sexes regarded each other with fixed eyes, and were drawn towards each other. Such as have loved each other had pieces of stone or clods of earth thrown at them by those who had not acted like them. The custom, therefore, of throwing rice, shoes, &c., at newly-married couples in our own day seems to have been derived from Buddhistic cosmogony. The couples afterwards searched after hiding-places, calling out, " Khyim, Khyim," [1] and built themselves houses.

[1] A shelter, a house ; in Tibetan, Khyim.

Then there arose the necessity of laying in stores of food for their wants; but on cutting down their rice-fields this time they perceived that the crops did not grow again, as was the case before. The animal beings—mankind—therefore gathered together to reflect on their former state. Some amongst them said, "We must mete out the land and assign a boundary to every man's property, saying, 'This is mine, and that is thine.'" It was done accordingly.

It happened afterwards that a certain individual took the salu (rice) of another without its being given to him; that is to say, he stole his brother's share. On this he was seized and dragged before the assembly, and was publicly reproved. Such instances occurred repeatedly.

Then they all assembled for the purpose of deliberation, and agreed to elect one who had a better complexion than themselves, more beautiful, was more fortunate and more renowned, and made him master and proprietor of all their fields.

They said, "He shall punish those who deserve punishment, and reward those to whom a reward is due. From the produce of the land he shall receive a certain portion."

They accordingly chose one and called him *Maha Sammata*, the Honoured by Men! Maha Sammata's family reigned for a long period. The last descendant was called Ikshwaku Virudhaka.

He had four sons. After his first wife's death he married again, this time a princess, his father-in-law insisting that his daughter's son should become heir to the throne.

The king agreed to this, and expelled his four sons from the kingdom.

The four brothers, taking their half-sisters with them, and accompanied by many followers, left the ancient capital, Potala, went towards Himalaya to settle on the banks of Bhagirathi, not far from the hermitage where Kapila the Rishi lived. By the advice and with the sanction of this hermit, they married their half-sisters and begat many children. The Rishi afterwards marked out a place for them, where a city was built, and in honour of this sainted man it was called Kapilavastu.

At Potala the king, thinking of his four sons, inquired on one occasion from his courtiers what had become of the princes, his sons? On this he was informed that after he had banished them they settled in the neighbourhood of the Himalaya, took their half-sisters for wives, and multiplied exceedingly.

The king, being much surprised on hearing this, exclaimed, "Shakya! Shakya! is it possible! is it possible!" And this is the origin of *the Shakya name.*

Thus ends the narration of Mongalyana. Shakya, the Bhagavan, approved of it, and recommended it to his followers.

VII.

MODE OF EXPRESSING NUMERALS IN TIBETAN.

Here the same system prevails as in Sanskrit. The printed Tibetan text has the dates in figure above, and then they are written in the body of the text, in symbolical words, so as to secure them against the danger of alteration. This system, in fact, gives the same safeguard against incertitude of figures that the mode of writing values and sums at length in European documents is intended to secure.

There are many astronomical and astrological treatises to be found in Tibet, which have not been embodied into the Kahgyur or Stangyur collections. Of these the most celebrated was written by a Viceroy at Lassa in the latter half of the seventeenth century A.D. In all works of this description symbolical names are used instead of numerals; as, for instance, lag, hand, for + 2; — mé, fire, for − 3; × chhu, water, for × 4; ÷ so, a tooth, for ÷ 32.

Besides the nine units and the zero, the following numerals have special expressions, namely, 10, 11, 12, 13, 14, 15, 16, 18, 24, 25, 27, and 32.

When dictating to an assistant in symbolical names what to write in characters, the pandit commences the operation from right to left, thus, if you say *Nyima*, sun, that means = 12; *mkhah*, void, means = 0; *mtsho*, a lake = 4, the copyist writes 4012. The very same method has been adopted in the Shastras.

As examples the following are cited :—

zla, *the moon,*	stands for	Number		1.
lag, *the hand,*	„	for	„	2.
mé, *fire,*	„	for	„	3.
chhu, *water,*	„	for	„	4
mdah, *an arrow,*	„	for	„	5.
dus, *time,*	„	for	„	6.
ri, *a hill,*	„	for	„	7.
sbrul, *a serpent,*	„	for	„	8.
srin-po, *a goblin,*	„	for	„	9.
phyogs, *a corner* (of the world),	„	for	„	10.
Dragpo, *the brave* (Rudra),	„	for	„	11.
Nyima, *sun,*	„	for	„	12.
hdod-pa, *lust, desire,*	„	for	„	13.
yid, *the mind,*	„	for	„	14.
tshes, nyin-zhag, *the 15th day of the lunar month,*	„	for	„	15.
Rgyalpo, *a king,*	„	for	„	16.
nyes-pa, *a blemish,*	„	for	„	18.
Rgyalva, *a Buddha,*	„	for	„	24.
de-nyid, *same self,*	„	for	„	25.
skar-ma, *a star,*	„	for	„	27.
so, *a tooth,*	„	for	„	32.

for zero, mkhah, *void space,* or : thig, *a spot or stain,* or : Stongpa, *the vacuum, a zero.*

It may be fitting to add here a few notes on the systems of reckoning time in use among the Tibetans, which the author noticed at page 147 of the appendix to his Grammar.

The Tibetans derived their astronomical and astrological knowledge, not from India only, but also from the Chinese people.

The mode of reckoning, according to the Indian system, is called by them "Karçis," that derived from China, "Nakçis." On both these systems are to be found numerous works in the Tibetan language.

The most common mode of reckoning time, especially in calculating the years of the present generation, or of determining the age of an individual, is that by the cycle of twelve years, in which each year is designated by the name of an animal, in this manner :—

Tibetan.	English.	Tibetan.	English.
1. byi-lo	the mouse-year.	7. rta-lo	the horse-year.
2. glang-lo	„ ox-year.	8. lug-lo	„ sheep-year.
3. stag-lo	„ tiger-year.	9. spré-lo	„ ape-year.
4. yos-lo	„ hare-year.	10. bya-lo	„ bird-year.
5. hbrug-lo	„ dragon-year.	11. khyi-lo	„ dog-year.
6. sbrul-lo	„ serpent-year.	12. phag-lo	„ hog-year.

But in books, in correspondence, and in every transaction of greater importance, the use of the cycle of *sixty* years has been adopted; and this system is twofold, the Indian and the Chinese.

The years of the Indian cycle, prevalent south of the Nermada river, exactly coincide with the Tibetan era, the Sanskrit names having been translated literally, but the Tibetans count the commencement of their first cycle from A.D. 1026; the Indians, on the contrary, date theirs from the Kalyyuga, and sometimes from the reign of Salivahana.

The Tibetans, like the Chinese, divide each year into lunar months, calling them first, second, third month, &c. During the period of each lunar cycle, which corresponds to nineteen solar years, they insert seven intercalary months, generally one in every third year, to make them agree with the solar years. In this manner the calculation exactly corresponds with the luni-solar system of the Hindus.

The *Indian* system differs from the Chinese in the mode of naming years. The Chinese nomenclature is made up by the names of *five* elements, and made *ten* by affixing the male and female termination to each, and this *series* is repeated six times; therefore 6 × 10 = 60.

The second series is made up of twelve zodiacal constellations, and is repeated five times, 5 × 12 = 60, thus making the cycle of sixty years.

The names of the five elements are as follows :—

Chinese.	Tibetan.	English.
1. kya.	shing pho.	wood, masculine.
2. yi.	shing mo.	wood, feminine.
3. ping.	mé pho.	fire, masculine.
4. ting.	mé mo.	fire, feminine.
5. vou.	sa pho.	earth, masculine.
6. kyi.	sa mo.	earth, feminine.
7. king	lchags pho.	iron, masculine.
8. zin.	lchags-mo.	iron, feminine.
9. zhin.	chhu po.	water, masculine.
10. kuhi.	chu-mo.	water, feminine.

The names of the twelve animals of the zodiac are these—

Chinese.	Tibetan.	English.
1. Tsi.	byi	Mouse.
2. Tshihu.	glang.	Ox.
3. Yin.	stag.	Tiger.
4. Mahu.	yos.	Hare.
5. Shin (Tshin ?).	hbrug.	Dragon.
6. Zi.	sbrul.	Serpent.
7. Hu (u).	rta.	Horse.
8. Wuhi.	lug.	Sheep.
9. Shing.	spré	Ape.
10. Yéhu.	bya.	Bird.
11. Zuhi.	khyi.	Dog.
12. Hahi.	phag.	Hog.

Thus the first cycle, consisting of ten years, is repeated six times.

The second cycle of twelve years is repeated five times, to make up the whole cycle of *sixty* years.

The list of the names of animals for each of the sixty years in a cycle, arranged in Chinese, Sanskrit, Tibetan, and English, is given in the text. See *op. cit.*, p. 151–154

VIII.

EXTRACTS FROM TIBETAN WORKS TRANSLATED.

1. *Tibetan Beau-ideal of a Wife.* (Kahgyur, MDo Kha, p. 106–7.)

The required qualities in a maiden who may aspire to be united in marriage with Shakya are thus defined by himself:

"No ordinary woman is suitable to my taste and habits, none who is incorrect in her behaviour, who has bad qualities, or who does not speak the truth. But such one alone will be pleasing and fit for me, who, exhilarating my mind, is chaste, young, of good complexion, and of a pure family and descent."

He indited a catalogue of these qualifications in verse, and said :—

"If there shall be found any girl with the virtues I have described, since I like not an unrestrained woman, let her be given to me in marriage. She who is young, well-proportioned, and elegant, yet not boastful of her beauty; who is affectionate towards her brother, sister, and mother; who, always rejoicing in giving alms, knoweth the proper manner how to bestow them on the priests and Brahmans; if there be found any such damsel, father! let her be brought to me. One who, being without arrogance, pride, and passion, has left off artifice, envy, and deceit, and is of an upright nature; who even in her dreams hath not lusted after any other man; who resteth content with her own husband, and is always submissive and chaste; who is firm and not wavering, who is not proud or haughty, but full of humility like a female slave; who has no excessive fondness of the vanity of sound, smell, taste (music, perfumes, and exquisite viands), nor for wine; who is void of cupidity, who has not a covetous heart, but is content with her own possessions; who, being upright, goeth not astray, is not fluctuating; is modest in her dress, and does not indulge in laughing and boasting; who is diligent in her moral duties without being righteous overmuch. Who is very clean and pure in her body, her speech, and her mind; who is not drowsy nor dull, proud nor stupid, but of good judgment, doth everything with due reflection; who hath for her father and mother-in-law equal reverence as for a spiritual teacher; who treateth her servants both male and female with constant mildness; who is as well versed as any courtesan in the rites and ceremonies described in the Shastras; who goeth last to sleep and riseth earliest from her couch; who maketh every endeavour with mildness, like a mother, without affectation. If there be any such maiden to be found, father! give her unto me as a wife."

Afterwards the King Shuddhodana directs his Brahman minister to go into the great city of Kapilavastu, and to inquire there in every house after a girl possessed with these good qualities, showing at the same time Shakya's letter, and uttering two verses of the following meaning :—"Bring hither that maiden who has the required qualities, whether she be of the royal tribe or of the Brahman caste, of the gentry or of the plebeian class. My son regardeth not tribe nor family extraction; his delight is in good qualities, truth and virtue alone."

The objections of the Buddhists to the seclusion of women may be gathered from the following imaginary conversation of Shakya's wife (extracted from Kahgyur, Do, Kha, vol. i., p. 120, 121). Sa-tsho-ma (Gopa), the wife of Shakya, upon hearing of her being upbraided by the domestics for not concealing her face when in company with others, expresses herself in some verses against the veil, the meaning of which is as follows :—

"Sitting, standing, and walking, those that are venerable are pleasing when not concealed. A bright gem will give more lustre if put on the top of the standard.

"The venerable are pleasing when they go; they are agreeable also when they come. They are so, whether they stand or whether they are sitting. In every manner the venerable are pleasing.

"They who put off all vices are venerable. Fools committing vices, how much soever they be adorned, are never pleasing.

"The venerable are always like a bowl full of milk and curd. It is a great happiness to see human nature capable of such purity.

"For such as have restrained their body, have suppressed the several defects of it, have refrained their speech and never used deceitful language, and having subdued the flesh are held in restraint by a pure conscience; for such, to what purpose is the veiling of the face?

"Moreover the great Lord (God), who is wise in knowing the hearts of others, yea, also the whole company of the gods, know my thoughts, my good morals, my virtues, my vows, chastity. Therefore why should I conceal my face?"

Shuddhodana, the father of Shakya, her father-in-law, was much pleased with these expressions, and presented her with several precious things. He uttered at the same time a sloka, the meaning of which is this :—

"My son being adorned with such qualities as he has, and my daughter-in-law having such virtuous qualifications as she describes: to see two such pure persons united, is like when butter and ghee are mixed together."

As breathing in accordance with the virtuous sentiments of

the above favourable specimen of the Tibetan sacred works, we may here extract a curious correspondence (but whether imaginary or real we will not pretend to say), stated to have taken place between a princess of Ceylon and the Buddhist Saint. This letter is very generally known and admired throughout Tibet, being introduced in every collection of epistolary forms for the instruction of youth.

Ratnavali's Letter to Shakya.

Ratnavali, a young princess of Ceylon, the daughter of King Singala, having been informed by some merchants from Central India of Buddha and of his doctrine, was much pleased with it; and as those merchants were about to return home, she sent some presents to Shakya (Chom-dan-dás), with a letter of the following contents :—

"Reverenced by Suras, Asuras, and men! really delivered from birth, sickness, and fear! Lord, who art greatly celebrated by thy far-extending renown from the sage's ambrosial portion, kindly grant me religious instruction and wisdom."

Shakya received this letter, and sent to the princess a picture of Buddha on cotton cloth, with some verses written above and below the image, containing the terms upon which refuge is obtained with Buddha, Dharma, and Sangha, and a few fundamental articles of the faith, together with two stanzas recommending Buddhism. The two stanzas are these :—

1. Arise, commence a new course of life,
   Turn to the religion of Buddha;
   Conquer the host of the lord of death, the passions,
   As an elephant subdues everything under his feet in a
       muddy lake.

2. Whoever has lived a pure life,
   According to the precept of this law,
   Shall be free from transmigration,
   And shall put an end to all his miseries.

In Tibetan, according to the pronunciation of the Lamas of Sikkim.

1. Tsampar chashing jungwar cha,
   Sangye tenla suppar cha;
   Dampü chimna longchen zhin,
   Chida deni zhonpar cha.

2. Kanshik raptu payö par
Chödul dela dögyur pa
Tyeöve khorua rappan sa
Dugnal thamar chopar gyur.

The compendium of the doctrine of Buddha in one sloka:—

In Tibetan.

Digpa chiyan minja te
Geba pünsum tsopa tsán
Rangi sempa yonsu dul
Thöni sangye tempa yin.

In English.

No vice is to be committed ;
Virtue must be perfectly practised ;
Subdue entirely your desires.
This is the doctrine of Buddha.

IX.

INTERPRETATION OF THE TIBETAN INSCRIPTION ON A BHOTIAN BANNER TAKEN IN ASSAM.

The following is the description of this trophy :—

It is a bit of plank, mounted on a staff, painted red, with an image of Buddha on one side and a Tibetan inscription on the other. The Demangiri Rajah always had it carried before him with great solemnity and under the special charge of a large guard of honour, who, however, in the affair of Subang-Kotta ran away without it, and it fell into our hands. A copy of the inscription was forwarded to Csoma for translation. With the exception of the salutation at the beginning and the conclusion and a few terms in the middle, the whole is in the Tibetan language. The purport of it was to obtain the favour and protection of several inferior divinities for the person and family for whom the ceremony had been performed and this magic emblem set up.

It may be that this flagstaff was carried before the Tibetan

N

chief in his march and so used as an ensign in war; but it is more probable that it may have belonged originally to the house-top or terrace of the Prince of Bhotan; because the houses of great personages in that country are generally decorated with such ensigns of victory.

The inscription, as already mentioned, is an invocation to several deities, and concludes thus: "Ye all! look on this emblem of Hu, the regent or governor (by whom, namely, it was set up). Ye divine principal Rakshákas, rulers of the world, I beseech you, that you will make this patron, the bestower of charitable gifts, obtain the fruit of his work and actions, who is very faithful to the doctrine of Shakya. May he, with his household and family, prosper more and more, and abound in life, fortune, honour, wealth—like the increasing face of the moon."

The text is given in the original with a literal translation.

X.

NOTE ON THE WHITE SATIN EMBROIDERED SCARFS OF THE TIBETAN PRIESTS.

(Translated by Csoma at Mayor Lloyd's request.)

These scarfs are almost indispensable in all religious offerings, and when distinguished strangers are presented at court, the master of ceremonies throws one of them across the shoulders of the visitor.

An inferior, on approaching a superior in rank, presents a white silk scarf, and when dismissed has in return one thrown over his neck. Equals exchange scarfs on meeting, bending towards each other. No intercourse whatever takes place without the intervention of a scarf. It always accompanies every letter sent by a messenger. Two colours are used for the manufacture, which is done in China; white and red. The latter is rather confined to the lower orders, the white is respectful in proportion to the purity and fineness of its material. There are various degrees in both.

This is the Tibetan text of the inscription in Roman. Characters :—

Nyin-mo bde-legs mts'han bde-legs
Nyin-mahi gung yang bde-legs shing
Nyin mts-han rag-tu brda-legs-pahi
Dkon-chag gsum-gyi bkrashis shog.

Translation.

Blessed the day, blessed the night,
The mid-day also being blessed ;
May the day and night always return (to us),
The special favour of the three holy ones.

XI.

NOTICES ON DIFFERENT SYSTEMS OF BUDDHISM EXTRACTED FROM TIBETAN AUTHORITIES.

Sángye is the generic name for expressing the Supreme Being or the Supreme Intelligence in the Buddhistic system. This word signifies "*the* most perfect Being," that is, pure and clean and free from all imperfections and abounding in all good qualities.

There are three distinctions with respect to the essence, the substance, or the body of Buddha, namely—

1. Dharma-Kaya.   This is the primary essence of all things, and is designated by the names of: Adi Buddha, Samanta Buddha, the Swabhàva, or the self - produced, self - existing. Dharmadhàtu, the root of all things, the Jina of Jinas; the origin of all things, existing without the three epochs, that is, without beginning, duration, and end.

2. Sambhoa-Kaya.   To this class or distinction belong the attendants of the Dharma-Kaya (the Adi Buddha) ; they are the Dhyani Buddhas, the chief of whom is Vairochana the Illuminator.

3. Nirmankaya.   To this distinction or class belong the

several incarnations of Buddha. Immense is the number of incarnations in past ages. The present age is called the happy one, and the number of incarnations is to amount to one thousand. The first four incarnations have already appeared, the rest are to follow. In the modern Buddhistic system Shakya is the last incarnate Buddha.

The systems of Buddhism known in Tibet are the following four, each having again a number of subdivisions.

The first is called Vaibashika, with four subdivisions, taken from the names of Shakya's four principal disciples. The followers of this system stand on the lowest degree of merit. They accept everything that is contained in the Scriptures, believe everything, and will not dispute.

The second system or school is Sutrátika, followers of the Sútras, with two subdivisions. The one will prove everything by scriptural authority, the other by argument.

The third system or school is the Yogáchárya, with nine subdivisions. Arya Sangha was its founder, in the seventh century A.D.

The fourth is the Madhyamika school; they keep the middle faith. This is the true philosophical school, formulated 700 years after Shakya's death, by Nagarjuna.

The two first systems are dogmatical; the two latter are philosophical, and are studied by the learned few.

There is another classification of Shakya's followers, namely, the Tri-yánam or the three vehicles; because all Buddhistic Scriptures are destined for the lowest, the middle, and the highest capacities. Some authors use the name of Lám-rim, classifying men under three degrees of intellectual capacity, according to this:

1. Men of a common capacity must believe that there is a God, that there is a future life, and that all will obtain, according to their deeds in this life, a reward hereafter.

2. Men of a middle degree of intellectual or moral capacity, in addition to the above doctrines, must understand that every compound thing is perishable; that there is no reality in things; that every imperfection causes suffering, and that deliverance from suffering, and eventually from bodily existence, is *final beatitude.*

2. Men of the highest capacities will know that between the

body and the supreme soul nothing exists by itself, nor can we prove whether the supreme soul will continue for ever, or absolutely cease ; because everything exists by a casual concatenation.

Concerning the Course of Life.

Those of common capacity are content with the observance of the Ten Commandments.

Those of the middle degree also endeavour to excel in morality, meditation, and wisdom.

Those of the highest capacities practise, besides the above, the six transcendental virtues as well.

Regarding Salvation.

Those of the first degree, seeing the miseries of those who, by virtue of the metempsychosis, suffer in the bad places of transmigration as beasts, &c., desire to be born again among men, or among angels (asuras), or among gods.

Those of the second class are not content with the lot of the former, and wish to be entirely delivered from all bodily existence.

The highest class, regarding existence, under whatever form, as suffering, crave for final emancipation, and by arriving at the supreme perfection, are enabled to assist others out of their miseries.

Several philosophical sects are mentioned, but the general principles of practical Buddhism are these :—

1. To take refuge only with Buddha.
2. To endeavour to arrive at the highest degree of perfection, and to be united with the Supreme Intelligence.
3. To adore Buddha.
4. To bring such offerings to Buddha's image as are pleasing to any of the six senses. Such offerings are : flowers, garlands, incense, perfume, eatables and drinkables raw or prepared, cloths for garments or ornamentation, curtains, etc.
5. To practise music or singing, and to utter praises to Buddha, extolling his person, or his love and mercy towards all.
6. To confess one's sins with a contrite heart, to ask forgiveness, and to repent sincerely.

7. To rejoice in the moral merits of all living beings.
8. To pray to those Buddhas who are now in the world,
   that they should teach religion, and not leave the earth
   but remain here for many Kalpas, *i.e.*, ages, to come.

XII.

ENUMERATION OF HISTORICAL AND GRAMMATICAL WORKS TO BE MET WITH IN TIBET.

The historical works are enumerated under seven classes :—

1. *Lo-gyus.* — Annals, chronicles, history ; fourteen works
   are classed under this head.
2. *Tam-Gyut.*—Tradition, oral history.
3. *Ch'Los-jung.* — Origin and progress of Buddhism ;
   several works are named.
4. *Tokzhot*—Means a judicious saying; memoir, biography
   containing many historical fragments and legends ;
   description of the fabulous country Shambhala.
5. *Nám-thár.*—Emancipation, biographical and legendary.
   Many historical works are noticed under this head
   referring to Shakya and to many of his disciples,
   how they were emancipated and acquired preter-
   natural faculties. In the Dulva there are notices
   of several princes, citizens, and illustrious persons.
6. *Grung.*—A fable, fabulous history, contains the history
   of Kesar, a fabulous king.
7. *Stan-çis.*—Chronology or astronomical calculation of some
   events occurring in the sacred volumes.

The Grammatical Works.

The Sanskrit grammatical works were known to ancient
Tibetans, and were partially translated into their tongue.

The names of such works have been given in the last
volume of Stangyur. The principal ones are *Páni-vyákarana*
in two thousand slokas.

Maha-bhána, a commentary on the previous work, in one
hundred thousand slokas.

A commentary on *chandrapá*, by Pandita Ratna Mali, in twelve thousand slokas, and many others are named besides. There are likewise in Tibet several works teaching how to read the Sanskrit texts, the Mantras, &c.

The most ancient grammatical work extant in the Tibetan tongue is that by Sambhota of the seventh century. Names of many authors are given; but there are yet other grammatical works of which no special mention is made in the essay under review.

XIII.

REMARKS ON AMULETS IN USE BY THE TRANS-HIMALAYAN BUDDHISTS.

The two scrolls procured at Rampúr, near Kotgarh, by Surgeon W. C. Carte of the 69th Regiment N.I., were forwarded to the Asiatic Society of Calcutta, where, at the request of the secretary, an explanation of them was furnished by the librarian, Mr. Alexander Csoma, who stated that they contained abstracts of some larger Tantrika or religious works in Tibetan, interspersed with Mantras in Sanskrit.

The first scroll, eight feet and a half long, is covered with figures to the extent of two feet. The rest of the paper bears printed text, containing 244 lines in Tibetan, each line being three and a half inches long. The figures are roughly traced, representing a victorious king, a tortoise with nine spots on the belly, showing the lucky and the unlucky periods, according as the moon is affected by the planets in her path. Afterwards come the twelve animals representing the twelve years of a cycle; then the zodiacal signs, the planets, sun and moon, &c., then the representations of the four, eight, and ten corners of the world. There is also seen the picture of a king with his minister, a horse, an elephant, a soldier, an eye, &c., then the head of a bird, and also certain Chinese symbolical figures, which appear to have been used under the Han dynasty 200 years before Christ. The Tibetans still use them extensively. After these symbolical representations follows the text, containing abridgments of five different Tantrika works.

The first is the salutation to the "Circle of Time," the Kalachakraya. Then come the regents of the year, month, day, and hour, and those of the planets and stars. The Nagas, imps, &c., are requested to be favourable to the person who wears these symbols and to the mystical prayers, that he may succeed in all his undertakings. All classes of divinities are requested not to hinder him in any of his occupations, but to give assistance that he may increase in prosperity.

The abstract of the second Tantrika work contains in Sanskrit short addresses to Shakya, Vagishwari, Manipadme, and others.

The third contains a sloka and a half in Tibetan to Manju Sri, the god of wisdom.

The fourth is called the venerable Sutra dispelling the darkness. The salutation is addressed to the God of Wisdom, to the ten Buddhas in the ten corners of the world. To each is addressed a short prayer thus: "If I go towards that corner over which you preside, after having obtained my aim, grant that I may quickly return."

The fifth is styled the Sutra of eight lights. The salutation is addressed to Buddha, to religion, and to the holy priests. There are several prayers in Sanskrit, asking to avert any unlucky year, month, day, and hour, and to counteract the influence of a malignant planet or star. Other mantras are written down, having the object of preventing any unlucky accident in the morning or in the afternoon, &c.

The second scroll, four feet eight inches long, contains twelve figures of animals representing the cycle of twelve years. The text covers 121 lines, each three inches in length. There are, besides, rough sketches of a tortoise with the nine mystical spots in a square, and the twelve animals of a cycle of twelve years.

This is the sum of the general contents of these two scrolls.

XIV.

REVIEW OF A TIBETAN MEDICAL WORK.

The principal work on medicine in the Tibetan language is called *r*Gyud *b*Zhi, in four parts. Its authorship is attributed to Shakya himself. The materials of the Tibetan treatise are derived from Sanskrit works. The learned Lama who made the analysis gave the following account of it to Csoma.

In the time of King Khri-srong Dehutsán, in the eighth or ninth century after Christ, a Tibetan interpreter, during his residence in Kashmir, with the assistance of a pandit who was himself a physician, made the translation into his native tongue, and presented the work to the said king. The treatise was subsequently revised and augmented by other learned men, and generally accepted as an authority. It is stated that besides this there are about forty other works on medicine in Tibet, not counting the five volumes embodied in the great encyclopædia the Stangyur.

The principal medical school of Tibet is in Chák-phuri, a monastery near Lassa. Two smaller ones, called Chák-Zúr are in the interior of the country.

A. *The First Part*

is called the *root* or basis of the medical treatise, and is divided into six chapters.

I. The first chapter describes how, in a forest abounding in medicinal plants, Shakya transformed himself into a chief physician, and there, in a magnificent palace, delivered his instructions, having for his pupils the gods, the sages, and a large number of orthodox men and also heretics.

II. In the second chapter Shakya speaks thus :—

Friends! be it known to you that every human creature who wishes to remain in health, and such also as desire to cure disease and to prolong life, must be instructed in the science of medicine. So also he that seeks after morality, virtue, wealth or happiness, and seeks to be delivered from the miseries of sickness, as also such a one as wishes to be honoured and respected by others, must be taught the art of healing. He must be instructed on the four parts of the medical science, which are as follows :—

The theory, the explanation, the instruction, and the manual operation requisite for the practice. He must likewise be specially instructed in the eight branches of healing, namely :—

1. The treatment of the body as a whole.
2. The treatment of diseases of childhood.
3. Of diseases of women.
4. Of diseases caused by evil spirits (mental diseases).
5. Of wounds inflicted with a knife or spear.
6. Of venomous or poisonous infections.
7. Of the infirmities of old age.
8. How to increase the power of manhood.

The number of chapters in the whole treatise amounts to 156.

III. In the third chapter the human constitution is illustrated by a simile taken from the Indian fig-tree; thus, there are to be considered three roots or trunks, nine stems, forty-seven branches, 224 leaves, two blossoms, and three fruits.

The seven fundamental supports of the body are described as those on which life depends, namely : the chyle, the blood, the flesh, the fat, bone, the marrow, and the semen.

The excretions are three : fœces, urine, and sweat.

The principal causes of disease are these three : lust, anger, and ignorance.

The accessory causes are four : a. the seasons, hot or cold; b. evil spirits; c. abuse of food; d. indiscreet or bad conduct.

The parts of the body capable of being affected by disease are said to be six : the skin, the flesh, the veins, the bones, the internal viscera, and the alimentary canal.

There are three humours : the phlegm, the bile, and the wind.

The fourth chapter treats of symptoms of diseases. Examination of the tongue and urine. Feeling of the pulse.

Inquiry into the origin of the disease, and its progress ; what food has agreed or disagreed? what pain is felt? The physician's twenty-nine questions, which are to be put to the patient, regarding food, exercise, previous history of the disease, &c., are here detailed.

The fifth chapter enumerates the means of curing diseases, and these are to be considered—

a. With respect to food.

b. The patient's mode of life, such as exercise, &c.

c. The therapeutics adapted to the three offending humours, viz., the phlegm, the bile, and the wind, which are fully discussed.

The varieties of medicines are such as assuage pain, or purge the bowels, or cause vomiting. Then there are remedies for flatulence, for anointing the body, embrocations, &c. Against bile, phlebotomy and bathing in cold water; against phlegm, warm applications are prescribed.

The sixth chapter contains recapitulation of subjects contained in the last three chapters.

Carrying on the metaphor of the Indian fig-tree, the two blossoms are, health and longevity; the three fruits, good morals, wealth, and happiness.

B. In the Second Part

four things are considered as to treatment of maladies, namely :—

1. What is to be treated?
2. What are the proper remedies?
3. In what manner the remedies are to be applied?
4. By whom are they to be applied?

The means of curing disease are enumerated thus: diet, exercise, medicine, and surgical operations. A chapter on the conception and the growth of the embryo is added, one chapter on bones, and another on nerves. Then the humours are fully considered. And the last chapter describes the requisite qualities of a physician, namely, that he should be well acquainted with the theory and practice of medicine, and be an unselfish, an upright, and a good-hearted man.

C. *The Third Part*

treats on separate diseases, and the following points are considered under each head :—

a. Primary causes ; *b.* accessory causes and effects ; *c.* subdivisions ; *d.* symptoms ; *e.* manner of treating disease.

The following is the list of maladies : swellings, dropsies, pulmonary diseases, including phthisis, fevers, wounds, and inflammation ; epidemic diseases, smallpox, ulcers, catarrh ; diseases of the eyes, of the ear, of the nose, of the mouth, of lips, tongue, palate, of the throat and teeth, with several distinctions under each ; diseases of the neck, of the chest, the heart, liver, spleen, kidneys, stomach, bowels ; diseases peculiar to women ; hæmorrhoids, erysipelas. Then follows the treatment of wounds, simple and poisoned. Diseases of old age are treated of, and the subject of virility is discussed.

D. *The Fourth Part*

contains details of the practice of medicine, such as examination of the pulse and urine ; varieties of medicaments, mixtures, pills, syrups, and powders. Nomenclature of medicinal plants. Description of purgatives, emetics, extracts, or elixirs.

The conclusion is this :—

Though there be 1200 ways of *examining* the heat and the cold, &c., in any given disease, they are all summed up in the following : examine the tongue and the urine, feel the pulse, and inquire into the history of the case. The remedies are said to be 1200 in number ; but they are reduced into the following four classes :—

a. Medicament ; *b.* manual operation ; *c.* diet ; *d.* exercise.

Medicaments either assuage pain or are depuratory. Manual operations are either gentle or violent. Food is either wholesome or noxious. Exercise is either violent or gentle.

There are said to be 360 practical ways of curing disease ; but they may be reduced to these three :—

1. Examination of the patient.
2. Rules of treatment.
3. The manner of applying remedies.

Hints are given how a physician can keep himself safe from any malignant or infectious disease.

XV.

A Brief Notice of Subháshita Ratna Nidhi of Saskya Pandita.

This paper was ready in 1833, but owing to the difficulties in the way of bringing out the Tibetan text with the translation, it was not published till eleven years after Csoma's death, and then it was accomplished through the kind assistance of Dr. A. Campbell.

This work was composed by the celebrated Sa-skya Pandita, who flourished in the thirteenth century of our era, in the time of Gengiz Khan and his successors. The author resided in the Sa-skya Monastery in Middle Tibet, in the province of Ts'ang, and was the uncle of a Great Lama. Many important Sanskrit books, brought thither from India, are still to be found in the monastery. The work begins thus :—

To the ten commandments[1] are to be added the following rules, which were enacted by a religious king of Tibet named Srong-b,tsaná (apostolic king, defender of faith, Dharma Raja). These rules are :—

1. Reverence God ; this is the first.
2. Exercise true religion ; this is the second.
3. Respect the learned.
4. Pay honour to your parents.
5. Show respect unto superiors and to the aged.
6. Show good-heartedness to a friend.
7. Be useful to your fellow-countrymen.
8. Be equitable and impartial.
9. Imitate excellent men.
10. Know how to enjoy rightly your worldly goods and wealth.
11. Return kindness for kindness.

---

[1] The ten commandments of Buddha are these :—

1. Not to kill. 2. Not to steal. 3. Not to commit adultery. 4. Not to tell falsehood. 5. Not to use abusive language. 6. Not to speak nonsense. 7. Not to slander. 8. Not to be covetous. 9. Not to bear malice. 10. Not to be stubborn in a wrong principle.

12. Avoid fraud in measures and weights.

13. Be always impartial and without envy.

14. Do not listen to the advice of woman.

15. Be affable in speaking, and be prudent in discourse.

16. Be of high principles and of a generous mind.

These are the sixteen rules. Subáshíta Ratna Nidhinama Shastra is the title of the work in Sanskrit.

Salutation to Manju Sri.

To the question: What is a "precious treasure of elegant sayings?" the following answer is given :—

It is the exhibition of judicious reflections upon all sorts of worldly affairs and upon the conduct of holy men, without offending against good morals. The following are the chapters :—

I. Reflections on the wise, with ten aphorisms.

II. On the excellent, the virtuous, and the good, with thirty-three sayings.

III. On the fool, the mean, and the wicked, with twenty-three aphorisms.

IV. On the mixed character of the wise and the foolish, with twenty-eight aphorisms.

V. On evil practices, with nineteen sayings.

VI. On good manners of men, with forty sayings.

VII. On unbecoming manners, with twenty-nine sayings.

VIII. On general conduct of men, with forty-four sayings.

IX. On the effect of religion on good morals, with twenty-three sayings, some of which are very striking, and we cite the following as examples :—

The wealth of a man who is contented with little, is inexhaustible; he who seeks always and is never satisfied, will have a continual rain of sorrow.

As children are loved by their parents, to the same degree they are not respected in return by their children.

He that is acquainted with the manners of the world, will exercise true religion. He that practises good morals is the living biography of a saint, &c.

This work contains 454 slókas in the original, but only 234 are given in this paper.

XVI.

A Dictionary of Sanskrit and Tibetan Words, Phrases, and Technical Terms.

We give the following resumé and index kindly furnished by Dr. Rajendrolála Mitra, of an extensive and most important work, which has already been referred to in these pages, but the existence of which is known at present to only a few, because since Csoma's decease Tibetan learning in India seems to have received no special attention. With some adaptation to the requirements of the present day and with the addition of a special index, this compilation, if rescued, as it deserves to be, from its manuscript condition, will form a most valuable help to the study of Buddhist writings, to which so many eminent and learned men in Europe are devoting their earnest attention. The MS. is in the library of the Asiatic Society of Bengal.

Note by Dr. Rajendrolála Mitra, dated 14th February 1883.

"The volume is a foolscap folio of 686 pages, with 20 pages of index and some blank pages, in a good state of preservation. Some sheets of the paper bear the water-mark of "Snelgrove, 1828," others of 1830. The writing, therefore, was not undertaken until 1831, when Csoma de Körös was in Calcutta, and he must have taken some time to complete it. The whole is in the handwriting of Csoma. From the general appearance of neatness and absence of erasures, corrections, and interlineations, it is evident that the volume is a fair copy. The matter is arranged in four columns, the first containing the serial number, next the Sanskrit word in English letters, then the Tibetan equivalent in Tibetan character, and lastly the English meaning. The words are grouped in classes, as shown in the index. The arrangements being according to classes and not alphabetical, it is difficult to use the volume for reference."

This is the index of the work, showing the several heads or titles under which Sanskrit and Tibetan words, proper names, phrases, technical terms, &c. &c., were collected or compiled by ancient learned Indian pandits and Tibetan Lotsavas (interpreters) or translators.

Note.—The number of titles shows the regular series in the original (though it has not been marked there); and the number of page indicates where the chapter under that head or title commences in this compilation.

Heads or Titles of Chapters.

No.		PAGE
1.	Names (epithets, attributes, &c. &c.) of Buddha (and also of Shakya)	1
2.	Names of different Tathagatas (or Buddhas) . . .	6
3.	Names of the mansions of Buddha (Buddha bhumi), of the five bodies or aggregates of those that are equal and of the unequalled (of Adi Buddha and the five Dhyani Buddhas), and the names of the three persons or bodies of Buddha (substances)	7
4.	Names of the ten powers of Tathagata (or Buddha) .	8
5.	Names of those four things in which a Tathagata is bold	495
6.	Names of the eighteen pure religious articles of Buddha	496
7.	Names of the thirty-two kinds of mercy of Tathagata .	499
8.	Names of the three kinds of clear recollection . .	505
9.	Names of four things in which a Tathagata is inculpable	506
10.	Names of the four kinds of discriminative knowledge .	507
11.	Names of the five kinds of eminent (special) knowledge	508
12.	Names originating with the occasion of the six special knowledges	508
13.	Names of the three miraculous transformations . .	514
14.	Names of the thirty-two characteristic signs of the great man (Maha Purusha)	181
15.	Names of the eighty points of beauty (on the body of a Tathagata)	184
16.	Names of the excellence of Tathagata according to the Sutras	171
17.	Names of the sixty branches (parts) of melody or harmony	166 167
18.	Names of deep meditations (or ecstsaies) according to the Sherchin or Prajna paramita system . . .	290
19.	General terms or names for a Bodhisatwa . . .	10

No.   PAGE
20. Names of different Bodhisatwas 11
21. Names of the deep meditations (ecstasies) of a Bodhisatwa   514
22. Names of the twelve dharanis (superhuman powers) of a
    Bodhisatwa 515
23. Names of the ten powers of a Bodhisatwa . . . 17
24. Names of those ten things which are in the power of a
    Bodhisatwa 517
25. Names of those four things of which a Bodhisatwa is not
    afraid 517
26. Names of the eighteen unmixed (pure) laws of a Bod-
    hisatwa 519
27. Names of the qualifications (or good qualities, perfections)
    of Bodhisatwas, according to the Sutras . . . 306
28. Names of the mansions (Bhumis) or the several degrees
    of perfection of the Bodhisatwas 18
29. Names of the ten kinds of religious practices . . . 19
30. Names of the ten transcendental (cardinal) virtues . 19
31. Names of those four things by which moral merit is
    acquired 523
32. Names of the three kinds of acquirement . . . 523
33. Names of the eighteen kinds of voidness or abstractedness
    (Shunyata) 20
34. Names of the four kinds of recollection 22
35. Names of those four things that must be entirely
    avoided 524
36. Names of four supernatural modes or means . . . 525
37. Names of the five organs 525
38. Names of the five faculties or powers 525
39. Names of the seven branches of perfect wisdom . . 23
40. Names of the eight branches of the sublime way . . 23
41. Names of the different degrees of self-sainted persons (as
    are the Rishis or hermits) (Prentyak Buddhas) . . 527
42. Names of the several degrees of perfection of the hearers
    or disciples of Buddha or Tathagata 24
43. Names of divers hearers or disciples (of Sakhya) . . 26
44. Names of the qualifications of (Sakhya's) hearers or dis-
    ciples 29
45. Names of the twelve kinds of rigid qualifications . . 74
46. Names of the several Bhumis (degrees of perfection) of
    the Hearers or disciples (of Buddha) 529
47. Names of six things that ought to be remembered . . 36
48. Names of unpleasant or disagreeable things . . . 528
49. Names of the several degrees of respiration (exhalation
    and inhalation) 529

* o

No.		PAGE
50.	Names of the four excellent truths divided into sixteen minor truths	535
51.	Names of the sixteen kinds of patience or forbearance in making reflections on or thinking of patience	577
52.	Names of the ten kinds of knowledge	579
53.	Four kinds of ways (or moments of actions)	540
54.	Names of the different kinds of vehicles (or principles)	36
54.	Names of the distinctions of mental organs (powers or faculties)	541
55.	Names of the five kinds of Buddhistic perfection	541
56.	Enumeration of the several kinds of Buddhistic scriptures	542
57.	Names relating to the turning of the wheel of the law (by Shakya)	546
58.	Names (or list) of religious tracts (current among the Buddhists)	152
59.	Names of several terms relating to the doctrine of Buddha, and the manner and form of delivering it to the hearers	162
60.	Names of the four kinds of meditation, &c.	549
61.	Names of ecstasies	552
62.	Names of the four immense things (in a Buddha)	555
63.	Names of the eight kinds of liberation or emancipation	556
64.	Names of the eight kinds of superior knowledge or conception	560
65.	Names of the twelve accomplished or perfect sentiments	567
66.	Names of the three doors of liberation or emancipation	569
67.	Names of those four things on which one may rely	569
68.	Names of the three kinds of wit or knowledge	151
69.	Names of the five classes of science	37
70.	Names of four moral maxims	570
71.	Names of the seven precious (or good) things	571
72.	Names of the most excellent six things	572
73.	Names of the six kinds of benediction	573
74.	Names of the nine good actions accompanied by great pleasure or delight	573
75.	Names of those six bad things from which one should come out	575
76.	Names of the four circles or kinds of goods and men	577
77.	Names of rigid practices of abstinence, &c.	577
78.	Names of abstract meditation on God, and the qualifications or perfections to be obtained by it	580
79.	Names of the four kinds of thriving, that is, speaking, teaching, and prophesying	582
80.	Names of the three kinds of criteria or definitions	582

No.		PAGE
81.	Names of the four kinds of thinking	583
82.	Names of the nine kinds of ironical thought or conception	583
83.	Names of being at rest and of seeing more, that is, the high degrees of fixed meditation	584
84.	Names of the ten immoral actions	192
85.	Names of the ten virtuous actions	192
86.	Names of those things by which one may acquire moral merit	193
87.	Names of true or real meaning of the Holy and True One	194
88.	Names of deliverance from pain	196
89.	Names of the several kinds of refuge and protection .	197
90.	Names of the several kinds of respect to be paid to a religious guide, &c.	198
91.	Names of assiduity and diligent application . .	201
92.	Names of the aggregate (the body), its regions and sensation, &c.	204
93.	Names of the division of the corporeal objects . .	204
94.	Names of the division of the aggregate of sensation .	211
95.	Names of the division of the aggregate of consciousness or perception	211
96.	Names of notions or ideas formed of animate and of inanimate existences or beings	211
97.	Names of the division of the aggregate, of equation, and of perfect knowledge	219
98.	Names of the twelve senses or the vehicles of perfection	219
99.	Names of the eighteen regions (of senses) . . .	220
100.	Names of the twenty-two organs	222
101.	Names of the several terms used on the occasion of explaining the aggregate, its regions, and the senses .	224
102.	Names of affection, passion, lust, desire, and longing .	585
103.	Names of the three kinds of sorrow or trouble . .	588
104.	Names of the eight kinds of sorrow	588
105.	Names of the twelve branches of causal concatenation or dependent contingency	39
106.	Names of the six causes	589
107.	Names of the four accessory causes or effects . .	590
108.	Names of the five fruits, viz., consequences, effects .	590
109.	Names of the four plans or ways of coming forth or being born	591
110.	Names of the four kinds of food	591
111.	Names of the nine places or abodes of animate existences	591

No.   PAGE

112. Names of the eight undesirable things 593
113. Names of the consequences of moral actions or works, of their coming to maturity 594
114. Names of the five boundless (most atrocious) acts . 596
115. Names of other five crimes approaching to the former . 597
116. Names of the five sorts of dregs or degenerations . . 597
117. Names of eight common maxims or sayings . . . 598
118. Names of all sorts of good qualities 599
119. Names of imperfections or defects 608
120. Names expressive of the chief Head of the pure, the liberated, or the emancipated 614
121. Names of being purified, liberated, or emancipated (purification or emancipation) 616
122. Names of relinquishing all imperfections and of becoming free 618
123. Names expressive of praise, blame, celebrity or renown 623
124. Names of opposite or contrary things 626
125. Names expressive of great, small, high, low, and similar adjectives 629
126. Names of the several degrees of acquaintance or familiarity 632
127. Names of virtue and blessings 634
128. Names expressive of speaking or hearing any religious tract ; names expressive of noise, sound, expression or utterance 636
129. Names of several examples illustrative of illusion or unreality 641
130. Names of charity or alms-giving, and of oblations and sacrifices 644
131. Names of the several kinds of advantage and utility . 647
132. Names of several terms expressive of the intellect, the understanding, the discrimination 648
133. Names expressive of the enumeration of the several sorts of learned men 649
134. Names of the enumeration of synonymous terms for profound or deep learning 651
135. Names of the enumeration of synonymous terms for joy or pleasure 652
136. Names expressive of anger of the several degrees of mischief or injury 654
137. Names of the four kinds of moral men 656
138. Names expressive of the life in this world and in the next ; death and transmigration 656
139. Names expressive of solitude and retirement . . 658

No.		PAGE
140.	Names of the four kinds of abiding, or the manner of living	658
141.	Names of the several degrees of shocks in an earthquake	282
142.	Names of brilliancy, light, or lustre	284
143.	Names of great and small powers	275
144.	Names of the four great fabulous continents . .	276
145.	Names of the several degrees of elevation of the three regions of the world	278
146.	Names of the gods in the region of cupidity (or in the realm of Cupid)	278
147.	Names of the mansion of the 1st degree of meditation .	279
148.	„ „ 2d degree of meditation .	280
149.	„ „ 3d degree of meditation .	280
150.	„ „ 4th degree of meditation	280
151.	Names of the pure (or holy) mansion	281
152.	Names of the incorporeal mansions	281
153.	Names of the gods inhabiting this or that world . .	317
154.	Names of the nine planets	322
155.	Names of the twenty moving stars (Nakshatras) . .	322
156.	Names of gods, Nagas, &c.	324
157.	Names of the Naga kings or princes	325
158.	Names of common or ordinary Nagas . . ' . .	331
159.	Names of the Yaksha king, or of the prince of the Yakshas	335
160.	Names of the prince of the Gandharas	336
161.	Names of the five gods, the Daityas, Titans, giants, Asuras	337
162.	Names of Vishnu's bird, the Garuda, the prince of the winged creation	338
163.	Names of the Prince of the Kinnaras	339
164.	Names of the prince of the Mahoragas	340
165.	Names of the Prince of the Kumbhándas . . .	342
166.	Names of the great Rishis	40
167.	Names of the ancient Buddhistic learned men in India	42
168.	Names of curious philosophical systems and sects .	44
169.	Names of the six Tirthika teachers (in Tibetan, Mu-stegs-pá-chen)	47
170.	Names of the series of the universal monarchs . .	47
171.	Names of the excellent qualities, and of the seven precious things of an universal monarch . . .	659
172.	Names of the sons or children of whom each universal monarch had a whole thousand	660
173.	Names of the four divisions of troops	662

No.   PAGE

174. Names of ordinary kings   52
175. Names of the Pandavas   53
176. Names of the several classes or ranks, dignities, occupa-
      tions, and professions among men   53
177. Names of different castes or tribes   66
178. Names of parentage, consanguinity, &c. . . . 68
179. Names of the several members and limbs of the body . 71
180. Names of the several degrees of the formation of the
      embryo and of several ages of men   79
181. Names of old age and sickness   81
182. Names of places, countries, cities, towns, &c., mentioned
      in Buddhistic works   82
183. Names of mountains, fabulous and real . .   85
184. Synonymous names for sea or ocean, rivers, &c. . . 86
185. Names of trees   135
186. Names of terms originating with the Tantrika system . 110
187. Names of signs for prognostication . . .   662
188. Names of dialectical and sophistical terms . .   664, 254
189. Names of terms originating with the Nyáya doctrine . 262
190.   „   „   Sankhya doctrine 264
191.   „   „   Mimansa   .   267
192.   „   „   Vaishishika school 268
193. Terms of different dialectical systems . . .   271, 667
194. Names of all sorts of theories   271
195. Names of fourteen theses that have not as yet been de-
      monstrated or proved   272
196. Names of several terms expressive of the soul according
      to the Tirthika teachers   274
197. Names of twenty positions relating to annihilation . 667
198. Names of grammatical terms   670
199. Inflections of a Sanskrit noun in the seven cases of all
      the three numbers   672
200. Names of the bad transmigrations or places of punish-
      ment after death   343
201. Names of several evil spirits (S. Preta. tib. Yidags, a
      ghost)   343
202. Names of all sorts of beasts into which bad or wicked
      men are supposed to transmigrate   344
203. Names of several Tartara, of the divisions of the hot
      Tartarus   354
204. Names of the several divisions of the cold Tartarus . 354
205. Names of the eighteen classes of science . . .   37
206. Names of mechanical arts and handicrafts . . . 356
207. Names of all sorts of musical instruments . . . 359

No.   PAGE
208. Names of the several tunes or parts of harmony . . 368
209. Names of the several kinds of dances, and the manner
     of dancing 361
210. Names of the literature and religious practices of the
     Brahmans. 39
211. Names of the six occupations of a Brahman . . . 362
212. Names of all sorts of words and phrases for such as wish
     to understand the Sanskrit language . . 362–382
213. Names of the dwelling-place or residence of the gods;
     names of the best, &c. 382
214. Names of all sorts of indeclinable words . . . 88
215. Names of castles, forts, and all sorts of dwelling-
     places 94
216. Names of the implements belonging to a cart or chariot 100
217. Names of all sorts of corn and pulse 384
218. Names of festivals or solemn days . . . 285
219. Names of curds, butter, and several kinds of food . 286
220. Names of drugs for curing diseases 385
221. Names of clothes or garments 390
222. Names of utensils, instruments, &c. 393
223. Names of pigments, paint, colours for painting and for
     dyeing stuffs 395
224. Names of precious things, as gems or jewels; gold,
     silver, &c. 397
225. Names of conchs or shells 400
226. Names of several sorts of ornaments 401
227. Names of all sorts of armour and weapon . . . 406
228. Names of all sorts of implements and ornamentations
     used on the occasion of oblations or sacrifices . . 409
229. Names of all sorts of flowers 411
230. Names of the several parts of flowers 417
231. Names of the excellence of some flowers . . . 419
232. Names of the incenses and perfumes 419
233. Names of all sorts of words, phrases (for the use of those
     who wish to understand the Sanskrit text) . . 229–253
234. The names of numerals, the definite and indefinite
     numbers, according to the Phal-chin division of the
     Kahgyur 673
235. Names occurring in the Sherchin Treatise of the Kah-
     gyur 676
236. Names originating with the Lalita Vistara, in the second
     vol. of the mDo class of the Kahgyur . . . 680
237. Names occurring in the mkong-mdsod or Sanskrit
     Abhidharma, of the Stangyur 684

No.　　　　　　　　　　　　　　　　　　　　　　　　　　　PAGE

238. Names of the common numerals, of the inhabitants of
　　　the world 421

239. Names of all sorts of quantities and measures of dis-
　　　tances from an atom to a Yojanam ; a measure of
　　　4000 fathoms 426

240. Names of the proportion of strength in a decimal pro-
　　　gression 428

241. Names of time, and its subdivisions and seasons . . 101

242. Names of the corners and cardinal points or quarters,
　　　and intermediate corners of the world . . . 107

243. Names of the ten advantages derived from learning and
　　　discipline 429

243. Names of the five classes of transgression, and of those
　　　of an indefinite character 430

244. Names of the four defects, or of the four great trans-
　　　gressions 431

245. Names of thirteen transgressions by which one is ren-
　　　dered a residue or dregs of the priests . . . 431

246. Names of thirty transgressions, committed by accepting
　　　and using unlawful things, the wearing or carrying
　　　of which should be avoided 432

247. Names of the ninety transgressions 435

248. Names of those four transgressions that must be con-
　　　fessed to obtain forgiveness 445

249. Names of many things to be learned and observed . 446

250. Names of seven terms for reconciling and settling dis-
　　　putes or quarrels 460

251. Names of punishment, chastisement, and correction . 460

252. Names of entreating, addressing, petitioning, praying
　　　the priesthood, and of performing some ceremonies
　　　on certain occasions 362

253. Names of taking refuge with the three Holy Ones . 465

254. Names of the eight fundamental articles to be learned
　　　and observed by those who enter into the religious
　　　order 466

255. Names of those four moral maxims that are repeated to
　　　him who will be made a Gelong (S. shramana) . 122

256. Names of all sorts of religious persons . . . 122

257. Names of several terms occurring in the Dulva, in the
　　　text entitled "The adopting of the religious order,
　　　or the taking of the religious character" . . . 126

258. Names of the thirteen implements or utensils (of a re-
　　　ligious person) 468

259. Names of utensils or implements of a Gelong . . 469

No.		PAGE
260.	Names of those twelve persons who perform several assigned duties on behalf of others . . .	477
261.	Names of the four classes of the Buddhists, together with their eighteen subdivisions	479
262.	The seventeen subjects or matters of the Dulva . .	481
263.	Names of the five sorts of water fit to be drunk by the priests	483
264.	Names of reproaching or rebuking a Buddhist priest (S. Shramana; Tib. Gelong), or any other religious person	484
265.	Names of a Bihar (sacred edifice), and several other places and things belonging to it	486
266.	Names of the material or stuff of which garments are made	487
267.	Some words and phrases taken or collected from the Dulva	137
268.	Names of those six persons among the disciples of Sakya, who were known under the name of the six Tribunes (in Sanskrit, Shadvargikah) . . .	150
269.	Names of the four kinds of nurses	151
270.	Names of diseases	109
271.	All sorts of distempers, diseases, or sickness . .	490

XVII.

A COMPARATIVE VOCABULARY OF SANSKRIT, HINDI, HUNGARIAN, &c., WORDS AND NAMES,

A Fragment.

NOT only in several memoranda of his friends, but in the preface of his Tibetan Dictionary, and also in the letters which Csoma addressed to Captain Kennedy in 1825, we find that the learned Hungarian had noticed, not merely a certain linguistic affinity between the Sanskrit and Hindi with the Hungarian tongue, but he discovered the existence of words and names, in the countries of South-East of Europe, which seem to point in that direction. Csoma has repeatedly given expression to such an opinion, the importance of which did not escape the notice of men like Wilson, Prinsep, Torrens, Campbell, and others. Yet, with the view to publication, he seemed always disinclined putting such memoranda on record,

because he had hoped, no doubt, that after arriving at Lassa he
would be able to present to the public something more tan-
gible and complete than what he could gather merely from
resources collected in India.

The ardent hope of his life, that of visiting Lassa and the
country beyond, was destined, however, never to be gratified.

A few pages of manuscript annotations in Csoma's own
handwriting are now in the possession of the Academy of
Sciences of Hungary. These annotations are presented
to the reader, however, it may be confessed, with some
diffidence. Desirous to do justice to Csoma's memory, we
wish to guard against the supposition that he would ever
have permitted this apparently unimportant vocabulary to
appear as we find it, because the most cursory examination of
it amply testifies that these memoranda are but casual annotations of words as they struck him in the course of his reading; still even so they will be considered as precious relics by
those who look with interest on Csoma's life and labours, as
the plank of a sunken vessel would be that a wave chanced
to throw upon a friendly shore.

With these preliminary remarks, and only under conditions
just described, do we feel justified in bringing to light this
hitherto unknown collection.

âtâ	आता H.	*father*	atya.
annada	अन्नद S.	*he who gives food*	enni adó.
annadânam	अन्नदानं S.	*the giving food*	enni adás.
ashita	अशित S.	*eaten*	ett, evett.
ash	अश् S.	*to eat*	enni.
ashanam	अशनं S.	*food*	ozsonya.
argha	अर्घे S.	*price, value*	ár, becs.
astam	अस्तं S.	*sunset* [*ing*	este.
(?) astamatî,	अस्तमती	*getting towards even-*	esteledik.
amutra	अमुत्र S.	*there*	amott.
agni	अग्नि S.	*fire*	(tüz égni.)
âlasa	आलस S.	*lazy*	aluszékony.
aswara	अस्वर S.	*having deficient voice*	szótalan.
ardati	अर्दति S.	*hurts*	árt.
alati	अलति S.	*prevents*	elöz, megelöz.

artha	अर्थ S.	*price*	érték.
arthajna	अर्थज्ञ	*understanding*	értelem.
aham	अहं S.	*I, yes*	én, ám.
arthayate	अर्थयते S.	*asks*	kérdez.
âm	आम् S.	*indeed*	ám.
arha	अर्ह S.	*value, price*	ár, becs.
arhati	अर्हति S.	*values*	becsül.
artham	अर्थं S.	*for*	—— ért.
		e.g., gurvartham, guruért.	
arthaka	अर्थक S.	*wealth*	érték, gazdagság.
arthavat	अर्थवत् S.	*wealthy*	értékes, gazdag.
âlasya	आलस्य S.	*sleepy, apathetic*	aluszékony, alu-
(?) akar		*he will*	akar. [szom.
ati	अति S.	*above, upper*	felette.
lâ	ला S.	{ *taking, occupying, conquering*	foglaló.
(?) Atila	अतिला (?)	{ Adi-la, *successful, great chief, conqueror*	elökelö, gyözelmes foglaló.
atala	अटल S.	*firm, solid*	állandó.
angikâ	अङ्गिका	*a shirt*	ümeg, ing.
argala	अर्गल S.	*a bolt*	horgoló, rekesz.
ativriddha	अतिवृद्ध S.	*very old*	megvénült.
asti	अस्ति S.	*is*	van, vagyon.
nâsti	नास्ति S.	*is not*	nincsen.
tejas	तेजस् S.	*fire, energy*	tüz, fény.
twish	त्विष् S.	*light, fire*	tüz.
tâta	तात S.	*father*	atya.
trâta	त्रात S.	*preserved*	megtartott.
trâyate	त्रायते S.	*preserves*	megtart.
tâdayati	ताडयति S.	*pushes*	taszit.
twam	त्वं S.	*thou*	te.
thâl, thâlâ, thâlî	{ थाल, थाला, थाली H.	{ *a dish*	tál.
talati	{ तल्लति S.		telni.
tâlayati	{ ताल्लयति S.	{ *to be full, complete*	tölteni.
talapayati	{ तल्लपयति(? S)		töltetni.

tasyati	तस्यति S.	*pushes, tosses*	taszit.
staryate	स्तर्यते S.	*spreads*	terjed, terjesz-
trâ, trâyate, trâpayate	ब्रा, बायते, बापयते S.	*to hold*	[kedik. tartani.
râga	राग S.	*anger*	harag.
râma	राम S.	*joy*	öröm.
raktam	रक्तं S.	*blood*	vér.
raktapa	रक्तप S.	*blood-sucker, a leech*	vérszopó [magú.
rakta-vîja	रक्तवीज S.	*pomegranate*	veres bélü, veres
râjati	राजति S.	*shines*	ragyog.
loka	लोक S.	*world*	világ.
loshta	लोष्ट S.	*rust*	rozsda.
lankâ	लङ्का S.	*a girl*	lyánka.
ghâs	घास H.	*grass*	gaz, fü.
bol	बोल H.	*speak thou*	szólj.
bolnâ	बोलना H.	*to speak*	szólni.
bulânâ	बुलाना H.	*to call*	szólitni.
bulwânâ	बुलवाना H.	*to cause to call*	szólittatni.
(?) bâlya	बास्य	*the family*	család.

N.B.—Magyar family names : Bala, Buda, Bodala, Barta, Bálya,
Bod, Bede, Binde, Vajna, Beder, Vida, Bardocz, Bihar,
Hari, Csorja, Sánta, Buja, Székely.

bandhu	बन्धु S.	*a friend*	barát.
bhrâtâ	भ्राता S.	*brother*	bátya
bhrátá me	भ्राता मे S.	*my brother*	bátyám.
bhogyâ	भोग्याS.	*a whore*	buja, bujálkodó.
bheka	भेक S.	*a frog*	béka.
briksha,vriksha	वृक्ष S.	*a tree*	bükkfa.
bhâshita	भाषित S.	*a discourse*	beszéd.
bhayânak	भयानक H.	*champion (terrific)*	bajnok
brikha, vrisha	बृक्ष H. वृष S.	*a bull*	bika.
vichâraka, bichârak	विचारक S. and H.	*the judge*	biró
balgati	वल्गति S.	*to tramp (to jump)*	ballagni.
Bharata	भरत S.	*younger brother of Râma, son of Dush- manta and Sakuntalâ.*	

—Magyar words : Barát, Barta, Bartos.

Budha	बुध S.	son of the moon, regent of the planet Mercury	bölcs. Buda.
bhâshe	भाषे S.	I talk	beszélek.
balavân	बल्बबान् S.	(?) an idol	bálvany.
eka	एक S. and H.	one	egy.
idam	इदं S.	this	ez.
hinsâ	हिंसा S.	injury	kinzás.
hinsati	हिंसति S.	injures	kinoz, kinzani.
hansa	हंस S.	a gander	gantzi.
hâsya	हास्य S.	laughter	kaczagás.
hazâr	हज़ार H. सहस्र S.	one thousand	ezer.
Himavat	हिमवत् S.	Himālaya range	havas.
himâgama	हिमागम S.	cold season	téli idöszak.
hikkati	हिक्कति S.	hiccoughs	csuklik (csuk-
hûṇa	हूण S.	a barbarian	hun. [lani).
hûnkâra	हूङ्कार S.	uttering the sound of a hûn	hun nyelven beszélni [bedni.
ûna (Hún?)	ऊन S.	to decrease	megfogyni, keves-
hasati	हसति S.	laughs	kaczag.
halabhṛit	हलभृत् S.	name of Balarāma	eke-tartó.
chashaka	चषक S.	a cup	csésze
chakra	चक्र S.	a wheel	kerék.

chakra; circus, circulus, cherk, in Russian; in Magyar: kerek, kerék, kör, kert, kerület, keritni, kerülni, kerités.

chhatra	छत्र S.	a parasol	sátor, ernyö.
chhala	छल S.	deceit	csalás.
chamû	चमू S.	multitude; an army	csomó, sokaság
chîkayati	चीकयति S.	touches, tickles	csikland.
chyâvayati	च्यावयति S.	scorns	csúfol.
chinoti	चिनोति S.	assembles, v.n.	gyül.
chayayati	चययति S.	assembles, v.a.	gyüjt.
chapayati	चपयति S.	assembles, v.c.	gyüjtet.
cheṭa, cheḍa	चेट, चेड S.	servant	cseléd.

garta	गर्तं S.	hole in the ground	gödör.
galhate	गल्हते S.	blames	gyaláz.
gohannam	गोच्चनं S.	cow-dung	ganéj.
ghagghati	घर्घति S.	derides	kaczag.
ghâtayan	घातयन् S.	killer	katona.
(îsh) îshṭe	(ईश्) ईष्टे S.	rules	uralkodik.
Îsha	ईंश S.	name of Siva	Siva isten neve.
îshîtâ	ईंशीता S.	superiority	uralkodás, felsöbbség.
îshitri, îshitâ	ईंशितृ, ईंशिता S.	owner	tulajdonos, úr.
Sikandar	सिकन्दर H.	Alexander	Sándor.
îḍ, îṭṭe	ईंड, ईंड्डे S.	praises, greets	üdvözöl.
îrte	ईंर्ते S.		
îrayati	ईंरयति S.	goes	jár.
îyate	ईंयते S.		
yâti	यांति S.	walks	jár.
yâ, yâti	या, यांति S.	to go	jár.
itastatas	इतस्ततः S.	here and there	ide's tova
îrayati	ईंरयति S.	lets go	jártat.
iti	इति S.	thus	igy.
îrshya	ईंर्ष्यं S.	envy	irigység.
îshṭe	ईंड्डे S.	rules (to be a god)	uralkodni, Isten,
ishṭam	इंडं S.	(the desired) God	Isten. [lenni.
yazdân	يزدان P.	God	Isten.

uru, vrihat	उरु, वृहत् S.	great, a giant	úr, hatalmas.
urvîsha	उर्वींश S.	proprietor	órias.
vahanam	वहनं S.	drawing, carrying	vinni, vonni.
vasanam, vastra	वसनं, वस्त्र S.	the cloth, linen	vászon.
varaṇa	वरण S.	defence	óltalom. Jegyz: Varna.
vâdayati	वादयति S.	accuses	vádol.
vachaknu	वचक्नु S.	gossiping	fecsegö.
-wâlâ	°वाला H.	belonging to a place or country	hová való.

vyâdha	बाघ S.	*a hunter*	vadász.
vṛika	हक S.	*a wolf*	farkas.
(?) utsa	उत्स ?	*street*	utcza.
uras	उरस् S.	*great*	nagy úr.
varyya	वर्य्य S.	*the chief*	vajda.
(?) varabala	वरबल S.	*powerful*	(?) verböltz.
jalnâ	अलना H.	*to ignite,* v.n.	gyúlni.
jalânâ	अलाना H.	*to ignite,* v.a.	gyujtani.
jalwânâ	अलवाना H.	*to burn,* v.c.	gyujtatni.
jwalati	व्वलति S.	*shines, burns*	fénylik, gyúl.
jwalana	व्वलन S.	*lighting*	meggyúl.
jayati	अयति S.	*conquers, is victo-rious*	gyöz, gyözelmes.
jaya	अय S.	*name of Yudishthira*	Gyözö, Geyza.
yavana	यवन S.	*a stranger*	jövevény.
yudh	युघ् S.	*war*	had, háború.
naḍa	नड S.	*a reed*	nád.
naḍvat	नड्वत् S.	*abounding in reeds*	nádas.
na	न S., H.	*no, not*	ne, nem.
nápi	नापि S.	*not even*	nem éppen.
nâma	नाम S.	*is it not !*	nem é ?
nacha	नच S.	*nor, neither*	nem is.
nanu	ननु S.	*is it not !*	nem e ?
nirarthaka	निरर्थक S.	*unmeaning*	érthetetlen.
mâyate, mâti	मायते माति S.	*measures*	mér.
mushka	मुष्क S.	*a strong man, a thief*	erös ember, tolvaj.
		N.B.—muszka.	
mṛiga	मृग S.	*deer*	szarvas, vad.
mṛigayati	मृगयति S.	*sports*	vadász.
mṛigayâ	मृगया S.	*a chase*	vadászat.
mṛigayu	मृगयु S.	*a hunter*	vadász.
mṛiduromavat	मृदुरोमवत् S.	*fine haired, a hare*	finom szörü, nyúl.
mǎyǎnâ	मयना H.	*a maina (Gracula religiosa)*	szajkó.
		N.B.—majom, majmolni·	
kansa	कंस S.	*goblet*	kancsó.

kupatha	कुपथ S.	*a hilly tract, a difficult path*	kárpát, hegyes.
kinchit	किश्चित् S.	*little*	kicsi.
kara	कर S.	*arm, hand*	kar, kéz.
kukkuṭa	कुक्कुट S.	*a cock*	kakas.
kashâya	कषाय S.	*bitter*	keserü.
kûpa	कूप S.	*a well*	kút.
kilâsa	किलास S.	*a boil*	kelés.
kiki	किकि S.	*a blue jay*	kék szajkó.
kukara	कुकर S.	*having a crooked arm*	görbe karú
kakkati.	कक्कति S.	*derides*	kaczag, gunyol.
(?) kikkati		*to cough*	köhögni.
koṛh	कोड़ H.	*leprosy*	kór.
kim	किम् S.	*who*	ki.
kshomam	क्षोमं S.	*silk*	selyem.
kapha	कफ S.	*phlegm, spittle*	köp.
karpûra	कर्पूर S.	*camphor*	kámfor.
kalasha	कलश S.	*a goblet*	kulacs.
khara-nakhara	खरनखर S.	*sharp-nailed*	köröm, körmös.
khyöd	(Tibetan)	*you*	kend, kegyelmed.
kashchit	कश्चित् S.	*who? what?*	kicsoda? micso-
kishora	किशोर S.	*a youth*	kis úr. [da?
kîrtita	कीर्तित S.	*celebrated*	hirdetett (meg-
kîrtti	कीर्ति S.	*fame*	hir. [kürtölt).
khatam	खतं S.	*a pond*	gödör.
kis kâ	किस का H.	*whose*	kié.
kis ko	किस को H.	*to whom*	kinek.
kula	कुल S.	*a family*	család.
sakula	सकुल S.	*belonging to the same family*	ugyan azon család-ból való, székely?
paṇa, dhana	पण, धन S.	*money, coin*]	pénz.
pachati	पचति S.		föni.
pachayati	पचयति S.	*to cook, to boil*	fözni.
pachayat	पचयत् S.		fözetni.
patati	पतति S.	*carries*	viszen, szál.
patayati	पतयति S.	*makes over (to)*	szálit.

pâtayati	पातयति S.	delivers	szálittat.
patha	पथ S.	road	út.
pathati	पथति S.	travels	utazik.
pathayati	पथयति S.	causes to travel	utaztat.
panthati	पन्थति S.	shows the way	utasít.
panthayati	पन्थयति S.		
pathin	पथिम् S.	traveller	utas
pathika	पथिक S.		utazó.
pathila	पथिल S.	wayfarer	utazó.
pathika santati	पथिकसन्तति S.	a caravan	utitársaság.
padika	पदिक S.	a footman / a pedestrian	gyalogos.
padâsanam	पदासनं S.	footstool	lábszék, zsámoly.
pachaka	पचक S.	a cook	szakács.
pachaka strî	पचकस्त्री S.	a female cook	fözö asszony.
(?) Pârthus	पार्षुः S.	a rebel	pártütö, pártos.

N.B.—Parthi exules Scytharum (Justinianus).

palâla	पलाल S.	straw, stubble	polyva, szalma.
pataka	पतक S.	that which falls or descends, a torrent	a mi esik, patak.
pachaka	पचक S.	earthen vessel	fazék.
pându	पाण्डु S.	clothed in yellow-ish white	(?) pandúr.
pata	पठ S.	cloth	posztó.

shîrshaka	शीर्षक S.	a helmet	sisak.
suta	सुत S.	a son	szülött, szülni.
sû	सू S.	parturition	szülés.
sauchika	सौचिक S.	a tailor	szabó.
sûchi	सूचि S.	a needle	tü (talán szöcs ?).
(sû) savanam	(सू) सवनं S.	to bring forth	szülni.
suhrita	सुहृत S.	a lover	szeretö.
sûta	सूत S.	born	szülte, szülött.
shakaṭa	शकट S.	a cart, carriage	szekér.
sabhâ	सभा S.	a gathering of people, a room	szoba.

* P

shobhâ	श्रोभा S.	*beauty*	szépség.
sankaṭa	सङ्कट S.	*narrow*	szük.
sevati	सेवति S.	*serves*	szolgál.
sûshati	सूषति S.	*brings forth*	szül.
skhadate	खदते S.	*tears*	szakad.
(?) sabdati		*to destroy, to defeat*	leszabdalni.
shwasati	श्वसति S.	*breathes*	szuszog.
sahate	सहते S.	*bears*	szül.
sau	सौ H.	*one hundred*	száz.
sa	स S.	*he*	az. ,
sabala	सवल S.	{ *one with an army, with a force or power* }	(?) szabolcs.
shikhâ	शिखा S.	{ *a stack or covered heap* }	(fedél) asztag.
(?) sakti		*island*	sziget.
sukrita	सुकृत S.	*virtuous*	erényes.
suhṛida	सुहृद S.	*lover, tender,*	} szeretö.
surata	सुरत S.	*compassionate*	
sûrya	सूर्य्य S.	*the sun*	nap.
sûryâvartta	सूर्य्यावर्त्त S.	*sunflower*	napraforgó
sevaka	सेवक S.	*servant*	szolga.
salavaṇa	सलवण S.	*salted*	szalonna.
dwâram	द्वारं S.	*a courtyard*	udvar.
dharati	धरति S.	*holds*	tart.
dadâti	ददाति S.	*gives, contributes*	adakozik.
dasha	दश S.	*ten*	tiz.
dhṛi	धृ S.	*to hold, to retain*	tartani.

N.B.—Examine these roots for all derivatives; *e.g.*, "dhrita-râshtra," the holder of a kingdom, a sovereign, a ruler, országtartó.

N.B.—dhar, in Hungarian: tart; tartani, tartozni, tartózkodni, tartás, tartomány, tartozó, tartatik, &c.

dhwani	ध्वनि S.	*a sound*	zaj, moraj.
		(?) Duna	Danube.

(?) lip	लिप	*to stride*	lépni.
	(Conjugate this verb.)		
Loma-pâda	लोमपाद S.	*King of Anga, Bhaugulpore is its*	
		capital.	
	*N.B.—*Árpád.		

Csoma affixed a remarkable note at the end of this paper, in the following words : *Materiam dedi, formam habetis, quærite gloriam si placet !*

INDEX.

AAVOR, 55
Abbot of Pukdal, 160
Abulferagius, 53
Abulfida, 53
Academy of Sciences of Hungary, 1, 106, 142, 167
Adrianople, 25
Afghanistan, 21, 32
Aga Mahdi Rafael, 29, 38
Agathyrsus, 54
Agram, 13, 25
Aleppo, 26, 32
Alexandria, 26, 32
Alexander & Co., 122
Allard and Ventura, 27, 32
Al-Mamun, 128
Al-Mansur, 128
Alphabetum Tibetanum, 19, 28, 36, 61, 127
Amara Kosha, 59
Amara Sinha, 59
Ambála, 23, 34, 71
America, 58
Amherst, Lord, 23, 76, 125
Amritsir, 28
Andkhoi, 101
Andrada, 96
Anga, 47
Appendix, 169
Arabic language, 52, 57, 155
Araris, 56
Asia Minor, 57
Asiatic Society of Bengal, 75, 76, 103, 104, 116, 117, 123, 130, 134, 135, 143, 144

Asoka, 109.
Assyria, 43, 57, 64
Austria, Emperor of, 24

BACCHUS, 54
Bactria, 59
Baghdad, 26, 32, 128
Balee (Bali) Ram, 70, 78
Balk, 27, 59
Baptist Mission Press, 115, 120
Bamian, 27, 32, 59
Belaspore, 30
Bellino, Mr., 26
Bengal, 49, 53
Bengali language, 155
Bentinck, Lord Cavendish, 125
Bernier, 21
Besarh, 18, 35, 68, 88
Bessarabia, 54
Bethlen College, 24
Beyrut, 26, 32
Bhadra Kalpika, 111
Bhagvan, 55, 58
Bhote, Bhutan, Bootan, 42, 144, 165, 193
Bihar, 56
Black Sea, 55
Blumenbach, 127
Boeotia, 56
Bokhara, 2, 27, 36, 101
Borysthenes, 54
Brahma, 44
Brahmaputra, 91
Bucharest, 25, 32
Bud, 59

Buda, 56
Budenz, 166
Budparast, 59
Bulgaria, 25, 55
Bunger, 55
Burmah, 53
Bushby, 145

CABOOL, see Kabúl
Cairo, 26
Calcutta, 2, 28, 35, 77, 112
Calder, 102
Campbell, 1, 15, 19, 22, 145, 155
Canterbury, Archbishop, 10
Carthage, 56
Catai Taikun, 61
Caspian Sea, 55
Cashmere, see Kashmir
Ceylon, 53
Champa, 43
Chandernagore, 50
Chandra Komi, 50
Charlemagne, 54, 128
Chatham's Letters, 12
Chepaul, 82
China, 26, 40, 61, 63
Chios, 26, 32
Chronology, Tibetan, 65
Chronos, 44
Collins, Dr., 165
Constantinople, 25
Crete, 57
Croatia, 25
Crozier, 117
Csoma's cousin, 3
Csoma's parents, 3
Csoma's tomb, 154
Csoma's travelling library, 161
Cunningham, General, 98
Cyprus, 26, 32

DACIA, DAKIA, 54, 56
Daka, 27, 32
Dala, 94
Dalai Lama, 40
Danube, 25, 32, 54
Darjeeling, 145

Delhi, 23, 24, 41
Deodar, 82
Depter Ningpo, 63
Derghe, 63
Dictionary, Tibetan, 114
Diodorus Siculus, 90
Dnieper, 54
mDo, 47, 49, 111
Döbrentei, 129, 130, 131
Dras, 19, 32
Dulva, 47
Durand, 2, 166

EBER, 55
Eden, Sir A., 166
Eichhorn, 6
Elliott, 41
English language, 57
Enos, 26, 32
Eötvös, Baron, 16, 17
Epitaph (Csoma's), 154
Eszterházy, Prince, 121, 130, 131,
    163
Etymology, Tibetan, 51
Euphrates, 57

FATALISM, 49
Fateh Ali Shah, 26
Fiorillo, 12
Fo-a-Xaca, 60
Forbes, 117
Forster, 21
Franks, 117
Francis Joseph of Austria, 161
Fraser, 80, 99, 100, 102
French language, 57, 155

GAULS, 54, 58
Gengiz Khan, 60, 63
Gerard, 19, 22, 39, 70, 76, 77, 80,
    98, 99, 102, 158
German, 54, 57, 59, 155
Getæ, 55, 56, 58
Gibbon, 61
Giorgi, see Alphabetum Tibetanum
Göcz Ilona, 3
Gogra, 91
Goths, 54, 59

Göttingen, 6, 117
Grammar, Tibetan, 114
Greek language, 57, 58
Griffith, 151
Grote, A., 164, 166
Guignes, de, 61
Gyakan, 63
Gyanak, 63
Gyud, Gyud-de, 48, 49
Gyulai, 166

Du Halde, 61
Hamadan, 26, 32
Hammer, von, 129
Hang, 69
Hanover, 24
Harun-al-Rashid, 128
Hebrew language, 52, 155
Heber, 55
Hegedüs, 4, 9, 36, 128
Henderson, 21
Herepei, 6
Hermanstadt, 25
Herries, Farquhar, & Co., 10
Himbabs, 28, 32
Hindú Kush, 36
Hindustani, 155
Hodgson, 106, 110, 112, 123, 140–147
Hor, 63
Horatius, P., 49
Horváth, Baron, 3, 166
Hügel, Baron, 16, 17, 20, 21
Hunfalvy, 157
Hungarian language, 52, 57
Hungs, 150
Huns, 40, 153, 155

Jacquemont, 21
Jamoo, 28
Jäschke, 124
Jat tribes of India, 55
Ichthyolites, 82
Jesus, 59
Imaus, 53
Indeterminists, 48
Indra, 44
Jones, Sir William, 53
Joobal, 82

Irkutsk, 13
Iswara, 44
Italian language, 57
Julpigorie, 136
Jupiter, 44
Justinianus, 56

Kabul, 27, 32, 59
Kalingah, 53
Kahgyur, 45, 46, 50, 52, 69, 107
Kalapsa, 63
Kalkas, 63
Kalmuks, 63
Kanaor, Kunawar, 18, 80, 81, 82,
   83, 94, 96, 97
Kaniska, 109
Kanum, 18, 69, 80, 82, 87, 95, 96,
   98, 104
Kashmir, 16, 21, 28, 29, 30, 49, 53
Katmandú, 59, 139, 140
Kenderessy, 7, 13
Kenderessy-Csoma scholarship, 13,
   160
Kennedy, 19, 21, 22, 23, 24, 34, 36,
   39, 71, 73, 76, 77, 102, 124
Kermanshah, 26, 32
Kezdi-Vásárhely, 160
Khalon, 29, 36
Kham, 150
Khamyul, 62
Kharpon, 69
Khorassan, 27, 32, 36, 53
Khri de Srongtsan, 128
Khri Srong débu tsan, 61, 128
King, Dr., 166
Kissengunj, 136
Klaproth, 11, 79, 149
Kongcho, 64
Körös, village of, 3
Körösi, 9
Kosala, 47
Kotgurh, 68, 69, 97
Kováts, 27
Kovászna, 3
Kulm, 27,
Kulu, 30, 68, 69
Kun-dgah-Snyingpo, 63

Kungavo, 47
Kylas, 91

LADAK, 28, 29, 35, 42, 123
Lahore, 28
Lahoul, 30, 69, 70
Lalita Vistara, 107
Larnica, 26
Lassa, 40, 42, 62, 102
Latakia, 26, 32
Latin language, 57
Leh, 21, 28, 29, 32, 35
Leitner, 160
Lloyd, 136, 138, 139, 154
Libera Mensa regia, 24
Literary Society at Pest. *See*
  Scientific Society
Limbus, 150

MACEDONIA, 25, 32, 54, 57
Macnaughten, 119, 133, 135
M'Cann, 166
M'Kenzie, 77, 92, 102
Magadha, 47, 53
Mahabharut, 85
Mahadeo, 91
Magyar, 55, 156, 157, 158
Mahomed Ali Mirza, 26
Mahomed Azim Khan, 27
Mahratta, 155
Maitreya, 43
Malan, 20, 64, 137, 142, 158, 166
Malda, 135
Marco Polo, 40
Mansarowar, 81, 91, 94
Maros, 14
Massagetæ, 55
Mauritius, Emperor, 6
Meer Izzut Oollah, 28, 29
Mer and Ser, 20
Mendee, 30
Merdin, 16, 32
Meshed, 32
Metcalfe, Sir C., 100, 102, 117
Mill, 117
Mithridates, 56
Mitscherlich, 8

Mivang, 62
Moldavia, 54, 59
Mongolia, 36, 88
Mongols, 40, 60
Monó village, 3
Moorcroft, 19, 21, 23, 28, 29, 30
  31, 32, 34, 41, 51, 67, 70, 75
Moorcroft's diary, 101
Moorcroft's tomb, 101
Mosul, 26, 32
Moscow, 13
Moses, 57
Mollah Eskander Csoma, 133
Mussurie (Masuri), 16

NAGY-ENYED, 4, 29
Nagy Szeben, 3
Naho, 69
Nami Srongtsan, 61
Narayana, 44
Narthang, 62
Nemzet, 3, 140
Nepal, 42-49, 59, 61, 63, 64, 110,
  112-123
Nesselrode, 29
Nicholson, 70
Niebuhr, 54
Ninus, 43, 64
Nirmankaya, 43
Nissung, 96
Niti Shastra, 50

ODEN, WODEN, 59
Odessa, 13
Olympus, 44
Orbán Baláza, Baron, 3, 161
Orfa, 26, 32
Orthoëpy, Tibetan, 51
Orthography, Tibetan, 51
Otantrapur, 52
Ovid, 55
Oxus, 55, 153

PADMA, 68, 69
Padmakarpo, 64
Pagan, 55-58
Paks-yul, 47

Palso, 35
Panchen Rinpoché, 62
Panjáb, 37
Pannonia, 54, 56
Parthians, 27, 56
Patna, 138
Pavie, 7, 140
Pearce, 115, 120
Pelasgi, 57
Pemberton, 140
Persia, 57, 60
Persian language, 155
Pest, 56
Petersburgh, 28
Philangi Dása, 160
Philippopolis, 25, 32
Phœnicia, 57
Piti (Spiti), 28, 69, 70, 96
Pliny, 90
Pohle, 125
Potchenpo, 63
Prinsep, 22, 115, 117, 119, 120, 129, 131, 133, 135
Prosody, 51
Ptolemy, 53
Pukdal, 18, 68, 69, 73, 101, 160
Pupil servants, 5
Pushtu, 155

QUARTERLY ORIENTAL MAGAZINE, 71, 74, 85, 90
Queen Anne of England, 10

RAFAEL AGA MAHDI, 29, 38
Rajendrolála Mitra, 66, 166
Rákóczy, 10
Ralpáchen, 128
Ralston, 15, 142, 157
Ranjit Sing, 16, 28
Rémusat, 11, 79, 123, 127, 149
Revue des deux Mondes, 7
Rheum palmatum, 97
Rhodes, 26, 32, 57
Rich (Mr.), 26
Rirap, 44
Rumelia, 25, 55
Royal Asiatic Society's Journal, 23

Rungpore, 145
Russian language, 155
Rustchuk, 25

SABATHÚ (Soobathu), 19, 23, 30, 37, 67, 68, 70, 73, 89, 90
Sakya (Shakya), 43, 47, 60
Saketee, 30
Samarcund, 54
Sassanian dynasty, 61
Sa-Skya, 63
Sanskrit, 17, 22, 155
Sarmatic, 55
Satsuma, 48
Schaefer, 125
Schoefft, 141
Sciences, five greater, 45
Sciences, five smaller, 46
Scientific Society (of Hungary), 16, 130, 134
Sclavonic language, 12, 24, 54, 57, 58
Scythæ, Scythians, 53, 55, 56
Sekunder Beg, 34
Seleucia, 61
Sembota, 61
Servia, 54
Shambala, 63
Shér-p'hyin (Sher-chin), 47
Sidon, 26, 32
Siculian nation, 24
Sihon, 63
Sikkim, 1, 138, 139, 144
Sikkim Raja, 136, 146
Simla, 68, 80
Sindhu, 49
Singhala, 53
Sita, 63
Skuno, 94, 96
Sokyul, 63
Sophia, 25, 32
Sopron, 140
Spanish language, 57
Speculum veritatis, 96
Spicker'sche Zeitung, 21
Srinaggar, 20, 33
Srongtsan Gambo, 61, 64

Sruan, 69, 70
Stacy, 19, 102
Stangyur, 45, 50, 60, 62, 69, 107
Stirling (Mr.), 67, 73, 79, 92
Sultanpore, 30
Sumeru, 44
Sungnam, 70, 96
Sutlej, 68, 80, 91
Sutra, 108
Swedish language, 57, 58
Swinton, 114
Swoboda, 26
Syntax, 51
Syrian language, 57
Szabó de Borgáta, 8, 117, 140
Szász, Bishop, 166
Széchényi, Béla, Count, 158
Székler, Székely, 3, 5, 9, 24, 160
Szent György, 161
Szolnok, Middle, 3

Taikún, 61
Tassin, 120
Tathagata, 55
Tauris, 26
Tebriz, 26
Teesa, 68, 70
Teheran, 19, 26, 32, 119
Temesvár, 24
Terai, 145
Thang, 61, 128
Theophylaktes Simocatta, 6
Thessaly, 57
Thewrewk de Ponor, 140, 166
Thong dynasty, 61
Thrace, 25, 54, 57
Thyrsus, 54
Tibetan language, 22, 57
Titalya, 138, 139, 140, 145
Tirhut, 123
Tirthika, 48
Tomi, 55
Torrens, Henry, 22, 110, 143, 153, 154, 158

Transylvania, 3, 12, 24, 26, 32, 54, 57
Transoxonia, 53
Trebeck, 21, 28, 29, 101
Trevelyan, 117
Tripoli, 26, 32
Tubgani Lama, 146
Turkestan, 36
Turkish language, 57
Turnour, 147
Tytler, 117

Ugrian, Ugric, 157
Ujain, 49
Uranos, 44

Vámbéry, 15, 34, 157
Ventura, 27, 32
Vigne, 21
Vishnú, 44

Wallachia, 25, 32, 54, 57, 58
Wallachian language, 57
Wallich, 117
Willock, Sir Henry, 26, 70, 119
Wilson, 11, 15, 37, 71, 76, 77, 86, 113, 114
Woden, 59
Wolff, 21
Wuzeers, 88

Yangla, 18, 29, 32, 36, 80, 83, 99
Yampu, 59
Yarkand, 22, 28, 34
Yates, 140
Yaxartes, 63
Yezdegird, 61
Yugars, Yoogurs, 63, 150
Yule, Colonel, 40

Zanskar, 18, 29, 30, 36, 69, 70, 83, 148
Zeus, 44
Zhu-hu-hou, 61
Zoroaster, 43, 64

PRINTED BY BALLANTYNE, HANSON AND CO.
EDINBURGH AND LONDON.

CPSIA information can be obtained
at www.ICGtesting.com
Printed in the USA
BVHW012244171221
624417BV00002B/69